CRITICAL RACE THEOLOGY

ETHICS AND INTERSECTIONALITY
An Orbis Series in Theological Ethics

SERIES EDITORS
MIGUEL A. DE LA TORRE
STACEY M. FLOYD-THOMAS
DAVID P. GUSHEE

Titles include:

Juan M. Floyd-Thomas, *Critical Race Theology: White Supremacy, American Christianity, and the Ongoing Culture Wars*
Melanie Jones Quarles, *Up Against a Crooked Gospel: Black Women's Bodies and the Politics of Redemption*

ETHICS AND INTERSECTIONALITY SERIES

Critical Race Theology

White Supremacy, American Christianity, and the Ongoing Culture Wars

Juan M. Floyd-Thomas

ORBIS BOOKS
Maryknoll, New York 10545

Founded in 1970, Orbis Books endeavors to publish works that enlighten the mind, nourish the spirit, and challenge the conscience. The publishing arm of the Maryknoll Fathers and Brothers, Orbis seeks to explore the global dimensions of the Christian faith and mission, to invite dialogue with diverse cultures and religious traditions, and to serve the cause of reconciliation and peace. The books published reflect the views of their authors and do not represent the official position of the Maryknoll Society. To learn more about Maryknoll and Orbis Books, please visit our website at www.orbisbooks.com

Dedicated to

Stacey M. Floyd-Thomas

Contents

Contents

Foreword:

Perfect Pitch

Michael Eric Dyson

When I was a kid in the ghetto of Detroit in the sixties and early seventies, I loved to watch Juan Marichal pitch. Dubbed "the Dominican Dandy," the San Francisco Giants righthander from the Dominican Republic became in 1983 the first player from his country, and the first foreign-born player, elected to the Baseball Hall of Fame. Marichal's style was sublime; in the parlance of baseball, he had great stuff. Unlike legendary power pitchers Bob Gibson and Sandy Koufax, both of whom overshadowed Juan, Marichal was a finesse artist on the mound who mastered his craft through precise control of his impressive repertoire of fastballs, curveballs, sliders, changeups, and screwballs. Marichal unerringly found the strike zone from a variety of angles, whether sidearm, over the top, or three-quarters. And his delivery was an athletic marvel: his high leg kick permitted him to hide the type of pitch he was set to throw until he fired away.

As an adult in the West End of Nashville, I love to watch Juan Marcial Floyd-Thomas hurl a variety of professorial pitches. His fastball is a rapid-fire riposte to a questionable assertion in sometimes melodic alliteration. His curveball produces a deliciously curious example, seemingly far afield, that sheds fresh light on well covered territory—for instance, citing rap music to illumine a discussion of American theology. His slider is an esoteric conversation that breaks suddenly into blissful vernacular, say, chasing elucidation of Kant with feigned exasperation curled up in the comically abbreviated proclamation, "I can't." His changeup is an apparent rush of information that arrives far more deliberately as he couches his views in mellow restraint.

And his screwball is unleashed when he appears to talk turkey but ends up talking trash. His delivery ranges from deadpan to operatic, in the most appealing of terms, and he kicks his intellectual leg high to mask the fire that pours from his mouth until he opens it to speak. Others at the Vanderbilt University Divinity School where he holds forth have bigger names and noisier titles, but he is, to my mind, the undisputed ace of the roster, the brightest brain in the academic dugout. He looks the part, too, what with his radiant brown skin and charismatic goatee, an irresistible chocolate Nietzsche.

The book you hold in your hand is ample proof of his great stuff. Floyd-Thomas is taking on a heady subject through a perspective he's helping to invent to bring relief to those suffering the multitude of oppressions he names. *Critical Race Theology* is a daring undertaking. Just as its conceptual mother, critical race theory, is under unprincipled assault in the racially charged public square, he goes and births a child—yes, men really can have babies—that will be just as bitterly denounced as her maternal inspiration. Perhaps even more so because God has been invited to the proceedings or shown to have been involved from the start.

Critical Race Theology joins a wealth of religious and spiritual and moral reflection to the complicated and virtuous abundance of ideas from the legal and historical side of things, from sociology and politics, too, for which critical race theory was known before it riled up the far right. The point is to think and act in ways that relieve the heartbreak endured by the true victims of a myriad of forces from race to class and gender.

Like another prophet from an earlier epoch, Floyd-Thomas doesn't merely want to understand the world but change it. He doesn't want to just do methodology; he doesn't just want to talk about the talk about the thing he wants—the transformation aimed at, the change desired, the shifts imagined and expressed. He wants to help bring them into existence. He wants to move from preparation to performance, or, in the vernacular, from "fixing to" to fixing up. Of course, he treasures the intellectual chops it will take to bring about this change. He's engaging big names, from Kimberlé Crenshaw to Derrick Bell. And he's not afraid to go toe to toe with icons.

His discussion of Reinhold Niebuhr's classic *Children of Light and Children of Darkness* offers grist for his mill of tackling the white supremacy that is the urgent undertow of the entire book: how to name it, nail it, and negate it. One might think the children of light and darkness are easy enough to identify, with evildoers and do gooders comfortably categorized. But he tethers the message of Niebuhr's Christian realism to Cheryl Lynn's "Got to Be Real" and turns that theological light back on its author and reminds us that all of us contain goodness and evil inside, and sometimes outside. White supremacy is a force to be reckoned with, whether in the eyes of a bigot or in the mind of a Black person who has succumbed to the harsh reality that James Baldwin said was true of his father: that he believed the lie of inferiority that the white world sold him, drilled into his Black brain.

Moreover, as Gen Z would have it, Floyd-Thomas is not here for the shenanigans, and he wants all the smoke. He admits Niebuhr's great ethical utility in grappling with the messy elements of democracy. But he acknowledges that Niebuhr falls far short in helping to combat the white supremacy that he barely speaks on, that Floyd-Thomas and other proponents of critical race theology seek to destroy. One of Floyd-Thomas's major aims is to show how white evangelical belief, white nationalist thought, and white religious ideology merge to reinforce and justify the unjust status quo that makes Black life on earth a hell of sorts.

As he puts Niebuhr in conversation with a rich heritage of Black thought that treasures Black life and insists that it matters, Floyd-Thomas comes upon what we might frame as a more lucid and useful binary: it is not the children of light against the children of darkness as much as it is the children who are light against the children who are dark. That is more than a clever turn of phrase; it is, instead, an insistence that grappling with a racial hierarchy that Niebuhr largely ignored might not only enrich his musings on a corrupted civilization but offer him, and us, far more effective tools in diagnosing its ills and healing its maladies.

Throughout *Critical Race Theology*, Floyd-Thomas connects the dots between seemingly disparate forms of thought and behavior. He argues that Francis Fukuyama is the child of Niebuhr. (There goes that screwball again, though one sees the parallels: both proffered a view of liberal democracy's triumph that lacked a crucial moderating element, for Niebuhr race, for Fukuyama the role of the church in civil society, which is ironic given that his father was a theologian at Chicago Theological Seminary where I once taught). He detects the metaphysical silences that swallow the Black voice while discerning the rich Black humanism that carries it forward in quarters untouched by believers. He artfully blends sacred and secular cultures into what might be termed a *sacrular* sensibility, one that lives at the intersections that enliven Critical Race Theology along several axes of personal and cultural identity.

Floyd-Thomas offers a rousing and complicated genealogy of the origins and evolution of violence in the name of God and government, and masterfully deconstructs the religious justifications of the use of weapons of all sorts – physical, psychological and moral – to bolster white supremacy. Yet, amid the vicious assaults on democracy from within, from some of its supposedly noble defenders, Floyd-Thomas not only manages to dissect their hypocrisy, but to outline a viable hope that is far more than a belief. It is, instead, an act, a sustained gesture, and a determined performance of possibility.

Critical Race Theology is a timely and brilliant intervention, just the book we need now, by the right person to write it for us. Only a thinker determined to act courageously can help us. Only a critic emboldened to tell the truth by the ancestors he channels can inspire us. Only a formidable scholar able to guide us through the thicket of dense critical reflection can enlighten us. Only a soldier of truth convinced of deep solidarity can help us go forward in hope with the expectation that we can make a difference and change the world. These are no platitudes. Rather they are principles of action inspired by a vital and dedicated theologian and activist who has pledged to help us transform our nation and the world by thinking right and doing better.

Introduction

Making America Possible Again: Toward a Critical Race Theology

In August 1790, President George Washington visited Newport, Rhode Island, in the hopes of generating popular support for the ratification of the Bill of Rights, which included protections for religious liberty. Countless members of the Newport community, including leaders and members of the city's religious denominations, crowded together to listen to the new president. In the audience gathered in Newport's public square that day were members of the city's Jewish congregation, Jeshu at Israel Synagogue (now known as Touro Synagogue). Moses Seixas, the Warden of Newport's synagogue, wrote a letter to Washington on behalf of the congregation and expressed the congregation's elation at having Washington as a leader as well as their joy in living under the political protection of a national Constitution that they were confident would not only prevent the establishment of a national church or religion but also finally guarantee true religious liberty to all people.

That visit occasioned a famous exchange of letters between Washington and the "Hebrew Congregations of Newport," in which the Jewish community of Newport addressed the first president of the newly formed American republic—and he replied. Four days after leaving Newport, Washington wrote a reply to the congregation. Extending beyond a concisely banal and quaintly polite acknowledgment of their letter, Washington's reply echoed the congregation's belief that the newly established United States was now a nation that would give "to bigotry no sanction, [and] to persecution no assistance" and continued to make a clear distinction that American society and culture's creation of the wall of separation enabled the United States to move from mere religious toleration to true religious liberty.

Religious toleration assumes that government can either give or take away the "privilege" of exercising one's religion. By contrast, religious liberty is an inalienable right that cannot be taken away by the civil state. Washington's letter to the Hebrew Congregation in Newport, Rhode Island, has come to be regarded as one of the most important pronouncements of a new philosophy concerning religion, namely, that government exists in part for the protection of religious liberty and matters of conscience. Throughout Washington's presidency, he deemed "religion and morality the indispensable supports of political prosperity and argued that religion was necessary for morality" within the ascendant political culture of the new nation.[1]

As Washington and many of his contemporaries presumed, the interplay between religion and morality can point us to knowledge, principles, and practices that extend beyond mundane human experience. Because of the corruptibility of institutions and the fallibility of human beings, religion and morality were deemed necessary to the social fabric so that each can benefit from incorporating ideas, frameworks, or habits of mind from the other. Above and beyond that, if religion serves as a fundamental cornerstone of both public and private life, it may lead people to intuit the will of the Divine while also inspiring one another to live better, more ethical mundane existences. Many people of this

---

[1] Martin E. Marty, *Pilgrims in Their Own Land: 500 Years of Religion in America* (New York: Penguin Books, 1985), 158.

era concluded that, if the state could constrain the civil power and privilege of established religion, it stands to reason that social equality and tolerance for human difference under the law among all peoples would prevail for churches and society alike.[2]

The disestablishment of a national church or religion in the United States is directly contrary to the contemporary claims of white Evangelicals and their conservative counterparts that America was a "Christian" nation from its inception. Despite the overall influence of the First Great Awakening and impact of the Enlightenment on the post-Revolutionary American society, we witness the emergence of a democratic republic that is neither completely secular nor sacred in its orientation. Upon its ratification in December 15, 1791, the First Amendment of the Bill of Rights read: "Congress shall make no law respecting an establishment of religion or prohibiting the free exercise thereof; or abridging the freedom of speech, or of the press; or the right of the people peaceably to assemble, and to petition the government for a redress of grievances." Given the immense worry over the Bill of Rights, the championing of religious liberty alongside these other civil rights, such as free speech, free press, and peaceful protest, as the bedrock of the new nation is a remarkable development.

Though these issues were and remain hotly debated at the state level, the premise that no religious denomination or church would receive explicit federal endorsement and the nation's government would not intervene in anyone's personal experience and public expression, including the right to worship, is quite an amazing promise.[3]

---

[2] Henry Steele Commager, *The Empire of Reason: How Europe Imagined and Europe Realised the Enlightenment* (London: Phoenix, 2000), 210–11.

[3] Nathan O. Hatch, *Democratization of American Christianity* (New Haven, CT: Yale University Press, 2011), 95; James P. Byrd and James Hudnut-Beumler, *The Story of Religion in America: An Introduction* (Louisville, KY: Westminster John Knox Press, 2021), 134; and John F. Wilson, "Religion, Government, and Power in the New American Nation," in

Several sentences from Washington's letter come to mind when faced with many of the dilemmas of our current moment:

> The citizens of the United States of America have a right to applaud themselves for having given to [humankind] examples of an enlarged and liberal policy—a policy worthy of imitation. All possess alike liberty of conscience and immunities of citizenship.

> It is now no more that toleration is spoken of as if it were the indulgence of one class of people that another enjoyed the exercise of their inherent natural rights, for, happily, the Government of the United States, which gives to bigotry no sanction, to persecution no assistance, requires only that they who live under its protection should demean themselves as good citizens in giving it on all occasions their effectual support.

> May the children of the stock of Abraham who dwell in this land continue to merit and enjoy the good will of the other inhabitants—while every one shall sit in safety under [their] own vine and fig tree and there shall be none to make [them] afraid.[4]

On the one hand, the grandiose exuberance that Washington displays of what we would herein call "American exceptionalism" echoes the best virtues and highest ideals of the newborn society. The idealism espoused by Washington's invocation—the imperative

Religion and American Politics: From the Colonial Period to the 1980s, ed. Mark A. Knoll (New York: Oxford University Press, 2007), 77–91.

[4] "From George Washington to the Hebrew Congregation in Newport, Rhode Island, 18 August 1790," Founders Online, National Archives, https://founders.archives.gov/documents/Washington/05-06-02-0135. [Original source: Mark A. Mastromarino, ed., *The Papers of George Washington, Presidential Series*, vol. 6, 1 July 1790–30 November 1790 (Charlottesville: University Press of Virginia, 1996), 284–86.]

that each person should be free and content to live "under their own vine and fig tree"—not only stated in this letter but repeated elsewhere in his writings, including his famous "Farewell Address," is concentrated in an oft-quoted passage from Hebrew Bible, Micah 4:4: "Everybody shall sit under their own vine and fig tree, and no one shall make them afraid"(see also 1 Kings 4:25; Zechariah 3:10).[5] In the wake of the American Revolution, Washington had a duty of care to calm the fears and distress of his fellow citizens of the newly established nation.

On the other hand, Washington's sentiments border on empty political platitudes for a national populace that both directly and indirectly experienced a history of prejudice and persecution. A few years earlier, during Washington's presidential inauguration, the idea of having the incoming president swear an oath on a borrowed Bible was an impromptu decision made by a special congressional committee mere hours before the ceremony. I emphasize the word *borrowed* here because, ironically or not, none of the lawmakers or leaders who made the decision actually possessed a copy of the Bible and had to scurry in madcap fashion to find one in order to accomplish this symbolic gesture.[6] This spontaneous move established a feature of this solemn ritual that has endured for more than two centuries and helped give rise to what sociologist Robert Bellah famously termed "civil religion."[7] Moreover, amid

---

[5] See Daniel L. Dreisbach, "'The 'Vine and Fig Tree' in George Washington's Letters: Reflections on a Biblical Motif in the Literature of the American Founding Era," *Anglican and Episcopal History* 76, no.3 (September 2007): 299–326; Walter Brueggemann, "'Vine and Fig Tree': A Case Study in Imagination and Criticism," *Catholic Biblical Quarterly* 43, no. 2 (April 1981): 199.

[6] Jill Lepore, *These Truths: A History of the United States* (New York: W. W. Norton, 2019), 133.

[7] Robert N. Bellah's "Civil Religion in America," *Daedalus* 96, no. 1, Religion in America [Winter 1967]: 1–21) sparked widespread multidisciplinary controversy within the scholarly arenas of religious

their congratulations and celebration of Washington's inauguration, members of the first Congress spoke of their fellow countrymen (note the gender exclusivity) as "the freest people on the face of the earth."[8] Of course, the visionary leaders of this newly formed government did not extend this same spirit of imagination, invention, and ingenuity to the abolition of chattel slavery, the equality of women, the sovereignty of Indigenous peoples, and a comprehensive pathway to citizenship for all immigrants.

Leaping forward to our historical moment, much of the discourse about the present state of our nation is permeated with questions and concerns about "white supremacy," "white Christian nationalism," and the "culture wars." First and foremost, what can and must be said about white supremacy? Philosopher Charles W. Mills asserts,

> White supremacy is the unnamed political system that has made the world what it is today … But though it covers more than two thousand years of Western political thought and runs the ostensible gamut of political systems, there will be no mention of the basic political system that has shaped the world for the past several hundred years.[9]

The recognition that this glaring omission is neither incidental nor accidental in nature haunts so much of our history. This is especially harrowing when giving deep consideration to how this manifests itself in our religious life as a people and a nation. As

---

studies, theology, US history, sociology, and American studies for roughly fifty years. See also Robert N. Bellah, Comment: [Twenty Years after Bellah: Whatever Happened to American Civil Religion?], *Sociological Analysis*, Thematic Issue: A Durkheimian Miscellany, 50, no. 2 (Summer 1989): 147.

[8] Eric Foner, *The Story of American Freedom* (New York: W. W. Norton, 1998), 42.

[9] Charles W. Mills, *The Racial Contract*, 25th anniversary ed. (Ithaca, NY: Cornell University Press, 2022), 1.

founder and CEO of the Public Religion Research Institute, Robert P. Jones, notes,

> American Christianity's theological core has been thoroughly structured by an interest in protecting white supremacy. While it may seem obvious to mainstream white Christians today that slavery, segregation, and overt declarations of white supremacy are antithetical to the teachings of Jesus, such a conviction is, in fact, recent and only partially conscious for most white American Christians and churches.

Furthermore, Jones states,

> The unsettling truth is that, for nearly all of American history, the Jesus conjured by most white congregations was not merely indifferent to the status quo of racial inequality; he demanded its defense and preservation as part of the natural, divinely ordained order of things.[10]

According to historian Lerone Martin, white Christian nationalism is "the impulse to make whiteness and conservative Christianity the foundation and guidepost of American governance and culture."[11] Over the course of three centuries—and especially its influence over the last half-century—the emergence of a vocal, virulent white Christian nationalism has animated the rising tide of oppression, exclusion, and even genocide of minority and marginalized groups while also securing privilege for white Protestants.[12]

---

[10] Robert P. Jones, *White Too Long: The Legacy of White Supremacy in American Christianity* (New York: Simon & Schuster, 2021), 6.

[11] Lerone Martin, *The Gospel of J. Edgar Hoover: How the FBI Aided and Abetted the Rise of White Christian Nationalism* (Princeton, NJ: Princeton University Press, 2023), 4.

[12] See Michelle Goldberg, *Kingdom Coming: The Rise of Christian Nationalism* (New York: W. W. Norton, 2007); Sarah Posner, *Unholy: How*

Before it took on its ubiquitous presence in public discourse, James Davison Hunter reframed the national debate over cultural politics in his 1991 book, *Culture Wars: The Struggle to Define America*. Hunter broached this subject as a raging battle between "traditionalists," who are committed to moral ideals inherited from the past, and "progressivists," who idealized societal transformation. These divergent worldviews, Hunter argues, were responsible for increasingly heated and politicized disputes over such sociocultural issues as affirmative action, abortion, immigration, economics, sexuality, and the overall role of religion in society.[13] Whereas there can be no doubt that there always have been (and probably always will be) dramatic debates and differences of opinion about important issues shaping the fate of the nation, one has to wonder whether a "culture war" must be both inevitable and intractable in nature.[14]

White Christian Nationalists Powered the Trump Presidency, and the Devastating Legacy They Left Behind (New York: Random House, 2021); Katherine Stewart, *The Power Worshippers: Inside the Dangerous Rise of Religious Nationalism* (New York: Bloomsbury Publishing, 2022); Andrew L. Whitehead and Samuel L. Perry, *Taking America Back for God: Christian Nationalism in the United States,* updated edition (New York: Oxford University Press, 2022); Carter Heyward, *The Seven Deadly Sins of White Christian Nationalism: A Call to Action* (Lanham, MD: Rowman & Littlefield, 2022); Philip S. Gorski and Samuel L. Perry, *The Flag and the Cross: White Christian Nationalism and the Threat to American Democracy* (New York: Oxford University Press, 2022); Pamela Cooper-White, *The Psychology of Christian Nationalism: Why People Are Drawn In and How to Talk Across the Divide* (Minneapolis: Fortress Press, 2022); Bradley Onishi, *Preparing for War: The Extremist History of White Christian Nationalism—And What Comes Next* (Minneapolis: Broadleaf Books, 2023).

[13] See E. J. Dionne Jr. and Michael Cromartie, eds., *Is There a Culture War? A Dialogue on Values and American Public Life* (Washington, DC: Brookings Institution and the Pew Research Center, 2007).

[14] James Davison Hunter, *Culture Wars: The Struggle to Define America*

As if speaking directly to contemporary fears of division, demonization, and exclusion, the late religious historian and activist Vincent Harding posed a critical question at the core of his classic text *Hope and History*: "Is America possible?" Framing this query, Harding states,

> For it is a question that has always been at the heart of the ... quest for democracy in this land. And wherever we have seen these freedom seekers, community organizers, artisans of democracy, standing their ground, calling others to the struggle, advancing into danger, creating new realities, it is clear that they are taking the question seriously, shaping their own answers, testing the possibilities of their dreams.[15]

Although speaking directly to the history of the civil rights movement, Harding contends that the true story that unfolded throughout much of his life at the nexus of academy, activism, and advocacy was dedicated to the steadfast belief that this saga "for freedom, democracy and transformation is a great, continuing human classic whose liberating lessons are available to all of us, especially those who are committed to work and sacrifice for the creation of a better country [and] a more hopeful world."[16] Despite the vehement disagreements between the Left and Right that have defined the past few decades, a movement to realign politics, faith, and culture in search of common ground is sorely needed.

(New York: Basic Books, 1991); Robert Wuthnow, *The Restructuring of American Religion: Society and Faith since World War II* (Princeton, NJ: Princeton University Press, 2021); Dionne Jr. and Cromartie, eds., *Is There a Culture War?*; Robert Wuthnow, *The Struggle for America's Soul: Evangelicals, Liberals, and Secularism* (Grand Rapids, MI: W. B. Eerdmans, 1989); Robert P. Jones, *The End of White Christian America* (New York: Simon & Schuster, 2017).

[15] Vincent Harding, *Hope and History: Why We Must Share the Story of the Movement* (Maryknoll, NY: Orbis Books, 1990), 177.

[16] Harding, *Hope and History*, 10.

Harding's question—"Is America possible?"—inspires and invites each of us to work, just as it reminds all of us of the painfully obvious: if any of us are to survive, we all must work toward creating a world where the lives on the margins are no longer intentionally targeted for disease, disaster, destruction, despair, and death. Why bother with hope? Amid the murder and menacing of countless innocent folks by the savagery of conservative politicians, predators, pariahs, law enforcement officers, vigilantes, mass shooters, bigots, and domestic terrorists, the moral imperative to affirm our contributions to this society is upon us. The moral imperative to affirm our humanity is upon us. The moral imperative to affirm our resilience because of—and not in spite of—our faith in the face of deadly modes of oppression is upon us.

I seek a new vision of the Social Gospel that embraces what I am calling *critical race theology*. In this regard, I find critical race theology to be intimately and inextricably linked to its analogue in the legal arena, critical race theory (CRT). Legal scholars, racial theorists, and other academic advocates of CRT have used their insights to focus on how the Constitution and the legal system have been used to perpetuate inequality and injustice throughout US history. In this fashion, CRT has provided a helpful framework for examining, explaining, and exposing how oppressive social dynamics have undermined our laws and societal institutions.

The progenitors and early proponents of CRT, legal scholars, such as Derrick Bell, Kimberlé Crenshaw, Patricia Williams, Mari Matsuda, Cheryl Harris, Richard Delgado, Gerald Torres, Charles Lawrence, and Angela Harris among others, emerged within the legal academy in the 1970s and 1980s.[17] Although they had their

---

[17] Writer Benjamin Wallace-Wells of the *New Yorker* magazine notes that the origin of CRT dates to roughly forty years ago and is "academic scholarship ... by a group of legal scholars who ... argued that the white supremacy of the past lived on in the laws and societal rules

own diverse perspectives and priorities, these pioneering figures were unified against the prevailing logic of the dominant system of American jurisprudence. Their work challenged the assumption that the law writ large was disconnected from the creation and cultivation of our society's racial hierarchies.

In his classic text *Faces at the Bottom of the Well*, Derrick Bell describes the core premise of CRT:

> I truly believe that analysis of legal developments through fiction, personal experiences, and the stories of people on the bottom illustrates how race and racism continue to dominate society. The techniques also help in assessing sexism, classism, homophobia, and other forms of oppression.[18]

This concept of the overlapping and interlocking nature of identities—race, gender, class, age, ethnicity, sexuality, ability, nationality, education, region, and, yes, religion—discrimination, and disadvantage speaks most directly to intersectionality, a concept developed by pioneering CRT scholar Kimberlé Crenshaw as a central framework for CRT analysis. According to Crenshaw, CRT explains that "the so-called American dilemma was not simply a matter of prejudice but a matter of structured disadvantages that stretched across American society."[19] By offering scrutiny to the vulnerabilities of women of color, specifically those

---

of the present." Benjamin Wallace-Wells, "How a Conservative Activist Invented the Conflict Over Critical Race Theory," *New Yorker*, June 18, 2021, https://www.newyorker.com/news/annals-of-inquiry/how-a-conservative-activist-invented-the-conflict-over-critical-race-theory.

[18] Derrick Bell, *Faces at the Bottom of the Well: The Permanence of Racism* (New York: Basic Books, 2018), 144.

[19] Faith Karimi, "What Critical Race Theory Is—And Isn't," *CNN* online, May 10, 2021, https://www.cnn.com/2020/10/01/us/critical-race-theory-explainer-trnd/index.html.

from immigrant and socially disadvantaged communities, Crenshaw "exposed and sought to dismantle the instantiations of marginalization that operated within institutionalized discourses that legitimized existing power relations (e.g., law) and at the same time, she placed into sharp relief how discourses of resistance (e.g., feminism and antiracism) could themselves function as sites that produced and legitimized marginalization."[20]

In early 2021, controversy rose about the role of CRT in contemporary US society. Marisa Iati writes that conservative pundits and politicians have used the term pejoratively as a "catchall phrase for nearly any examination of systemic racism in the present."[21] For instance, the *Washington Post* reports that, whereas the phrase *critical race theory* was mentioned about 132 times on Fox News shows in 2020, it was mentioned 1,860 times between January 1 and June 24, 2021.[22] The sensationalism fostered by right-wing pundits and politicians has led to a frenzy of anti-CRT localized protests, as well as numerous bills proposed by Republican legislators in over fifteen states, that would force school districts to end initiatives to acknowledge individual and institutional acts of racism within their curricula.[23] This outrage

---

[20] Devon W. Carbado, Kimberlé Williams Crenshaw, Vickie M. Mays, and Barbara Tomlinson, "Intersectionality: Mapping the Movements of a Theory," *Du Bois Review: Social Science Research on Race* 10, no. 2 (2013): 304.

[21] Marisa Iati, "What Is Critical Race Theory, and Why Do Republicans Want to Ban It in Schools?" *Washington Post*, May 29, 2021, https://www.washingtonpost.com/education/2021/05/29/critical-race-theory-bans-schools/.

[22] Jeremy Barr, "Critical Race Theory Is the Hottest Topic on Fox News. And It's Only Getting Hotter," *Washington Post*, June 24, 2021, https://www.washingtonpost.com/media/2021/06/24/critical-race-theory-fox-news.

[23] Nicquel Terry Ellis and Boris Sanchez, "Turmoil Erupts In School District after Claims that Critical Race Theory and Transgender Policy Are Being Pushed," *CNN*, June 24, 2021, https://www.cnn.com/2021/06/24/

has been given voice on conservative cable news channels like Fox News, One America Network, and Newsmax. CRT has been condemned on social media outlets spearheaded by the likes of Christopher Rufo, Dick Morris, Steve K. Bannon, and Ben Shapiro. CRT has been portrayed in right-wing media circles as "the basis of race-conscious policies, diversity trainings and education about racism, regardless of how much the academic concept actually affects those efforts."[24]

In 2022, dozens of state legislatures and governors—most of them Republican-dominated—proposed laws and executive orders banning the teaching of CRT; "woke ideology"; or, more broadly, aggressively defunding diversity, equity, and inclusion (DEI) initiatives. Perhaps most noteworthy was newly elected Virginia Governor Glenn Youngkin's "day one" executive order banning the teaching of CRT and other allegedly "divisive concepts" that are vaguely targeted in this conservative outcry. When the phrase *critical race theory* was evoked by right-wing politicians and conservative media pundits, it was "intentionally used as a scare tactic to appeal to that base," William H. Frey argues.[25]

---

us/loudoun-county-school-board-meeting/index.html; Eesha Pendharkar, "Efforts to Root Out Racism in Schools Would Unravel Under 'Critical Race Theory' Bills," *Education Week*, May 26, 2021, https://www.edweek. org/leadership/efforts-to-root-out-racism-in-schools-would-unravel-under-critical-race-theory-bills/2021/05.

[24] Ben Mathias-Lilley, "The Problem Isn't that Some Republicans Don't Know What 'Critical Race Theory' Is. It's That Many of Them Do." *Slate*, June 25, 2021, https://slate.com/news-and-politics/2021/06/critical-race-theory-republicans-desantis-ben-shapiro.html; Marisa Iati, "What Is Critical Race Theory, and Why Do Republicans Want to Ban It in Schools?"

[25] William H. Frey, "Anti-CRT Bills Are Aimed to Incite The GOP Base—Not Parents," *Brookings*, March 30, 2022, https://www.brookings.edu/articles/anti-crt-bills-are-aimed-to-incite-the-gop-base-not-parents/; Bryan Anderson, "Critical Race Theory Is a Flashpoint for Conservatives, But What

Many high-profile GOP officials are also actively pushing to erode key safeguards at public universities that previously shielded professors from political interference. For example, Texas Lieutenant Governor Dan Patrick, another outspoken conservative, openly has threatened to terminate tenure at the University of Texas after the faculty leadership reaffirmed their belief in academic freedom as well as the right to teach about racial equality and gender justice.[26] Right-wing groups also have launched defamatory campaigns against school leaders, educators, librarians, and teachers' unions to derail efforts.[27] During a January 2023 inaugural event, Florida Governor Ron DeSantis proudly declared that his state "is where woke goes to die."[28] In the following month, DeSantis stacked the Board of Governors of New College of Florida, a well-known liberal arts college, with right-wing ideologues and has directed universities to report their DEI efforts and CRT classes to his office.[29]

Does It Mean?," *PBS NewHour*, November 4, 2021, https://www.pbs.org/newshour/education/so-much-buzz-but-what-is-critical-race-theory.

[26] Andrew Schneider, "Dan Patrick's Plan to End Tenure at Texas Universities Could Have Dire Consequences, Experts Warn," *Houston Public Media: inDepth Politics*, March 28, 2022, https://www.houstonpublicmedia.org/articles/news/in-depth/2022/03/28/421924/patricks-plan-to-eliminate-tenure-at-texas-state-universities-could-have-dire-consequences-experts-warn/.

[27] Tyler Kingkade, "In Rare Move, School Librarian Fights Back in Court Against Conservative Activists," *NBC News*, August 13, 2022, https://www.nbcnews.com/news/us-news/rare-move-school-librarian-fights-back-court-conservative-activists-rcna42800.

[28] Emily Mae Czachor, "'Florida Is Where Woke Goes to Die,' Gov. Ron DeSantis Says after Reelection Victory," *CBS News*, November 9, 2022, https://www.cbsnews.com/news/ron-desantis-florida-where-woke-goes-to-die-midterm-election-win/.

[29] Jonathan Feingold, "Florida Gov. DeSantis Leads the GOP's National Charge against Public Education that Includes Lessons on

Governor Ron DeSantis and Florida's GOP lawmakers worked together to pass the Florida's HB 7, also known as the Stop Wrongs Against Our Kids and Employees (Stop W.O.K.E. Act). This law prohibits educators from teaching or even expressing viewpoints on racial or gender discrimination, especially in addressing the legacies of American slavery, white privilege, sexism, and anti-LGBTQIA+ bias.[30] Following a lawsuit led by a multiracial group, including the American Civil Liberties Union (ACLU) and the Legal Defense Fund (LDF), in late 2022, a federal judge issued an order immediately blocking the Stop W.O.K.E. Act based on its violation the First and Fourteenth Amendments of the Constitution.

Why does any of this appreciation of intersectional realities matter? It matters because it is vitally important to understanding what it means to be fully and freely human. When trying to make sense of the various dynamics and dilemmas that shape people's lives on an individual or collective basis, it is insufficient to view people strictly through an external lens that gazes upon superficial distinctions while ignoring the myriad permutations and possibilities that brought them into existence and truly define their sense of being. We must be ever mindful of what shortcomings and omissions happen when the worldviews of women have always only been dictated by the experiences of men, the historic achievements of non-white racial ethnic people solely defined by whites, the terms of

---

Race and Sexual Orientation," *The Conversation*, January 18, 2023, https://theconversation.com/florida-gov-desantis-leads-the-gops-national-charge-against-public-education-that-includes-lessons-on-race-and-sexual-orientation-196369.

[30] American Civil Liberties Union, "Judge Blocks Florida's 'Stop W.O.K.E.' Censorship Bill from Taking Effect in Higher Education," *ACLU: Press Releases*, November 17, 2022, https://www.aclu.org/press-releases/judge-blocks-floridas-stop-woke-censorship-bill-taking-effect-higher-education#:%7E:text=The%20court%20order%20found%20the,expression%20of%20the%20opposite%20viewpoints.

happy, meaningful lives for LGBTQIA+ folks derived solely from the perspective of cis-gendered, heteronormative folks, and the most basic functioning of society for the working poor and needy determined by and favoring the rich and greedy.

As will be discussed in this book, this is not an attempt to advance a saga of retrograde notions of the overly simplistic markers of identity that serve to make us one-trick ponies. Rather, I recognize the complex humanity and messy spirituality that dwells within every one of us if we dare look within ourselves and our fellow humans. Recognizing and regarding intersectionality for the marginalized and oppressed creates a bulwark against the dominant culture's desire to enact its "divide and conquer" mandate even in the attempts to set each person against their very own soul. As Black feminist philosopher Audre Lorde succinctly states, "There is no thing as a single-issue struggle because we do not live single-issue lives." Acknowledgment of shared histories, similar struggles, and systemic exclusion is the first and most vital step in repairing the damage done by a dominant society that has sought to eradicate the bodies and erase the memories of those who have been trampled underfoot by the powerful.

The scholarship of Derrick Bell is pivotal to envisioning the synergy between law and religion that makes CRT not just feasible but fertile. As the first tenured Black professor at Harvard Law School and godfather of CRT, Bell was a towering figure in the burgeoning field of CRT, dedicating his writing and teaching career to bearing witness to how people of color, especially Black folks, were consistently marginalized and oppressed by practically every metric and index of social well-being. In his final law review article, "Law as a Religion," Bell states that many people hold superficial beliefs about religion and law but fail to question where these ideas come from or whether they are worthy of respect.[31] Advocating

---

[31] Derrick Bell, "Law as a Religion," *Case Western Reserve Law Review* 69 (2018): 265. Also, see George H. Taylor, "Racism as 'The Nation's

the value and vitality of both sides, Bell contends "religion and law are each great and mostly unacknowledged mysteries. People gain basic religious beliefs at an early age and simply accept what they are taught. Some recognition of law comes later but again there is more learning than challenging" of established doctrines.[32] He was driven by the conviction that religious values and spiritual virtue inform the overall quality of public life in America, especially within our political culture, and he worked to stop the terrible drift away from both common ground and common sense.

As Reinhold Niebuhr once declared, "The sad duty of politics is to establish justice in a sinful world." Religion and the law have been the two great ordering principles of human experience, yet Bell firmly believed these two forces needed to keep their safe distance from one another for the good of society in a responsible and respectful manner. Bell attests that advocates of both religion and law

> claim to elevate human conduct. Law claims to pursue justice (including racial justice) while religion claims to inspire love and good will among humans (including racial good will). Each also relies on blind faith that it achieves its fundamental goals. It calls upon this faith in defiance of evidence and reason. We know, for example, that the Resurrection of Christ could not and did not happen as a matter of science; yet, Christian religion calls upon the faithful to accept the Resurrection. Similarly, we know from history and experience that law will never deliver justice and that law in America will

---

Crucial Sin': Theology and Derrick Bell," *Michigan Journal of Race and Law* 9, no. 2 (2004); George H. Taylor, "Race, Religion and Law: The Tension Between Spirit and Its Institutionalization," *University of Maryland Law Journal of Race, Religion, Gender, and Class* 6, no. 1 (2006); Jean Stefancic, "Law, Religion, and Racial Justice: A Comment on Derrick Bell's Last Article," *Case Western Reserve Law Review* 69 (2018).

[32] Derrick Bell, "Law as a Religion," 265.

never deliver racial justice; yet, we are called upon to believe somehow justice is just around the corner.[33]

In the case of both CRT and critical race theology, the power of narrative is a central driving force for both of them.

The proliferation of scholarship on race, racism, and religion over the last half century provides much of the *raison d'être* for this present study. Though I arrived at this concept on my own terms, the phrase *critical race theology* is not original to me alone. In his 2017 doctoral dissertation, "A God Worth Worshiping: Toward a Critical Race Theology," Duane Terrence Loynes Sr. asserts a precondition of critical race theology, contending,

> Any theology that seeks to speak to the marginalization of people and systems of inequity—especially when these conditions are interwoven with particular narratives of Christianity—*must* be avowedly and unapologetically political … Critical race theology, like all theology should be, is concerned with a faithful explication of the Christian Scriptures that is accountable to the Christian tradition. However, it does not see its prophetic task in challenging racism to be in any conflict with its alethic aims.[34]

As will be addressed throughout this text, it will be useful to interrogate this concept of alethic truth—that there is an objective reality in the world above and beyond the scope of subjectivity.[35] According to Loynes, there are at least two key features that are integral to the overall project. First, critical race theology is

---

[33] Derrick Bell, "Law as a Religion," 265.

[34] Duane Terrence Loynes, "A God Worth Worshiping: Toward a Critical Race Theology," Marquette University, Milwaukee, WI (ProQuest Dissertations Publishing, 2017), 8.

[35] See Ruth Groff, "The Truth of the Matter: Roy Bhaskar's Critical Realism and the Concept of Alethic Truth," *Philosophy of the Social Sciences* 30, no. 3 (2000): 407–35.

necessary because normative theology and the theologians who advance its goals "fail to name the pervasive ways in which White supremacy has shaped and sustained the Christian theological tradition, they are unaware of and unable to halt the theological perpetuation of a racially hierarchized culture." Second and more importantly, because normative theologians have not only been inattentive to this problem but are largely indebted to its propagation, Loynes argues, "They do not (indeed, cannot) engage in the liberating project of systematically reimagining theology in a manner that includes those who were formerly marginalized."[36]

Recognizing these conditions, we must also recognize how there has been a default mode of thinking that the attention to racial inequality and social injustice is somehow incompatible with the "real" work of normative Christian theology. Issues of human differences and diverse identities are always being kept at arm's length rather than wholeheartedly embraced as a means of overturning oppression and ensuring empowerment for our fellow humans. If any consideration is given to these pressing social concerns at all, they are dismissively dubbed as "contextual theology" and rendered as a lesser, subordinate form of theological writing and thought, or they are reframed as a subfield of ethics as if theology and ethics are mutually exclusive. While Christianity upholds belief in one God, so-called contextual theology at least recognizes that there are infinitely different ways that people of diverse backgrounds may understand and relate to God based on their own cultural perception and historical experiences. Arguably, any theology that ignores these realities would ring false and cannot be seen as valid.

Historian of religion Charles Long reminds us,

> Theologies are about power, the power of God, but equally about the power of specific forms of discourse

---

[36] Loynes, "A God Worth Worshiping: Toward a Critical Race Theology," 5.

about power. These discourses are about the hegemony
of power—the distribution and economy of this power in
heaven and on earth—whether in the ecclesiastical locus
of a pope or, more generally since the modern period,
the center of this power in the modern Western world.
It is this kind of power which is attacked in the opaque
theologies, for this power has justified and sanctified the
oppression rendering vast numbers of persons and several
cultures subject to economic-military oppression and
transparent to the knowledge of the West.[37]

Whereas the original iteration by Loynes understands this power
implicitly, the "fierce urgency of now" demands that we recognize
the uses and abuses of said power explicitly and directly. To this
point, postmodern theorist Michel Foucault reminds us that
"power is tolerable only on condition that it masks a substantial
part of itself. Its success is proportional to an ability to hide its own
mechanisms."[38] While the initial iteration of critical race theology
has been envisioned as theological methodology, this book is loudly
and proudly a work of moral theology. In this regard, dealing with
critical race theology according to the presumable standard goals of
theological discourse as "God-talk," we can recognize how so much
of the constructions of theological responses are preoccupied
with how we talk about these crises rather than deliberately and
decisively debating the crises themselves.[39]

---

[37] Charles H. Long, *Significations: Signs, Symbols, and Images in the Interpretation of Religion* (Philadelphia: Fortress Press, 1986), 209.

[38] Michel Foucault, *The History of Sexuality I: An Introduction* (New York: Vintage Books, 1990).

[39] This assessment corresponds to Theodore Jennings's insight that "there is a growing danger that the work of theology is being replaced by the work of preparing to do theology." Theodore W. Jennings, *The Vocation of the Theologian* (Philadelphia: Fortress Press, 1985), 2–3.

Advancing critical race theology as a specific mode of moral theology pays strict attention to the actual convergence of theology and ethics as an attempt at positive societal transformation rather than scholarly lip service. As an academic discipline, moral theology studies the nexus of human thought, being, and action. The emphasis here is on deliberate acts, development of moral principles and ethical norms, and their application to human actions in general, as well as in particular situations, in light of divine revelation and human reason.

By reframing critical race theology to focus on the moral rather than methodological dimensions, I argue that we contend with *why* critical race theology operates as a mode of discourse instead of *how* it operates. This reorientation serves as the basis for an informed dialogue about human freedom, justice, equality, and dignity as the crux of Christianity as a liberating faith. In Luke 4:18–19, there is a simple but direct prophetic command to all so-called followers of Christ: "The Spirit of the Lord is on me, because [God] has anointed me to preach good news to the poor. [God] has sent me to proclaim freedom for the prisoners and recovery of sight for the blind, to release the oppressed, to proclaim the year of the Lord's favor." In his reflections on the nature and task of Christian theology, James Cone instructs us:

> Christian theology is a theology of liberation. It is a rational study of the being of God in the world in light of the existential situation of an oppressed community, relating the forces of liberation to the essence of the gospel, which is Jesus Christ. This means that its sole reason for existence is to put into ordered speech the meaning of God's activity in the world, so that the community of the oppressed will recognize that its inner thrust for liberation is not only consistent with the gospel but is the gospel of Jesus Christ. There can be no Christian theology that is not identified unreservedly with those who

are humiliated and abused. In fact, theology ceases to be a theology of the gospel when it fails to arise out of the community of the oppressed.[40]

As troubling as the CRT debate has been within the broader society, it has become an equally pernicious dilemma within the church. Contrary to serving as a divinely inspired beacon of hope to guide us toward a better, brighter future, it appears that the contemporary church is sliding into the muck and mire of the world without a clear vision of how to save anyone from despair, including itself. Communications scholar and pastor Andre E. Johnson observes, "The belief that CRT and Intersectionality are problematic comes not only from a lack of understanding of the terms, but how conservatives and white evangelicals have positioned them as anti-faith—and more particularly, anti-Christian."[41] To Johnson's point, many of the folks fighting so ardently against CRT seem to be doing so not because it is inconsistent with the actual life, lessons, and legacy of Jesus Christ, but rather because it is inconvenient to how they preach, teach, and do outreach based on their interpretation of the faith. In times like these, I often reflect on the English writer G. K. Chesterton's refrain: "The Christian ideal has not been tried and found wanting; it has been found difficult and left untried."[42]

The narrowmindedness on race and ethnicity in many US ecclesial settings mirrors a similar animus by predominantly white

---

[40] James H. Cone, *A Black Theology of Liberation* (Maryknoll, NY: Orbis Books, 2010), 1.

[41] Andre E. Johnson, "Where Did White Evangelicalism's Hatred of Critical Race Theory Really Begin?" *Religion Dispatches*, June 23, 2021, https://religiondispatches.org/where-did-white-evangelicalisms-hatred-of-critical-race-theory-really-begin/.

[42] G. K. Chesterton, "The Unfinished Temple," in *What's Wrong with the World* (1910), https://www.gutenberg.org/files/1717/1717-h/1717-h.htm#link2H_4_0006.

male leadership toward gender and sexuality. Put another way, if the church can be shamelessly racist in the name of God, it is not mutually exclusive that we have also been self-righteously sexist.

Unfortunately, the constant ways that conservatives misinterpret, manipulate, and mangle the Holy Bible and the US Constitution to justify beliefs and behaviors not addressed in either text are the chief resemblances between the Holy Bible and the US Constitution in too many of our public debates. Derrick Bell argues that, far too often, "both the Bible and the Constitution are more honored than read, more accepted than understood, more quoted than respected."[43] In the face of the sociopolitical transformation that recently led to Trumpism, a resilient spirit of social justice has been rooted in the recognition that every human being should have an undeniable right to share in the common good of God's creation. Toward that end, this book is an effort to imagine and proclaim a reawakening of the social gospel, one intending to redeem American Christianity in our time.

Henry David Thoreau argued, "To speak practically and as a citizen, unlike those who call themselves no-government men, I ask for, not at once no government, but at once a better government. Let every [one] make known what kind of government would command [his/her] respect, and that will be one step toward obtaining it."[44] I write an invitation to reclaim the soul of a people and a nation. Even now, we are still struggling to give voice to a grounded public theology that fully recognizes the deep yearning for what Harding recognizes in Langston Hughes's phrase "the land that has never been yet."[45]

---

[43] Derrick Bell, "Law as a Religion," 269.

[44] Henry David Thoreau, "Civil Disobedience" (1849).

[45] Vincent Harding, "The America That Has Not Yet Been, Trying to Be Born" (lecture, Ikeda Center for Peace, Learning, and Dialogue, Cambridge, MA, September 20, 2008), https://www.ikedacenter.org/resources/vincent-harding-america-has-not-yet-been-trying-be-born.

As the visionary leader of a much earlier Social Gospel movement, Walter Rauschenbusch declared,

> The social gospel . . . is the religious reaction on the historic advent of democracy. It seeks to put the democratic spirit, which the Church inherited from Jesus and the prophets, once more in control of the institutions and teachings of the Church. The social gospel is the old message of salvation, but enlarged and intensified. The individualistic gospel has taught us to see the sinfulness of every human heart and has inspired us with faith in the willingness and power of God to save every soul . . . But it has not given us an adequate understanding of the sinfulness of the social order and its share in the sins of all individuals within it. It has not evoked faith in the will and power of God to redeem the permanent institutions of human society from their inherited guilt of oppression and extortion.[46]

As such, Rauschenbusch proclaims, "The social gospel seeks to bring [people] under repentance for their collective sins and to create a more sensitive and more modern conscience."[47] We must remain hypervigilant of our total well-being at micro- and macrolevels in these chaotic times. Susan Hill Lindley gives a more recent definition of the Social Gospel that challenges Rauschenbusch's theological vision and hopes to change it into a more holistic and total gospel of well-being. Lindley explains, "The Social Gospel was distinguished, on the one hand, from general charity and humanitarian work by the religious motivation behind its ideas and activities and its insistence on connecting social ideals with the Kingdom of God, at least partially realizable in the world."[48] Toward this end, she

---

[46] Walter Rauschenbusch, *A Theology for the Social Gospel*, reprint ed. (1917; Nashville: Abingdon Press, 1987), 4–5.

[47] Walter Rauschenbusch, *A Theology for the Social Gospel*, 5.

[48] Susan Hill Lindley, "Deciding Who Counts: Towards a Revised

strives to recognize the merit of the Social Gospel's earliest iteration while also demonstrating the need for historical integrity and the inclusion of previously neglected and ignored voices. Much like their counterparts in the ranks of the American Evangelical movement, Lindley observes that newly recovered perspectives of more diverse social gospellers beyond the white church-based urban labor activists, Christian socialists, and theological liberals would ostensibly have to be woven into the traditional narrative so that it became "a new story for all, not simply the old story with a few more footnotes."[49] This new social gospel is a proactive, if not preventative, measure and is born out of a duty of care for ourselves and all others with whom we share God's gift of Creation.

Church leadership from every walk of life must confront white supremacy and its cognate forms of oppression everywhere they manifest in our so-called civil society, most especially within our churches. Despite the tidal wave of frustration and fears the very idea of this confrontation might incite for some readers, we must combat white supremacy, white Christian nationalism, and their progeny at work in American society because they have done a great deal in terms of undoing our declarations of the unconditional love and acceptance of God for all human beings. As many scholars of race and racism in the United States context have argued, the persistent and pernicious roots of "America's original sin" sadly continues to define our society's investment in systematic and systemic modes of oppression that still haunt us to this very day.[50] It seems that the dogged persistence of racial inequality and

---

Definition of the Social Gospel," in *The Social Gospel Today*, ed. Christopher Hodge Evans (Louisville, KY: Westminster John Knox Press, 2001), 24.

[49] Lindley, "Deciding Who Counts," 17–26.

[50] Although countless African American scholars, clergy, journalists, artist, political leaders, and activists have espoused and advanced this concept of racism as "America's original sin" for generations, this idea has been popularized by White antiracist scholarship such as Gunnar Myrdal,

social injustice within "Christian America" remains a mandatory hypocrisy embedded within our fragile democracy.

Toward this end, it is incumbent upon white clergy and theologians to help break the silent complicity about white supremacy within church, academy, and broader society. Throughout American society, we often find it incredibly difficult to engage in conversations much less resolve conflicts based on matters of human difference and cultural diversity. Thus, white supremacy will never vanish from society until white people see it as their own peril that needs to be addressed for their salvation rather than a plight befalling people of color that whites need to empathize with for their own liking. Confronting this reality vis-à-vis critical race theology gives clergy, scholars, and laity opportunities to develop antiracist theologies that go beyond simply condemning racism in a distant, dispassionate manner. Antiracism, feminism, and other liberationist endeavors are works of love and justice because they engage in labor that enhances our humanity.[51]

There needs to be a similar, if not greater, effort to pursue an antiracism enterprise within the related fields of religion and theology. Toward this end, the *critical race theology project* outlined herein is influenced by the prolific work of critical race theorists (thus no longer making it the exclusive or rarified property

---

An American Dilemma: The Negro Problem and Modern Democracy, 2 vols. (New York: McGraw-Hill, 1964); Jennifer Harvey, *Whiteness and Morality: Pursuing Racial Justice through Reparations and Sovereignty* (New York: Palgrave Macmillan, 2007); Chris Crass, *Towards the "Other America": Anti-Racist Resources for White People Taking Action for Black Lives Matter* (St. Louis: Chalice Press, 2015); Jim Wallis, *America's Original Sin: Racism, White Privilege, and the Bridge to a New America* (Grand Rapids: Brazos, 2016); Jones, *White Too Long*; Khyati Y. Joshi, *White Christian Privilege: The Illusion of Religious Equality in America* (New York: New York University Press, 2020).

[51] James H. Cone, "Theology's Great Sin: Silence in the Face of White Supremacy," *Black Theology* 2, no. 2 (2004): 139–52.

of legal scholars) and infused with the pioneering efforts of Black liberationist, womanist, feminist, and queer theologians. As such, critical race theology is concerned with the ways in which the scripture and our churches have been responsible for perpetuating oppression and exclusion. Both in form and function, critical race theology demands that church scholars, ordained ministers, and lay leaders interrogate how oppressive social dynamics have corrupted the mission and ministries of our ecclesiastical institutions to the detriment of both church and society. Furthermore, critical race theology welcomes all adherents of the gospel who are moved by true conscience and a liberating faith—especially white Christians—to be contributors and collaborators to advancing a renewed vision of the Social Gospel that emphasizes all modes of human difference, particularly racial–ethnic diversity, as a blessing rather than a burden within the contemporary church.

What do race and religion *together* have to do with being "American"? Since its inception as a nation, the identities of Americans as a people have been constituted through ever-evolving religious and racial imaginaries, conflicts, and lineages: forging ideological stances, symbols, and myths that rival traditional "religions." The ability to teach, to write, to discuss, and even to think about what and how we coexist with one another as part of God's Creation within US society thoroughly depends upon the ability to embrace the freedoms established in the Constitution's First Amendment. The ability to voluntarily assemble in a peaceful and productive manner, independently select and share the resources and references deemed most significant and substantive for examining, exploring, and expanding the intellectual capabilities of our fellow human beings as active, engaged learners who also expect to be citizen-leaders in the world, should never be taken for granted. And yet these enlightened enterprises are being further complicated by the intrusion of politicized debates and performative debacles of the "cultural wars" in classrooms, courtrooms, convention centers, and congregational spaces in ways that must be addressed in a strenuous, straightforward manner.

Using a moral historical approach, this book explores the racial and religious imperatives encapsulated within concepts of "Americanness" and the racial ideas and religious ideals that define the cultural, historical, and sociopolitical boundaries of American identities. In addition to examining how claims to American identities have altered the religiosity of historically marginalized racial "Others," we will also consider the ways racial concepts have resembled and drawn upon religious forms in their operations in America. This is especially important in a society and culture defined by freedom of religion as it has been embedded in both the US Constitution and multiculturalism typified by *E Pluribus Unum* ("Out of many, one"). Finally, we will discuss how people's responses to racial and religious imperatives challenge, nuance, and expand concepts of the American nation-state and the American as a citizen-subject. At root, too many folks—scholars and nonscholars alike, are either afraid or ashamed to admit that, if they look too closely at the substance of their heavenly faith, they may also be staring at the scene of a horrible crime.

Embracing one's yearning to live in accordance with the will of the revealed and yet-still-revealing God entails confronting honestly and condemning wholeheartedly the biological descendants and behavioral dependents of white supremacy and white Christian nationalism in all their varieties based on prophetic witness and urgent utterances. Those who believe that the Divine still has miracles and mysteries beyond measure will also recognize that the aforementioned challenge is the desperately necessary work of our present era.

1

"Let Us Make Humankind in Our Image"

Racial Hierarchy and
Religious Hegemony in American Theology

Norman Rockwell's fabled artwork is so iconic that the very mention of his name is synonymous with the notion of Americana. One of the most acclaimed and successful American artists of the twentieth century, Rockwell strove to create art with meaningful messages beyond simple comfort and casual aesthetic pleasure. In 1961, he painted "Golden Rule," wherein he portrayed a glorious gathering of men, women, and children of different races, religions, and ethnicities all standing in prayerful, penitent poses. Emblazoned as superscript onto this tableau is a simple but universal phrase inspired by Matthew 7:12: "Do unto Others as You Would Have Them Do unto You." The phrase reflected Rockwell's personal philosophy, and the painting captured Rockwell as a cosmopolitan figure who proudly traveled around the world for both work and pleasure and was welcomed wherever he went.[1] "I'd been reading up on comparative religion. The thing is that all major religions have the Golden Rule in common," he

---

[1] "The Golden Rule," *United Nations: Gifts* (1985), https://www.un.org/ungifts/golden-rule.

said.[2] "'Do unto others as you would have them do unto you.' Not always the same words but the same meaning."[3]

In equal measures, the painting revealed a great deal about the artist and the context in which it was created. Writing contemporaneously about the relationship among world religions, historian of religion Huston Smith observed that at least one of the possible aims of such interreligious encounters "is powered by the hope that there may someday be a single world religion."[4] Smith also warned that "if we were to find ourselves with a single religion tomorrow, it is likely that there would be two the day after."[5]

On the first day of my "Race and Religion in America" course, I have shown the image of this Rockwell painting to the students and asked their opinion of it. Aside from serving as an icebreaker to jumpstart a class discussion even before the students have begun tackling the required texts and assignments outlined in the course, it allows the students a chance to express themselves in a free associative, *sui generis* fashion. This exercise is a nice way to introduce key issues that will be relevant throughout the semester such as nuances of finding descriptive imagery as well as analyzing the relationship between creator and creation. Regardless of their different backgrounds, perspectives, and academic interests, students appreciate Rockwell's work and point out some key issues with the painting. They note that many of the older, visibly "white" figures were more centrally situated in the picture's foreground while many of the darker-hued figures appeared younger in age and were more peripheral. Though Rockwell was trying to disrupt issues of prejudice, preference, and privilege via a departure

---

[2] Norman Rockwell, *The Norman Rockwell Album* (1961), https://www.nrm.org/images/mobile-app/gr/gr.html#dynamicContent.

[3] Norman Rockwell, *The Norman Rockwell Album*.

[4] Huston Smith, *The World's Religions*, rev. and updated ed. (1958: New York: Harper Collins, 1991), 385–86.

[5] Huston Smith, *The World's Religions*, 385–86.

from whiteness, it appears that the artist was unable to escape its subliminal grasp.

This classroom exercise has been a useful way to explore a phenomenon known as implicit bias. According to insights from the Harvard Implicit Association Tests (IAT), perhaps the most salient examples of implicit bias involve race and religion across a variety of scientific perspectives.[6] In addition to study participants' voluntary responses, researchers believe that the amount of time it takes individuals to react and respond to different combinations of stimuli in the test also sheds light on the mental associations and split-second decisions they make—even when they are not consciously aware of those thoughts and their deeper motivations. For more than twenty years, millions of people have used this online test to probe attitudes they did not realize they had. During this period, the IAT has led to the examination of unconscious modes of discrimination and automatic, often instantaneous thought processes among people of various backgrounds in different contexts, including employers, police officers, jurors, voters, and educators.[7]

Thanks to the nonstop barrage of traditional and social media in contemporary American society, the average person now sees more mediated and manufactured images in one day than a person saw during their entire lifetime over a century ago. Over the past twenty to thirty years, the technologies of simulation and visualization have transformed the ways of experiencing and being in the world, demanding new modes of literacy and

---

[6] See the Harvard Implicit Association Tests (IAT) website, https://implicit.harvard.edu/implicit/takeatest.html.

[7] Jesse Singal, "Psychology's Favorite Tool for Measuring Racism Isn't Up to the Job: Almost Two Decades after Its Introduction, the Implicit Association Test Has Failed to Deliver on Its Lofty Promises," *New York Magazine: The Cut*, January 2017, https://www.thecut.com/2017/01/psychologys-racism-measuring-tool-isnt-up-to-the-job.html.

cultural competencies in terms of reading signs and symbols. Artificial intelligence–powered "virtual rappers" like FN Meka allow technology and music companies to traffic in gross racist stereotypes, donning a digital blackface and trivializing mass incarceration, gun violence, and police brutality both in visual and audio presentations.[8] The transformation of the word *woke* from the gatherings of young Republicans known as "Wide Awakes" that helped propel Abraham Lincoln to the US presidency, through countless iterations within English-speaking Black communities over nearly 150 years, to a target of racist backlash, fueled by sensationalist conservative white ignorance, today demonstrates the mind-bending ways that our very language is a technology of world transformation. Marcus Garvey bellowed the summons: "Wake up, Ethiopia! Wake up, Africa!," and Huddie "Lead Belly" Ledbetter responded to the wrongful arrests, trials, and convictions of the Scottsboro Boys by singing an exhortation to Black people to "stay woke ... keep your eyes open" as they traveled through Alabama and the Deep South. Martin Luther King Jr. often developed the theme that "there is nothing more tragic than to sleep through a revolution."[9] In the late twentieth and early twenty-first century, the theme of staying woke has been developed by figures from Spike Lee to Erykah Badu to Childish Gambino, and, by the time

---

[8] Murray Stassen, "This Robot Rapper has 9M Followers on TikTok. The Company that Created Him Thinks Traditional A&R Is 'Inefficient and Unreliable'," *MusicBusiness Worldwide*, April 1, 2021, https://www.musicbusinessworldwide.com/this-robot-rapper-has-9-million-followers-on-tiktok-his-creator-thinks-traditional-ar-is-inefficient-and-unreliable/; Joe Coscarelli, "Capitol Drops 'Virtual Rapper' FN Meka after Backlash Over Stereotypes," *New York Times*, August 23, 2022, https://www.nytimes.com/2022/08/23/arts/music/fn-meka-dropped-capitol-records.amp.html.

[9] Martin Luther King Jr., "Remaining Awake Through a Great Revolution," Commencement Address, Oberlin College, June 1965, https://www2.oberlin.edu/external/EOG/BlackHistoryMonth/MLK/CommAddress.html.

of the police killing of Black teenager Michael Brown in Ferguson, Missouri, the word had skyrocketed to prominence in the Black Lives Matter protests. While these complex cultural meanings and uses perdure, US conservatives have misconstrued and abused "wokeness" in a covert and clumsy way of saying "those non-whites" and/or "un-American" people. They have co-opted the word in such a way that transforms the notorious slur—the N-word—into an umbrella term that includes other people of color, feminists, LGBTQ+ people, white social justice allies, and other marginalized groups.

So-called accent-matching software developed by Sanas AI claims to offer modification of different accents with the push or pull of a slide. However, this invitation to "hear the magic" belies the fact that the working demonstration only ever featured the digital modification of an Indian accent being transformed into a bland white American accent that was bereft of any regional dialect.[10] Millions of dollars' worth of funding and investment pour into the multifarious and nefarious transformations of our world and our experience in and of it. The dystopian satirical plot of Boots Riley's 2018 debut film *Sorry to Bother You* may be closer to fact than fiction. In that film, the Black protagonist's ability to put on a "white" voice on the phone as a telemarketer allows him to advance rapidly up the corporate ladder, passing his former co-workers. Whereas Riley's film frames this ability to "pass sonically" as leading to internecine tension and deep resentment within the workplace that eventually compromises the drive for unionization and multiracial working-class solidarity, the alleged "empowerment" promised by today's technological "advances" appears to be another means of recolonizing already subjugated,

---

[10]　Edward Ongweso Jr., "This Startup Is Selling Tech to Make Call Center Workers Sound Like White Americans," *Vice*, August 24, 2022, https://www.vice.com/en/article/akek7g/this-startup-is-selling-tech-to-make-call-center-workers-sound-like-white-americans.

subaltern people for the sheer comfort and convenience of ethnocentric consumers.

These technological moves speak to the importance of the human voice in how humans image their world. Volker Küster has recognized the image-driven dimensions of contemporary Christianity around the globe and how intercultural Christology was always already primed to meet our peculiar moment:

> In the West, this hybrid stereotype, an orientalizing image of Jesus the Jew with the face of a white man, is still present despite ongoing secularization. But Christology seems to have long since faded in favor of a liquid theism. What remains is the man Jesus, who is still the subject of various films and books of varying quality, but most of which are produced outside of ecclesiastical contexts or even theological seminaries. The question "Who do you say that I am?" apparently threatens to fade away without the contextual pressure and biographical involvement with which the first generation of contextual theologians ... set about their work of Christological deconstructions and reconstructions. The contextual theologies would then enter an age of epigones that has long paralyzed Western academic theology.... Contexts have changed, but questions of social justice in its intersectionality of race, class, and gender, as well as the challenges of cultural-religious pluralism, have become more acute and are now disrupting North Atlantic societies.[11]

In June 2023, a rather unique social experiment took place at the biennial gathering of the German Evangelical Protestant Church Congress in Germany. With deep fascination, the experiment furthers the attention to image and provokes important

---

[11] Volker Küster, *The Many Faces of Jesus Christ: Intercultural Christology*, rev. ed. (Maryknoll, NY: Orbis Books, 2023), xxxv.

questions for a critical race theology. An artificial intelligence chatbot "led" worship.

> The artificial intelligence chatbot asked the believers in the fully packed St. Paul's church in the Bavarian town of Fuerth to rise from the pews and praise the Lord. The ChatGPT chatbot, personified by an avatar of a bearded Black man on a huge screen above the altar, then began preaching to the more than 300 people who had shown up … for an experimental Lutheran church service almost entirely generated by AI.[12]

As worship began, the computer-generated avatar greeted the conference attendees with an expressionless countenance and monotonous voice, saying, "Dear friends, it is an honor for me to stand here and preach to you as the first artificial intelligence at this year's convention of Protestants in Germany."[13] The forty-minute service included a sermon, prayers, and music. It was created by Jonas Simmerlein, a theologian and philosopher from the University of Vienna, with the ample assistance of ChatGPT. The twenty-nine-year-old scholar told the Associated Press, "I conceived this service—but actually I rather accompanied it, because I would say about 98% comes from the machine."[14] In the subsequent weeks and months, Simmerlein has received an unfathomable amount of offensive and threatening correspondence from those thinking that he did this as a "woke" social experiment rather than a worthwhile spiritual experience.

---

[12] Kristen Grieshaber, "Can a Chatbot Preach a Good Sermon? Hundreds Attend Church Service Generated by ChatGPT to Find Out," *Los Angeles Times,* June 10, 2023, https://www.latimes.com/world-nation/story/2023-06-10/can-a-chatbot-preach-a-good-sermon-hundreds-attend-church-service-generated-by-chatgpt-to-find-out.

[13] Grieshaber, "Can a Chatbot Preach a Good Sermon?"

[14] Grieshaber, "Can a Chatbot Preach a Good Sermon?"

In this and countless other examples, the prevailing logic of implicit bias or innate fears of change more broadly leads even the most unassuming person to imagine when, where, how, and why what we imagine to be holy and sacred might shift and transform with time. It might be helpful to remember that, at the height of the Middle Ages, stained-glass windows were utilized in most European chapels and cathedrals not merely as beautiful architectural elements and artistic flourishes. They were educational tools to help illustrate biblical teachings to the largely illiterate churchgoers of the era. Much like the other instances mentioned earlier, both the content and construction of this ChatGPT worship service depict some of the most poignant ideas and powerful images in the Christian tradition that were ultimately and undeniably brought into existence by human heads, hearts, and hands.

White supremacy leads even the most unassuming person to imagine that a God who can do anything but fail somehow made a cosmic mistake by making non-white people into racial–ethnic Others. While there seemingly would be some consolation in blaming the horrid offenses on artificial intelligence, all of this can be attributed to the natural idiocy of human beings. Historian Mark M. Smith argues that, in the US South, white southerners spent several centuries utilizing all their senses—not merely eyesight— to define race, construe racial differences, and disseminate racist opinions. "Understanding the sensory history of race allows us to understand how and why the clumped notions of 'black' and 'white,' of binary notions of racial identity, gained such social currency," Smith contends.[15] "The senses were central to the creation of that clumsy world even as it was belied by everyday contingencies, compromises, and complications."[16] Unfortunately,

---

[15] Mark M. Smith, *How Race Is Made: Slavery, Segregation, and the Senses* (Chapel Hill: University of North Carolina Press, 2008), 9.

[16] Smith, *How Race Is Made*, xviii.

this phenomenon never remained in the Deep South, becoming part and parcel of global culture. As Paul Gilroy observes, "The human sensorium has had to be educated to the appreciation of racial differences."[17] Rodgers and Hammerstein put it more lyrically in their musical "South Pacific": "To hate all the people your relatives hate / You've got to be carefully taught."[18]

The examples listed above lend themselves to the premise that one's perception *of* reality can drastically morph into a state of being wherein perception *is* reality. Self-awareness, the ability to objectively evaluate the self, ought to compel us to question our own instincts, behavioral patterns, and assumptions. Yet we are prone to *oiêsis*, a Greek term that translates to self-deception or arrogant and unchallenged opinion. Consequently, we must hold all our opinions up to hard scrutiny, even when our senses might deceive us. It can be alarming to be forced to realize that one cannot even trust one's own senses. Or, one could take it another way: because our senses are often wrong, especially when trying to comprehend and overcome human differences, our emotions so easily overwhelmed, our projections overly optimistic, we are better off not jumping to conclusions about anything.

It can be easy enough for many of us to dismiss offenses such as those depicted by the IAT, FN Meka, the Sanas "sonic whitening" software, the German ChatGPT worship service, and even, to a certain extent, Rockwell's painting, as glimpses of how technology has failed to help human beings rise above our shortcomings. But has contemporary theology fared any better?

---

[17] Paul Gilroy, *Against Race: Imagining Political Culture beyond the Color Line* (Cambridge, MA: Belknap Press of Harvard University Press, 2001), 7–8.

[18] Andrea Most, "'You've Got to Be Carefully Taught': The Politics of Race in Rodgers and Hammerstein's 'South Pacific.'" *Theatre Journal* 52, no. 3 (2000): 307–37.

It is notable how many congregations have felt the need to insert coded descriptions, such as "community," "open," "welcoming," and "affirming," in their names, road signs, and publicity materials to ensure vulnerable populations that these congregations and houses of worship might provide security, solace, and satiety for those brave enough to cross the sanctuary's threshold. Such proclamations were a promise implied within the concept of *koinonia* (κοινωνία), a term Christianity has putatively embraced unto itself, referring to a community of believers called together to participate in shared religious values, principled commitments, and spiritual fellowship. More than anything, this display of language's power (or, more accurately, power's language) is gauged by who is part of our community and how we assure our personhood within that frame.

Here, it is important to assert how much critical race theology concurs with the proponents of critical race theory (CRT), contending that race is a social construction to establish differentiation among groups of people rather than serving as a determination of God and genetics. Racism, then, is one form of oppression among an entire intersectional and interlocking matrix of categorical oppressions rather than some natural phenomenon of separation. Additionally, it is important to note that people racialized and identified as white must understand that "race" in and of itself is equally applicable to them as it is to the so-called racial–ethnic "minorities."[19]

Much attention has been given to the demographic predictions that racial–ethnic minorities are set to become the majority in the United States by 2042.[20] As much as paranoia and panic have largely

---

[19] Ian F. Haney-Lopez, "The Social Construction of Race," in *Critical Race Theory: The Cutting Edge*, ed. Richard Delgado (Philadelphia: Temple University Press, 2013), 191–203.

[20] Sam Roberts, "Minorities in U.S. Set to Become Majority by 2042,"

crystallized into the noxious claims of the "great replacement theory" for some portion of America's white populace, white people's growing despair at being stamped with minority status could be derived from some awareness of how groups called minorities have been excluded, mistreated, exploited, and disrespected throughout our nation's history thus far.[21] As Indian American comedian Hari Kondabolu once joked, "Saying that I'm obsessed with race and racism in America is like saying that I'm obsessed with swimming while I'm drowning."[22]

In subsequent chapters, I explore reasons why the socially constructed racial categories of "white" and "Black" exist among humans despite having no correlation with God's original intent. Ignoring the underlying rationale of white supremacy maintains the "diseased social imagination," the problem of theological perspective that persists at the heart of contemporary Christianity.[23]

New York Times, August 14, 2008, https://www.nytimes.com/2008/08/14/world/americas/14iht-census.1.15284537.html.

[21] Jason Wilson and Aaron Flanagan, "The Racist 'Great Replacement' Conspiracy Theory Explained," *Southern Poverty Law Center: Hate Watch*, May 17, 2022, https://www.splcenter.org/hatewatch/2022/05/17/racist-great-replacement-conspiracy-theory-explained; Dustin Jones, "What Is the 'Great Replacement' and How Is It Tied to the Buffalo Shooting Suspect?" *National Public Radio*, May 16, 2022, https://www.npr.org/2022/05/16/1099034094/what-is-the-great-replacement-theory; Steve Rose, "A Deadly Ideology: How the 'Great Replacement Theory' Went Mainstream," *The Guardian*, June 8, 2022, https://www.theguardian.com/world/2022/jun/08/a-deadly-ideology-how-the-great-replacement-theory-went-mainstream.

[22] Sarah Sahim, "Hari Kondabolu: 'My Comedy Is Very American. It's Aggressive'," *The Guardian*, December 11, 2015, https://www.theguardian.com/stage/2015/dec/11/hari-kondabolu-comedy-american-race-issues-interview.

[23] Willie James Jennings, *The Christian Imagination: Theology and the Origins of Race* (New Haven, CT: Yale University Press, 2010), 6.

Indeed, the very idea of "race" was invented to establish, inculcate, and normalize the twin fallacies of racial hierarchy and religious hegemony as God-given mandates that, in turn, have led to several centuries of unequal social relationships between people perceived to be at the top and the bottom of global scales.

Considering these twin fallacies, theology stands to benefit greatly from the ways that CRT directly challenges classic liberal ideology and legal practice, especially their allegiance to claims of objectivity, neutrality, impartiality, and color blindness. Not only have these concepts been weaponized by conservatives to protect the status quo from making needed changes, but they also have been questioned increasingly by progressives as shibboleths within the law as it relates to the furtherance of social injustice and undue misery. When left unchecked, perceptions of this sort normalize discrimination and perpetuate suffering by ostensibly allowing opponents of social progress to ignore the existence of racial inequalities that infuse and direct the structural foundations of myriad forms of oppression. Recognizing the intersectional nature of oppression is one thing, but living under the crushing weight of all these multiple modes of deadly dehumanization diminishes the importance and pernicious persistence of the endemic and foundational legacy of race upon which this country was founded, and the significant effect of racism on all our lives. Even more, failure to tackle openly and honestly how race has been used to negatively impact all human lives eventually discounts the behaviors and beliefs that continually support and drive our nation's social fabric and overall identity.

Avoidance and/or silence around racial issues does not make them go away. Talking about "social construction of identity" is an explanation but NOT an excuse for ending oppression. Race and racism are neither synonymous nor interchangeable facts of life. Racism results from an "unholy trinity" of prejudice, privilege, and power being treated as a protected right and rite of whiteness. The constituencies who have experienced prejudice, deprivation, and abuse in American society and culture historically and contemporaneously had racial–ethnic identities within the United States that were of Indigenous/First Nation, African, Mesoamerican, and Asian descent. Within the American context, these are core groups against whom racism has been defined and developed.

White supremacy is not only a problem for people of color, affecting also white people. It is a false assumption to think that eliminating any reflection on diversity and difference among humans singlehandedly could end conflict. Conversely, when we have problems about human differences, the general presumption that we need to have a "conversation" about it immediately might also fly in the face of conventional wisdom, since any unthoughtful, reflexive mention of "race" tends to blow up every argument.

The most enduring explorations of human experience recognize that our focus moves from the specific to the universal. Ultimately, human difference is supposed to be a gift to the world and not a curse. Information about the historical racism experienced by these core groups provides a foundation for better understanding the continuing individual and systemic discriminatory treatment of all peoples of color. Over time, the mold has shifted and changed, and the mold of racism has now incorporated other peoples of color who have immigrated to the United States. Ignoring the history of racism with respect to these core groups discounts the extent to which white privilege and dominance have historically defined this country. To deny and/or misconstrue the existence of racism minimizes the social and psychological importance of racism in the development of the United States on both individual and institutional levels, and allows for the perpetuation of the false perceptions that there is racial equality in this country. We once believed humans were created in God's image, but modernity has remade us in the imagination of racial hierarchy and religious hegemony. In the remainder of this chapter, I explore the nexus of racial hierarchy and religious hegemony currently at work in American theology.

Viewing humanity through the prism of Genesis 1:26—"Then God said 'Let us make humankind in our image, according to our likeness'"—forces us to grapple with a crucial contradiction white supremacy imposes on Christian theology. Reading the Book of Genesis from a marginalized and decolonized perspective, as ethicist Miguel De La Torre reminds us, "seems more to be a testimony of the goodness of God's creation in spite of the shortcomings of humanity."[24] The reading and rendering of Genesis as dictated by theological precepts that frame the trajectory of human existence as a downward spiral ought to be challenged. While much of Western Christian thought is dependent upon the repentance of the moral agent as a reasonable and responsible participation in God's salvific love, grace, and mercy, is there any true pathway or even possibility for redemption of the non-white, non-Christian Other in a worldview dominated by whiteness? Said another way, does whiteness make it impossible to even recognize—much less rescue or repair—a divinely created soul that just so happens to be enshrined in dark flesh? As recent works have indicated, the answer to that query for too many white Christians might have always already been "yes."[25]

---

[24] Miguel De La Torre, *Genesis* (Louisville, KY: Westminster John Knox Press, 2011), 7.

[25] Jon Sensbach, *A Separate Canaan: The Making of an Afro-Moravian World in North Carolina, 1763–1840* (Chapel Hill: University of North Carolina Press, 1998); Travis Glasson, *Mastering Christianity: Missionary Anglicanism and Slavery in the Atlantic World* (Oxford: Oxford University Press, 2012); Richard Bailey, *Race and Redemption in Puritan New England* (Oxford: Oxford University Press, 2011); Rebecca Anne Goetz, *The Baptism of Early Virginia: How Christianity Created Race* (Baltimore: Johns Hopkins University Press, 2012); Heather Miyano Kopelson, *Faithful Bodies: Performing Religion and Race in the Puritan Atlantic* (New York: New York

In 2020, Laura McTighe wrote in the *Journal of the American Academy of Religion*: "Religious studies has a race problem."[26] It is remarkable how a deceptively simple declaration can unveil a complex and persistent problem within the larger scholarly enterprise. While the academic study of religion and theology has been exceedingly hesitant to engage with the nexus of race, culture, and power, in the same regard as CRT, American Studies, Ethnic Studies, and similar disciplines conversely have been pallid in their overall explorations of religion and theology during the past sixty or so years. Critical race theology considers its questions at the nexus of race, religion, and nation shaped in the forge of modernity while also drawing upon the wisdom of our many religious traditions. On an individual as well as institutional level, for believers and nonbelievers alike, critical race theology is intended for those gripped by questions that are immense and intense in their scope. Dismantling racial hierarchy and religious hegemony that have ensconced themselves within American theology writ large is a day-by-day struggle of speculating, doubting, questioning, weighing

University Press, 2014); Christopher Cameron, *To Plead Our Own Cause: African Americans in Massachusetts and the Making of the Antislavery Movement* (Kent, OH: Kent State University Press, 2014); Kathryn Gin Lum, "The Historyless Heathen and the Stagnating Pagan: History as Non-Native Category?," *Religion and American Culture: A Journal of Interpretation* 28, no. 1 (2018): 52–91; Khyati Y. Joshi, *White Christian Privilege: The Illusion of Religious Equality in America* (New York: New York University Press, 2020); Katherine McKittrick, *Demonic Grounds: Black Women and the Cartographies of Struggle* (Minneapolis: University of Minnesota Press, 2006); Alexis S. Wells-Oghoghomeh, *The Souls of Womenfolk: The Religious Cultures of Enslaved Women in the Lower South* (Chapel Hill: University of North Carolina Press, 2021).

[26] Laura McTighe, "Introduction: 'Religio-Racial Identity' as Challenge and Critique, *Journal of the American Academy of Religion* 88 (2020): 299.

options, studying, debating, wondering, listening, contemplating, believing, discerning, and deciding with all sorts of influences—both sacred and secular—coming to bear on this matter. Throughout much of American history, as Judith Weisenfeld notes, African Americans seem to be "the only group burdened with race."[27] Critical race theology challenges us to recognize that, while Blackness is too often rendered hypervisible and prone to intense scrutiny, whiteness has tended to remain largely unseen and uninterrogated for several centuries in the modern world.

The multidisciplinary insights of W. E. B. Du Bois, easily one of the most impressive and important scholars this nation has ever produced, remain an influential paradigm about race more than one hundred years later. In his "The Conservation of Races" speech from March 5, 1897, Du Bois weaves together his own scholarly analysis of history, sociology, religion, and philosophy, and proposes a pioneering theoretical concept of racial identity wherein he proffers a sociohistorical rather than biological explanation for the distinctive character of a race's spiritual contribution to humanity. While not trying to alienate the ideas and issues connected to race held by many of his elders, especially his idol, the Episcopal priest, scholar, and activist Alexander Crummell, the remarks also reflect the expanding and evolving nature of Du Bois's thoughts on the matter of race as a world-historical phenomenon.

In the landmark essay that developed from the speech, Du Bois declares,

> While these subtle forces have generally followed the natural cleavage of common blood, descent and physical peculiarities, they have at other times swept across and ignored these. At all times, however, they have divided human beings into races, which, while they perhaps

---

[27] Edward Blum et al., "Forum: American Religion and 'Whiteness,'" *Religion and American Culture: A Journal of Interpretation* 19 (2009): 28.

transcend scientific definition, nevertheless, are clearly defined to the eye of the historian and sociologist.

If this be true, then the history of the world is the history, not of individuals, but of groups, not of nations, but of races, and [anyone] who ignores or seeks to override the race idea in human history ignores and overrides the central thought of all history. What, then, is a race? It is a vast family of human beings, generally of common blood and language, always of common history, traditions and impulses, who are both voluntarily and involuntarily striving together for the accomplishment of certain more or less vividly conceived ideals of life.[28]

In many ways, Du Bois's essay can be read as a philosophical precursor to his subsequent and more significant exploration of African American spirituality in *The Souls of Black Folk* (1903). But, much like his later work, Du Bois is attentive to both the structural and spiritual dimensions of race in the modern world. Moreover, this identification of a racial "spirit" that extends beyond phenotypical and genotypical traits lends itself to understanding race in a phenomenological and generative key. Presaging the advent of race's social construction, Du Bois's proposal has nevertheless stirred considerable debate.

Philosopher Kwame Anthony Appiah critiqued Du Bois's perspective as a racialist one that merged the scientific and sociohistorical factors to assert that races are realities, that racial identities are valuable and undeniable properties of human beings, and that racial solidarity can help realize such goals as

---

[28] W. E. B. Du Bois, "The Conservation of Races," The American Negro Academy. Occasional Papers No. 2, The Project Gutenberg eBook of The Conservation of Races, by W. E. Burghardt Du Bois, March 13, 2024, https://www.gutenberg.org/cache/epub/31254/pg31254-images.html.

self-actualization, human equality, and empowerment.[29] By contrast, philosopher Paul C. Taylor contends Appiah is arguably a "racial eliminativist," who, among other things, "believes races do not exist, that acting as if they do is metaphysically indefensible and morally dangerous, and, as a result, that eliminating 'race' from our metaphysical vocabularies is an important step toward ... a rational and just ... world-view."[30] Even Appiah admits that Du Bois is "to have thought longer, more engagedly, and more publicly about race than any other social theorist of [the twentieth] century."[31] Whether consciously or not, everyone has their own particular encounter with race in today's world, navigating the messy middle road between the polar extremes of "race is everything" (Du Bois's racialism) and "race is nothing" (Appiah's eliminativism) that define contemporary society.

Though racism is neither isolated nor peculiar to the United States alone, the United States has had its own uniquely mutable and durable form of racism that is rooted and embedded in this nation's genesis. To better understand racism in its US manifestations, critical race theology recognizes three important insights about racism that can help navigate this messy middle road. First, race and racism are neither synonymous nor interchangeable facts of life. Said another way, contrary to popular logic, every mention of race is *not* automatically a conversation about racism. Second, when and where racism is the topic of conversation, racism most commonly results from an "unholy trinity" consisting of prejudice, privilege, and power manifesting itself as the protected right and rite of whiteness. Third, racism—as just one facet or outgrowth of white

---

[29] Kwame Anthony Appiah, "The Uncompleted Argument: Du Bois and the Illusion of Race" *Critical Inquiry* 12, no. 1 (Autumn 1985): 21–37.

[30] Paul C. Taylor, "Appiah's Uncompleted Argument: W. E. B. Du Bois and the Reality of Race," *Social Theory and Practice* 26, no. 1 (Spring 2000): 103–4.

[31] Appiah, "The Uncompleted Argument," 22.

supremacy—is a problem for people of color *and* affects white people with detrimental and deadly consequences. "Race" is every bit as important to people who have been racialized as white as it is to the so-called racial minorities. There are reasons why the socially constructed category "white" exists, and ignoring the reasoning that undergirds whiteness maintains the crux of our problem.

The impact and influence of racism have long been recognized, and the racial perceptions of years past are dynamic and still occurring today. Though discourse around issues of race and racism has expanded over the past half century since the high watermark of what sociologist John Skrentny calls "the minority rights revolution," the most recognized mode of racism in the US context is generally still limited to understanding racism as personal prejudice and intentional bias in interpersonal interactions across different racial–ethnic groups.[32] Despite this individualist approach, we must reckon with the fact that racism exists within a multifaceted and structured hierarchy of interconnected oppressions. Contrary to popular belief, individual acts of racism are symptomatic of a more fundamental schema of racism. This emerging explanation of racism contends that an array of cultural norms as well as institutional policies and practices routinely produces racially inequitable outcomes, often without individual intent or personal malice.

This typology of oppression is beholden to a dreadful nexus of white supremacy, Christian nationalism, and cultural politics. To envision this framework, one can imagine four expanding concentric rings, beginning with the most familiar type of racialized antipathy, individual racism. As the phrase suggests, this antagonism is personally mediated and is often intense, immediate, and interpersonal in nature. Whether practicing racial microaggressions, uttering racist slurs or insensitive jokes, or

---

[32] See John D. Skrentny, *The Minority Rights Revolution* (Cambridge, MA: Harvard University Press, 2002).

executing hate crimes and intolerant acts, this is the bias that occurs when individuals interact with others and their personal racial beliefs affect their quotidian public exchanges. Moving one level beyond the individual, institutional racism refers to unfair policies and discriminatory practices, such as miseducation, residential redlining, the school-to-prison pipeline, predatory lending, racial profiling, hiring discrimination, and health care disparities, by societal institutions, such as banks, hospitals, police departments, schools, workplaces, legislatures, and ecclesial organizations, that consistently produce negative outcomes for people of color while ensuring advantages for white people. Individuals operate and exist within institutions and take on the power of said institutions when they reinforce racial inequality and other forms of inequities through these institutional structures. Although it might seem counterintuitive, the next and penultimate level in this framework is the internalized racism that lies within the psyches of those individuals impacted by the steady diet of oppression as a lived experience. This type of racism permeates the innermost being with self-destructive personal beliefs and private biases about race, influenced by a prevalent culture of degradation and despair. When left unchecked, the seemingly endless encounter with disdain and disrespect can take many different forms of prejudice among different racial–ethnic groups, including anxiety, tokenism, victim-shaming, self-hatred, paranoia, pathology, and rage. The internalization of this oppression hinges on the damaging beliefs of inferiority about oneself that are inculcated within people of color in contrast to self-aggrandizing senses of entitlement, privilege, and superiority adopted by white people. Finally, inspired racism is the most extreme form within this framework. As a gestalt function of racialized bias, "inspired" racism transcends individualized actions, institutional forces, and internalized views. It is a preponderance of cumulative, compounding effects to lead one to assume that white supremacy in all its forms is an undeniable part of God's plan for humanity. When viewed against how modes of white supremacy have been woven through the histories, cultures, ideologies, and interactions of various human societies around and over numerous generations—Curse of Ham, Manifest Destiny, One Drop Rule, White Man's Burden, etc.—one could almost believe that the extant racial hierarchy that systematically privileges white people and disadvantages people of color was a divine creation rather than a human contrivance.

Bearing in mind this typology of racism, critical race theology proposes an alternate definition: race is not only about skin color and perceptible variances in shared physical characteristics and embodied human differences (such as skin hue, hair texture, eye shape, etc.). Race is also a concept that signifies spiritual struggles symbolized by competing historical narratives, social interests, and cultural elements.

If the concept of race is so hazy and haphazard in its function, why can't we simply get rid it? Put another way, can we "do without" race already, especially in the supposedly more "enlightened" contemporary era? Michael Omi and Howard Winant's concept of racial formation is useful for understanding better how race has been made by and for humans. According to Omi and Winant, racial formation is defined as "the sociohistorical process by which racial identities are created, lived out, transformed, and destroyed."[33] The process of racial formation highlights the ways that "race" is socially constructed, specifically and intentionally in furtherance of white supremacy. The seemingly invisible and innocuous processes connected to social, economic, political, cultural, and even religious power shape and have been shaped by the contours and conditions by which racial categories and hierarchies are formed. "The hallmark of [American] history has

---

[33] Michael Omi and Howard Winant, *Racial Formation in the United States*, 3rd ed. (1986; London: Routledge, 2014), 109.

been racism," not the abstract "ethos of equality," Omi and Winant insist.[34] "While groups of color have been treated differently, all can bear witness to the tragic consequences of racial oppression. The United States has confronted each group with a unique form of despotism and degradation."[35]

Furthermore, Omi and Winant help clarify a key concern about how Americans have come to think about race as a fundamental element of the identity and, ultimately, reality of people who are recognizable and categorized by race. Their racial theory centers on the concept of the "racial project." "Race" in and of itself, they argue, is a notional and negotiated narrative by which people have constructed these imagined categories ("the races") and then sorted humanity into these varied groupings. As it has commonly been described in our contemporary parlance, "race" neither occurs as an unswerving constant in nature nor does it exist as a consistent categorical concept over the course of human history.[36] Instead, human beings over time and space have envisaged race and partaken in the formation of racial categories and their uses creatively. In racial formation, "racial projects" are configured to see the various ways that people have been assigned membership within the categories of race. For instance, when we look at

---

[34] Omi and Winant, *Racial Formation in the United States*, 8.

[35] Omi and Winant, *Racial Formation in the United States*, 8.

[36] See Charles Hirschman, "The Origins and Demise of the Concept of Race," *Population and Development Review* (September 2004); 385–415; Evelyn B. Higginbotham, "African-American Women and the Metalanguage of Race," *Signs* 17, no. 2 (Winter 1992): 251–74; Frank M. Snowden Jr., *Before Color Prejudice: The Ancient View of Blacks* (Cambridge, MA: Harvard University Press, 1991); Steve Olson, *Mapping Human History: Genes, Race, and Our Common Origins* (New York: Mariner Books, 2003); Charles Mills, *The Racial Contract*, 25th anniv. ed. (Ithaca, NY: Cornell University Press, 2022); Paul C. Taylor, *Race: A Philosophical Introduction*, 3rd ed. (London: Polity, 2022).

the racial–ethnic categories utilized by the US Census Bureau across time, terms, such as "white," "Black/African American," "American Indian/Alaska Native," "Asian," and "Native Hawaiian/ Other Pacific Islander," are incomplete and inconclusive in nature. Additionally, these terms have only recently emerged into regular usage as they are deemed worthwhile in our everyday vernacular. Yet, as Khyati Y. Joshi asserts, categories of free, white, and Christian "have been superimposed to form mutually supporting advantages based on the co-construction of religion, race, and national origin."[37]

This racial project culminates in the presumed and putative normativity of white racial identity and Christianity in the United States, which empowers structural Christian privilege and societal power specifically encoded to align with whiteness. The focus here, however, is not just the primacy of Christian principles and practices in some benign or bucolic privilege. Rather, critical race theology emphasizes how the religion of Jesus has been wedded to whiteness vis-à-vis racial formation through centuries of endorsing and embracing white supremacy. Omi and Winant rightfully contend that "race has been understood as a sign of God's pleasure or displeasure" within the human condition.[38] Paying sharp attention to white Christian supremacy in broad scope, Joshi is especially helpful in the current effort to chart a critical race theology by taking an intersectional approach to this coalescing of race and religion, because "White racial superiority and Christian religious superiority have augmented and magnified each other."[39]

The scholarly enterprise of religion and theology is embodied and socially embedded work. Critical race theology is broadly shaped by the experiences of Black, Indigenous, and People of

---

[37] Joshi, *White Christian Privilege*, 2.

[38] Omi and Winant, *Racial Formation in the United States*, 4.

[39] Joshi, *White Christian Privilege*, 25.

Color (BIPOC) in this country and more specifically shaped by my own identity as a first-generation American son of Afro-Caribbean immigrants. My Jamaican and Cuban ancestral roots imbue me with "glocal"—a merger of global and local—sympathies and solidarities that shape how I approach this work. At once, I am immersed in overlapping, diasporic communities and yet also always perpetually situated as someone else's other to the extent that I am (to borrow a phrase from the title of comedic actor Aasif Mandvi's memoir) "No land's man."

In this overlapping, diasporic, no-landed-ness, understanding race more fully must be made to envision it as an unstable, "decentered" complex of social meanings constantly being transformed as much by political struggle and pious standpoint as well as prejudicial stereotype. Decentered in this way, racism "avoids being recognized as such because it is able to line up 'race' with nationhood, patriotism, and nationalism."[40] In this important shift, "racism . . . has taken a necessary distance from crude ideas of biological inferiority and superiority and now seeks to present an imaginary definition of the nation as a unified *cultural* community."[41] Gilroy recognizes that racism in this mode "constructs and defends an image of national culture—homogenous in its whiteness yet precarious and perpetually vulnerable to attack from enemies within and without."[42] From Gilroy, critical race theology can recognize consequences and instances of racism's instability and perpetual vulnerability throughout US society.

For instance, most experimental psychologists will attest that the "universal" basis for their research projects is based on

---

[40] Paul Gilroy, "The End of Antiracism," in "*Race," Culture and Difference*, ed. James Donald and Ali Rattansi (London: Sage Publications, 1992), 53.

[41] Gilroy, "The End of Antiracism," 53.

[42] Gilroy, "The End of Antiracism," 53.

the assessment of people who can be called WEIRD (Western, Educated, Industrialized, Rich, and Democratic) in comparison to the vast majority of the world's populace.[43] There is a sizable disconnect, then, between generalized knowledge of psychological and emotional experiences affecting most human beings based on inferences, insights, and information derived from a quite rarefied and highly selective sample of the global population that invariably skews all such data against those who fall outside the bounds of Western normativity.

More than a fair share of our mistakes and misgivings about the well-being of our fellow human beings can be attributed to viewing the world through the perspective of WEIRD people. Yet, as Audre Lorde declares,

> I cannot afford the luxury of fighting one form of oppression only. I cannot afford to believe that freedom from intolerance is the right of only one particular group. And I cannot afford to choose between the fronts upon which I must battle these forces of discrimination, wherever they appear to destroy me. And when they appear to destroy me, it will not be long before they appear to destroy you.[44]

---

[43] Oliver Burkeman, "This Column Will Change Your Life: Weirdness Just Got Weirder," *The Guardian*, September 17, 2010, https://www.theguardian.com/lifeandstyle/2010/sep/18/change-your-life-weird-burkeman?CMP=Share_iOSApp_Other; The Daily Dish, "Western, Educated, Industrialized, Rich, and Democratic," *The Atlantic: Daily Dish*, October 4, 2010, https://www.theatlantic.com/daily-dish/archive/2010/10/western-educated-industrialized-rich-and-democratic/181667/?utm_source=copy-link&utm_medium=social&utm_campaign=share.

[44] Audre Lorde, "There Is No Hierarchy of Oppression," in *Homophobia and Education* (New York: Council on Interracial Books for Children, 1983).

Such an approach has facilitated understanding of a whole range of contemporary controversies and dilemmas involving racial difference, including the shifting nature of racism, the relationship of race to other forms of oppression (such as misogyny, elitism, xenophobia, homophobia, and transphobia), and the current dilemmas of nationalism today.[45] The objective in this regard is to overturn racial hierarchy in lieu of racial transparency.

Critical race theology deals with both the racial and religious hegemonic functions in US society and culture. Sociologist Will Herberg's classic book *Protestant—Catholic—Jew* (1955) formulated a new religious paradigm for American society and culture in the mid-twentieth century. As the title suggests, he argues for a three-religion status quo of American life—Catholic, Protestant, and Jewish. "The newcomer," he wrote, "is expected to change many things about him as he becomes an American—nationality, language, culture. One thing, however, he is not expected to change—and that is religion."[46] In the prosperous mass consumerism and burgeoning suburbanization of the post–World War II era, Herberg identified these three traditions as the principal religious groups within the United States, reflecting an American common religion. Considering the robust anti-Catholicism and anti-Semitism of the recent past, Herberg's book strenuously asserts that the 1950s signaled that members of these faith communities—many of whom were first-and second-generation immigrants—had become "assimilated" within American society. By this account, religious identity had superseded ethnic identity among white-identified Americans.[47]

---

[45] Michael Omi and Howard Winant, *Racial Formation in the United States: From the 1960s to the 1990s*, 2nd ed. (New York: Routledge, 1994), pp. 55–56.

[46] Will Herberg, *Protestant—Catholic—Jew: An Essay in American Religious Sociology* (Garden City, NY: Anchor Books, 1960), 23.

[47] James P. Byrd and James Hudnut-Beumler, *The Story of Religion in*

Overall, following the trials and travails of the early half of the twentieth century, religious identification during the 1950s was on a massive upsurge. Consensus rather than conscientiousness occupied a more unwavering place at the heart of the nation's religious self-definition. A driving concern for Herberg was to explore how America simultaneously could be "at once the most religious and the most secular of nations."[48] Inclusion of the phrase *under God* in the Pledge of Allegiance in 1954 reflects President Dwight Eisenhower's concerns that "our form of government has no sense unless it is founded in a deeply felt religious faith, and I don't care what it is."[49] Based on contemporaneous polling data, approximately 95 percent of Americans identified as "religious,"[50] with a further distribution of 68 percent Protestant, 23 percent Catholic, and 4 percent Jewish. For Herberg, religious identification and affiliation were quantitatively and qualitatively measurable. The former was shown by demographic growth in the number of believers. The latter was represented by qualitative achievements of greater prevalence in civil participation and national identity, though the latter often masqueraded as patriotism. According to sociologist Robert Wuthnow, the resonant idea in the American public square during this particular era was that "a deep religious faith"—whether Catholic, Protestant, or Jewish in Herberg's tripartite view—"gave the individual moral strength, conviction, the will to do what was right."[51] Yet, even as this

---

America: An Introduction (Louisville, KY: Westminster John Knox Press, 2021), 310.

[48] Herberg, *Protestant—Catholic—Jew*, 3.

[49] Dwight D. Eisenhower, *Address at the Freedoms Foundation*, Waldorf-Astoria, New York City, New York, December 22, 1952.

[50] George H. Gallup Jr., "Americans More Religious Now Than Ten Years Ago, but Less So Than in 1950s and 1960s," *Gallup* (March 29, 2001), https://news.gallup.com/poll/1858/americans-more-religious-now-than-ten-years-ago-less-than.aspx.

[51] Robert Wuthnow, "*Quid Obscurum:* The Changing Terrain of

conjoined understanding of the religious and political was considered "fundamental" to the values and behavior that defined good moral character in the mid-twentieth century, it was also beginning to unravel and be questioned.

Presaging Robert Bellah's subsequent landmark work on "civil religion" in the 1960s, Herberg's concept of "common religion" included stronger bonds than any religious differences, than the "American Way of Life," a set of ideas, rituals, and symbols that define the "overarching sense of unity" within civil society. In this respect, being an American equals a sacred worldview replete with the following elements: democracy, "free enterprise" capitalism, individualism, and an idealistic, moralistic impulse. Conversely, the religious differences among Americans were taken for granted. For Herberg, religious pluralism was not simply a fact, but "an essential part of the American Way of Life, and therefore an aspect of religious belief."[52] According to David J. O'Brien, Herberg argued that, whether Catholic, Protestant, or Jewish, Americans "tend to think of their church as a denomination existing side by side with other denominations in a pluralistic harmony that is felt."[53]

Whereas Herberg's research was once treated as cutting-edge scholarship, there are a great many ways it now resembles wishful thinking. By advancing such an oversimplified vision of religious life in American society, he gave short shrift to the rich plethora of diverse religious communities beyond the Catholics–Protestants–Jews matrix and to the deep complexity within the three traditions themselves. There is a way in which the seedbed for Herberg's model was deeply rooted in his own personal journey, emanating from "the 'passionate atheism' of his parents, to his

---

Church-State Relations," in *Religion and American Politics: From the Colonial Period to the 1980s*, ed. Mark A. Noll (New York: Oxford University Press, 1990), 348.

[52] Herberg, *Protestant—Catholic—Jew*, 85.

[53] David J. O'Brien, "Will Herberg: The Religions, or Religion, of America," *U.S. Catholic Historian* 23, no. 1 (2005): 41–49.

youthful Marxist commitments, and, finally, to his own version of Judaism."[54] It is also necessary here to mention there is a significant difference between religious diversity and pluralism in the public square. While the two concepts are clearly related, they are compatible but should not be confused as being commensurate to one another. Diversity is a state of coexistence with and around dissimilar people and communities of faith, while pluralism requires the active engagement that genuinely recognizes and even reveres the common ground shared by all the variety and vitality of human experience in one's midst.[55]

At this point, it is important to link the formation of racial identities to the evolution of hegemony, the way in which human bodies and social structures are represented, organized, and controlled in society in processes many religious scholars and theologians refer to as "meaning-making." Religion is central in the ongoing process of hegemony.[56] Whether thinking of religious faith in terms of William James's "unseen order," Rudolf Otto's "Holy Other," or Paul Tillich's "ultimate concern," such ruminations often hover around the mystical and somewhat nebulous nature of religiosity at work in our mundane lives. While I endorse the transcendent, contemplative, and esoteric dimensions of religion, much of our contemporary academic discourse about religion and theology has a furtive, almost forlorn approach to talking about the realistic impositions of religion upon human identities and

---

[54] Rebecca Kneale Gould, "'Protestant, Catholic, Jew' at Fifty: An Historian's Perspective," *U.S. Catholic Historian* 23, no. 1 (Winter 2005), 79.

[55] Diana L. Eck, *A New Religious America: How a "Christian Country" Has Become the World's Most Religiously Diverse Nation* (New York: HarperOne, 2002); Stephen Prothero, *Religious Literacy: What Every American Needs to Know—And Doesn't* (San Francisco: HarperSanFrancisco, 2007).

[56] Antonio Gramsci, *Selections from the Prison Notebooks* (London: Lawrence & Wishart, 1971), 57–58; Perry Anderson, "The Antinomies of Antonio Gramsci," *New Left Review* 100 (1976–77): 26.

interactions. Paul Kivel defines hegemony "as the predominant and pervasive influence of one state, religion, region, class, or group . . . A hegemonic society functions not just to establish a homogeneous way of thinking, but also to try to make any alternative disappear."[57] If taken at its most specific sense, religion as a holistic way of life in American society and culture works to align humanity with spiritual concerns, but its hegemonic function has been redefined to decipher the means for the demarcation of earthly power vis-à-vis structural relationships and societal resources.[58]

All the chatter about America's religious diversity, both old and new, does not instantly and inevitably bring about pluralism. In a growing metropolis like Nashville, Tennessee, with a population of roughly 715,000 inhabitants, there are more than 700 established denominational buildings, especially serving as the headquarters for the Southern Baptist Convention and a major hub for American Methodism. Nashville might rightfully claim one of its nicknames as the "City of Churches" or, as a former colleague referred to it, "the buckle of the Bible Belt." Amid the city's preponderance of white, conservative-leaning mainline and Evangelical Christian congregations, one can also witness Jewish synagogues, Korean Presbyterian churches, a Muslim Community Center, Latinx Pentecostal churches, a Unitarian Universalist church, an African American Roman Catholic church, a Cambodian Buddhist temple, a Church of Scientology, a Hindu temple, and even the Sunday Assembly Nashville, a secular humanist congregation, across the metro Nashville area.[59] These communities coexist within this

---

[57] Paul Kivel, *Living in the Shadow of the Cross: Understanding and Resisting the Power and Privilege of Christian Hegemony* (Gabriola Island, BC: New Society Publishers, 2013), 2.

[58] Jeannine Hill Fletcher, "Warrants for Reconstruction: Christian Hegemony, White Supremacy," *Journal of Ecumenical Studies* 51, no. 1 (Winter 2016), 54–79.

[59] Paul Griffith, "A Different Kind of Church," *Nashville Scene*, March

varied and vibrant religious landscape, representing great degrees of diversity, particularly in a thriving city in the American South. This does not reflect an example of genuine pluralism by any stretch of the imagination, if there is an absence of any significant interactions or sustained relationships among these different assemblies.

Situating this important distinction between diversity and pluralism within the process of hegemony, critical race theology can argue that, even within a society and culture that endorses freedom of religion as a key benchmark of civic personhood and national identity, liberty is still positioned within its proximity to Christianity. To wit, the ways in which legalistic discourse on the interplay of religion and politics functions in American society is still predicated on the concept of "church–state relations" in a nation where our recognition of sacred communities can and should be more multifarious than envisioned by that construction. Nevertheless, among the plethora of issues we routinely encounter is Christianity's tendency within the United States to overshadow and dominate its faith counterparts. By positioning a co-opted, cajoled, cherry-picked, and even corrupted vision of American Christianity as being superior to its comparable religious traditions, Christianity has demonstrated itself to be incredibly bruising in the way it encounters the perspectives, principles, and pathways by which our fellow human beings can find a better, brighter meaning in life. This malformed, misappropriated vision of the religion of Jesus remains inextricably yoked to a normative American identity.

There is no repudiating Christianity's moral ambiguities, complexities, and contradictions on American soil. In light of Christian theology's inability to heed charitable criticism and constructive chastisement, Willie James Jennings notes that it presently operates "without the ability to discern how its intellectual and pedagogical performances reflect and fuel the problem, further

---

27, 2003, https://www.nashvillescene.com/news/a-different-kind-of-church/article_ee5729c3-74cf-5cea-a034-d40ed2fe722f.html.

crippling the communities it serves."[60] Without question, I have so often wrestled with the conflicting and contradictory realities of our history, culture, and faith within the nation's sociopolitical culture as much as its spiritual contours as they impose themselves on every human life. Faced with all of that, it is this core premise that drives me in my scholarly and spiritual pursuits to contemplate how the corrosive and coercive elements of a conjoined concept of white supremacy and Christian hegemony in our nation has undermined the humanity of those who exist both literally and figuratively beyond the pale.

In a worldview governed by Christianity as supremacist rather than a sympathetic tradition, it is easy to acknowledge that some portion of the American populace feels threatened by or even downright hostile to all modes of diversity, particularly with regard to religion. Since the desire for assimilation emerging in the wake of the Second World War, many people have looked forward to the magical, magnificent, and magisterial day when all human differences would simply fade away into the proverbial "melting pot" of a predominantly Christian mainstream American culture. Moving from welcoming diversity of religions to fostering a workable model of religious pluralism will mean engaging people of different faiths and cultures in the creation of a common society. From a historical standpoint, however, the movement away from hegemony to pluralism as the teleological trajectory of religious diversity is not a foregone conclusion but an ideal achievement.

The constraints barring the possibility of pluralism in response to widening cultural and religious diversity taking shape in American life have perennially been defined by either exclusion or assimilation. Historian R. Laurence Moore observes,

> If we cannot count on God's plan to tell us what is or is not "mainline" in American history, and if we now recognize

---

[60] Jennings, *The Christian Imagination*, 6–7.

that the purported size of denominations does not by itself tell us which religious beliefs excited the most popular interest, then what guides do we have to tell us what was important? Are all religious groups, no matter what their size, no matter how ephemeral, equally significant in accounts of American religion? Do the concepts "normal" and "deviant" tell us nothing about how to characterize the behavior of various religious groups? . . . Is the notion of Protestant hegemony a myth?[61]

A joint research effort by Ligonier Ministries and LifeWay Research, their biennial "State of Theology" survey aims "to evaluate the theological temperature" of the American Evangelical church in relation to the mainstream culture for the purposes of future ministry and discipleship. The "State of Theology" survey defines "Evangelical" as a Christian believer who satisfies the four following criteria: the Bible is the highest authority for what someone believes; that it is important for non-Christians to trust Jesus Christ as their savior; Jesus's death on the cross is the only sacrifice that removes the penalty of humanity's sin; and only those who trust in God alone receive God's free gift of eternal salvation.[62]

Of those polled,[63] some 95 percent of the respondents agreed steadfastly with the statement that "the Bible is 100 percent accurate in all that it teaches." Yet, according to data compiled in their 2022 report, nearly half (48 percent) of

---

[61] R. Laurence Moore, *Religious Outsiders and the Making of Americans* (New York: Oxford University Press, 1986), 21.

[62] John Stonestreet and Kasey Leander, "What 'the State of Theology' Tells Us," *Voices*, September 27, 2022, https://www.christianpost.com/voices/what-the-state-of-theology-tells-us.html.

[63] The data in this paragraph is taken from key findings and more information on "State of Theology" survey. See https://thestateoftheology.com/.

Evangelicals agreed that God "learns and adapts to different circumstances," a claim that stands in stark contrast to the biblical doctrine of God's immutability (unchanging nature of the Divine). Sixty-five percent of Evangelicals denied the doctrine of original sin, which, for better or worse, stands as the very bedrock rationale within Western Christian tradition for why people need salvation in the first place. Some 56 percent of Evangelicals agreed with the idea that "God accepts the worship of all religions, including Christianity, Judaism, and Islam." When the survey asked whether the respondents believed "Jesus was a great teacher ... but not God," 43 percent of American Evangelicals answered yes, up 13 percent from just two years earlier in terms of conservative Christians' overall belief and embrace of Jesus Christ's divinity. Conversely, 94 percent of Evangelicals admonished extramarital sex as a sin, roughly 91 percent of Evangelicals agreed that abortion is a sin, 94 percent agreed that sex outside of traditional marriage is a sin, and another 28 percent of Evangelicals agreed that scripture's condemnation of homosexuality "doesn't apply today."

It is fascinating the extent to which Evangelicals, whose brand within American Christianity hovers around their unwavering, unmitigated faith stance, seem more than a bit conflicted regarding core tenets of Christianity such as original sin, God's immutability, and the divinity of Jesus Christ. While not trying to reopen theological debates that easily predated the Protestant Reformation by at least a thousand years or more, it seems that actual fundamental church doctrine and creedal dogma do not seem to matter in a major way for contemporary Evangelicals. While the respondents wrestled with these spiritual issues, it was surprising that nearly nine out of ten Evangelicals polled had ironclad opinions on social issues, particularly those pertaining to gender and sexuality. To this point, a Christian leader once quipped at a meeting, "If we could just get all the Christians saved, we'd be in good shape."[64] Yet, on that basis, one could reasonably argue that the Evangelicals are far more dedicated and devoted to being culture warriors than the most conservative of other churchgoers.

Critical race theology is grounded and informed by my embrace of a prophetic Black Christianity that encompasses but is not limited to liberationist, womanist, and decolonial perspectives. Any human activity, intellectual or otherwise, that is not dedicated to promoting some aspect of freedom, justice, equality, and dignity for yourself and others is guaranteeing the continuation of the status quo. "It is not an oversimplification to say that the Christian story is the tension between the promise of justice and liberation and the unjust and oppressive patterns in our daily lived experiences," Cole Arthur Riley notes.[65]

As I write these words, I do so in full knowledge that I am advancing a counternarrative of a proud and prolonged struggle for human fulfillment and flourishing that, while far from being perfect, has been striving toward the goal of life and liberation. As I have always upheld, it has been both an academic and an activist concern that links divine justice to social justice so that ALL people in every part of God's dream of creation can enjoy freedom, justice, and equality with dignity and decency. As developed by historian Judith Weisenfeld, the concept of "religio-racial identity" hinges on an incisive critique of how white Christian normative categories and narratives of religion are persistently naturalized in both the related fields of religious studies and theology as well as our society and culture.[66] Furthermore, as a contribution to theory and method

---

[64] Stonestreet and Leander, "What 'the State of Theology' Tells Us."

[65] Cole Arthur Riley, *This Here Flesh: Spirituality, Liberation, and the Stories That Make Us* (New York: Convergent Books, 2022), 128–29.

[66] See Judith Weisenfeld, *New World A-Coming: Black Religion and Racial Identity during the Great Migration* (New York: New York University Press, 2017).

in the study of religion, "religio-racial identity" challenges us to put aside the seeming universality of these categories and to do so by specifically centering the voices, viewpoints, agency, and theoretical contributions of BIPOC communities. Put simply, we as scholars need to be taking more from Weisenfeld than the term *religio-racial identity*. We need to be extending the method of study through which she produced it.

In my effort to give voice to the desperate, disinherited, disadvantaged, and dispossessed peoples of God's creation, I find it no shame to admit that I am totally biased in favor of divine grace and social justice, making their lives shiny examples of human freedom and flourishing. Anything else should be unacceptable for an avowed believer in a living and loving God. I share my own religio-racial identity as an attempt to expand rather than narrow channels of communication regarding the possibilities for critical race theology. Unlike the inordinate number of mainstream white theologians and scholars of religion who, either by dint of their temperament or through training, have approached their particular discipline in a distant and detached manner while assuming the ubiquity of Christocentric principles and practices, I operate from Olympic experience that has witnessed the works of beauty as well as the brutality at the hands of those who professed to be working in accordance with God's will.

Part of the urgent work within critical race theology is to repair the damage wrought by an unchecked vision of American Christianity wedded to power and privilege. We do so while acknowledging that God's baseline expectation of our profession of faith is that we do justice, love kindness, and walk humbly with our God (Micah 6:8). The constant existential struggle of our time is to not abdicate the entirety of our identity and worldview to the worst practitioners and most misguided representatives. "What is bothering me incessantly," Dietrich Bonhoeffer reflects in his *Letters from Prison*, "is the question of what Christianity really is, or indeed who Christ really is, for us today. The time when people could be told everything by means of words, whether theological or pious, is over, and so is the time of inwardness and conscience—and that means the time of religion in general."[67] Approaching his conundrum from an altogether different angle, the writer Garrison Keillor remarks, "Anyone who thinks sitting in church can make you a Christian must also think that sitting in a garage can make you a car."[68]

I am both personally and professionally inclined to view Christianity in connection and conversation with faith traditions and belief systems. In my humble efforts to be my fullest, freest self, I embrace Jesus Christ as the Holy Other in whom I have all the divinity I could ever want or need, but I also recognize that everyone else has the right and need to find a wholly other "Holy Other" for themselves. This does not diminish the greatness of God for Christians, but rather demands that we do not take the primacy of a white Western model of Christianity as the be-all and end-all of our discourse. "The Christian ideal has not been tried and found wanting," according to English writer G. K. Chesterton, but rather "it has been found difficult and left untried."[69]

As a scholar of Black religious experiences and expressions, the intersectional, interreligious, and international possibilities for critical race theology are readily apparent to me. In my capacity as a professor and scholar for more than two decades, I have

---

[67] "Letter To Eberhard Bethage, April, 1944," Dietrich Bonhoeffer, *Letters and Papers from Prison* (London: SCM Press, 1971), 279.

[68] Cable Neuhaus, "Garrison Keillor on the Joys of Aging," *Saturday Evening Post*, April 18, 2022, https://www.saturdayeveningpost.com/2022/04/garrison-keillor-2/.

[69] G. K. Chesterton, "The Unfinished Temple," in *What's Wrong with the World* (1910), https://www.gutenberg.org/files/1717/1717-h/1717-h.htm#link2H_4_0006.

developed some degree of familiarity—maybe even facility—in comparing many of the world's religions. Nevertheless, I have found that I am best able to speak in the most compelling and compassionate manner possible about other traditions by first plumbing the depths of what I find best within my own. Likewise, although I am advancing critical race theology from a prophetic Black Christian perspective, this can and should extend beyond this frame of reference. Much like CRT eventually spawned LatCrit, AsianCrit, TribalCrit, and DisCrit among other offshoots, critical race theology should afford those committed to social justice principles and praxis the necessary cognitive space not only within a Christian viewpoint but also from Jewish, Muslim, Buddhist, Hindu, Taoist, Yoruba, Santero, or humanist perspectives.

By examining court cases, laws, human rights reports, and related materials, the legal challenges faced by adherents of the most widely practiced African-derived religions in the twenty-first century such as Santería, Lucumi, Haitian Vodou, Candomblé, Umbanda, Islam, Rastafari, and Obeah, Danielle N. Boaz's scholarly research on religious racism indicates promising future directions for this sort of enterprise. According to Boaz, "religious racism" is a term that originates from Brazil, where devotees of African diaspora religions have been experiencing increasingly pervasive intolerance over the past several years, underscoring that discrimination against African-based religions is more than mere prejudice against a faith or group of faiths; it is the intersection of religious intolerance and racism.[70] Goldschmidt and McAlister's analysis further enriches our attempts to make sense of the correlation of race, nation, and religion in American life. They write,

> Even when racism is condemned in unambiguous terms and nationalism subjected to searching critique ... a troubling conceptual divide remains. Non-western others

---

[70] See Danielle N. Boaz, *Banning Black Gods: Law and Religions of the African Diaspora* (University Park: Pennsylvania State University Press, 2021).

are thought to act in terms of "religion"—to base their identities and politics on beliefs about the supernatural world that we in the west implicitly or explicitly deem unfounded or rational. Yet Americans are thought to act in terms of "race" and "nation"—to base our identity and politics, for better or worse, on rational analysis of social or scientific facts or belief in a secular modern world that remains largely secure despite our growing fear of non-modern religious others.

Religion has been inextricably woven into both racial and national identities, to such an extent that "race," "nation," and "religion" have each defined the others. These seemingly distinct discourses of difference have at times borrowed and at times contested each other's rhetorical authority, reinforcing and undercutting each other's social hierarchies, mixing and mingling in unresolved dialectics irreducible to any one term.[71]

In the final analysis, this is where critical race theology comes into view.

---

[71] Henry Goldschmidt and Elizabeth A. McAlister, eds., *Race, Nation, and Religion in the Americas* (New York: Oxford University Press, 2004), 4, 5.

2

"One Nation under God"?

White Christian Nationalism and
the Divided States of America

I have been asked repeatedly, in one form or another, "Is the United States of America a nation based on 'Judeo-Christian' values?"[1] A sizable number of Christians would answer this question in a knee-jerk fashion, with a hale and hearty "Yes," based largely on the tropes and trappings of what sociologist of religion Robert Bellah once famously called civil religion. In ways large and small, we routinely encounter somewhat shallow symbols of overtly simplistic expression of American Christianity as state religion: exchanging paper money and coins emblazoned with the phrase *In God we trust*; uttering the Pledge of Allegiance to "one nation under God" in

---

[1] I use quotes around "Judeo-Christian" as a phrase in the recognition that a singular Judeo-Christian tradition does not exist and has never existed. If a dominant tradition of use can be discerned, it is a mid-twentieth-century phrase in the United States that originated in the 1930s and rose to prominence in the early Cold War as a way to simultaneously identify white, capitalist, US nuclear family practices as "holy" and against Soviet "godlessness" while also attempting to absolve US consciences from their complicity in the anti-Semitism of the previous decades, particularly the atrocities of the Holocaust.

public schools and major sporting events; placing one's right hand on a Bible to swear oaths of fidelity to "God and country" in our courthouses and other halls of government; and one of the nation's most patriotic songs is entitled "God Bless America."[2]

Sadly, there is a bitter irony associated with the phrase *civil religion*. Despite the best of intentions, the elements of civil religion are often the more fractious and contentious issues in public life. With those basic slogans and symbols clearly in mind, we may be able to explore the numerous problems and challenges at the intersection of faith, culture, and politics in twenty-first-century American society, gaining insight into how and why we must engage in the contemporary culture wars. Focusing on white Christian nationalism and how this movement divides the world into a struggle of good and evil are critically important concerns. This chapter reveals and explores how white Christian nationalism threatens to limit our communal vision and expose the fragility of our civic virtues.

In 1990, Maya Angelou's poem "These Yet to Be United States" struck a particular nerve in addressing the nation's zeitgeist. The poem profoundly indicts the nation's name as being a misnomer at its best and an outright lie at its worst. This is particularly evident in the poem's fifth stanza, wherein Angelou writes, "They kneel alone in terror / with dread in every glance. / Their rights are threatened daily / by a grim inheritance."[3] Answering the earlier stanza's question, "Why do your children cry?" those who kneel in terror are young people in the United States. With words like *terror, dread, threaten,* and *grim,* she prophetically depicted a present as well

---

[2] Juan M. Floyd-Thomas, Stacey M. Floyd-Thomas, and Mark G. Toulouse, *The Altars Where We Worship: The Religious Significance of Popular Culture* (Louisville, KY: Westminster John Knox Press, 2016), 98–129.

[3] Maya Angelou, "These Yet-to-Be-United States," *Los Angeles Times,* June 3, 1990, https://www.latimes.com/archives/la-xpm-1990-06-03-bk-967-story.html.

as a future that are undesirable, unenviable, and decidedly negative. This divided nation is the home of children who shed far too many tears because they are not looking forward to what the future may promise. Defining the nation more by those who were excluded than included into its broken and beleaguered body politic, the concept of being "united" appears to be a gross mockery of its best intentions. Angelou foresaw how the "United States" was entering the twenty-first century internally divided by self-inflicted wounds that infected its people with a pervasive, paralyzing fear of its future and a bitter callousness toward the victims of its destruction.

White Christian nationalism has emerged through this fear and callousness as a potential weapon of mass destruction in the culture wars. Toward the end of Barack Obama's presidency, many in academia and mainstream media were sounding the death knell of white Christian America's influence over our nation's political affairs. In 2016, scholars, journalists, and political pundits offered diagnoses and prognostications about the impact of shifting national demographics. Republicans could no longer rely solely on the white Christian vote that had protected them for so long; *U.S. News and World Report* used the term *the powerless religion voter*.[4] Prior to the 2016 election, Robert P. Jones, CEO of the Public Religion Research Institute, released a book titled *The End of White Christian America*, which offered a historical look at the varieties of white Christian identity. Ultimately, many liberal and progressive media figures cited the book, welcoming the imminent demise of a white Evangelical stranglehold on American politics. Others argued that conservative Christians were simply too diffuse to muster the power they once had in the public sphere.

---

[4] Lindsey Cook, "The Powerless Religious Voter: White Christian America Doesn't Hold the Same Sway in Elections as It Used to," *U.S. News & World Report*, July 19, 2016, https://www.usnews.com/news/articles/2016-07-19/the-gop-cant-rely-religious-voters-to-win-anymore.

Yet, in terms of its racial–ethnic and religious identifications, the one group whose electoral and cultural support for Donald Trump never wavered was white Evangelical voters. Despite Trump's myriad personal flaws and professional failures (or possibly because of them), he enjoyed a sharply improved performance among this demographic over his political rival, Hillary Rodham Clinton, in the 2016 presidential race. Dissecting and debating the key reasons why Trump's overall share of the electoral vote among white Evangelical voters—including those who claimed to have been "evangelical" all along, as well as those who began identifying as evangelical in the period between 2016 and 2020—ticked upward from 77 percent in 2016 to 84 percent in 2020 has been one of the great challenges of the past few years.[5]

---

[5] Gregory A. Smith, "More White Americans Adopted Than Shed Evangelical Label during Trump Presidency, Especially His Supporters," *Pew Research Center*, September 15, 2021, https://www.pewresearch.org/short-reads/2021/09/15/more-white-americans-adopted-than-shed-evangelical-label-during-trump-presidency-especially-his-supporters/; Jason Husser, "Why Trump Is Reliant on White Evangelicals," *Brookings: Commentary*, April 6, 2020, https://www.brookings.edu/articles/why-trump-is-reliant-on-white-evangelicals/; Jeff Brumley, "From 2016 to 2020, Trump Grew in Support from White Evangelicals," *Baptist News Global*, September 20, 2021, https://baptistnews.com/article/from-2016-to-2020-trump-grew-in-support-from-white-evangelicals/; Gene Demby, Shereen Marisol Meraji, "The White Elephants in the Room," *National Public Radio: Code Switch*, November 18, 2020, https://www.npr.org/2020/11/17/935910276/the-white-elephants-in-the-room; Dick Hannah, "Not without Precedent: Populist White Evangelical Support for Trump," *Berkeley Journal of Sociology* 61 (2017): 26–31; Harriet Sherwood, "White Evangelical Christians Stick by Trump Again, Exit Polls Show," *The Guardian*, November 6, 2020, https://www.theguardian.com/us-news/2020/nov/06/white-evangelical-christians-supported-trump; Ed Stetzer and Andrew MacDonald, "Why Evangelicals Voted Trump: Debunking the 81%," *Christianity Today*, October 18, 2018, https://www.

How did a Christocentric constituency who so proudly proclaimed itself as the standard-bearer for religious belief and moral integrity select an individual so markedly cruel, corrupt, and contemptuous to be the most appropriate avatar for its principles and priorities?

Although this voting bloc proved insufficient to garner their chosen candidate the political victory in the popular vote, it is both telling and jarring that this constituency supports this very specific person for the US presidency so strenuously.[6] Approximately 80 percent of white Evangelical voters consistently approved of President Trump's performance in utter contradistinction to principles, proclamations, and practices akin to Jesus Christ over the four years of his presidency—the failed effort to implement a federal Muslim travel ban; the disastrous "Unite the Right" Alt-Right rally in Charlottesville; declaring African and Caribbean nations to be "sh**hole countries"; the intentional separation of tens of thousands of Latin American migrant children from their families at US–Mexico border crossings; multiple credible accusations of him committing adultery and sexual assault; and the Trump administration's grossly negligent response to the COVID-19 pandemic.

While their numbers have dwindled from 21 percent to 15 percent of the US population, white Evangelicals still have remained a formidable force in politics. This segment makes up a little over a third of Republicans, yet they have an outsized impact on elections, making up about a quarter of *overall* voters. More simply put, approximately 15 percent of Americans account for about 25 percent of those who "turn out to vote" in the most

---

christianitytoday.com/ct/2018/october/why-evangelicals-trump-vote-81-percent-2016-election.html.

[6] Jack Jenkins, "Why Christian Nationalists Love Trump: God and Country," *ThinkProgress*, August 7, 2017, https://archive.thinkprogress.org/trumps-christian-nationalism-c6fe206e40cc/.

recent US elections. "In these twilight years of white Christian America, for those still within the veil, the strain of holding these contradictions can lead to a dissociative state, where self-reflection becomes treasonous and self-delusion a necessity," Robert P. Jones argues. "The fruits of this spirit are abundant. Empathy signals weakness, and disdain strength. Prophets are shunned, and authoritarians embraced. Truth is exchanged for a lie."[7]

As performative outbursts and politicized uprisings occur throughout the country, including in the halls of government, we experience a seemingly endless torrent of concern about how this alleged zenith of our current world system has put "polarization" and "tribalism" at the center of our zeitgeist. On a granular level, this reductionist and vague "polarization" narrative has become a beloved lamentation among our media and political elite as they attempt to rationalize why so many Americans lack the ability to "get things done" and "come together" with a "shared reality." In the spirit of bothsidesism, we are told that both the Right and the Left have grown too radically extreme on the political spectrum. "Becoming too polarized" is a superficially appealing, albeit appalling, motif in American public life. It is at once nostalgic for a nonspecified previous era defined by the "reasonable" centrism of the mythic American mainstream while also being noncommittal about the overall erosion of conscious and compassionate compromise as a core civic virtue toward an idealistic vision of consensus building.

Yet, both "sides" are not the same. One side, evidently, wants to establish a fascistic theocracy with unquestioned dominion over the lives and livelihoods of nonwhite, non-Christian, nonnormative, and noncitizen peoples while unfettered political and economic clout is amassed and sparingly doled out by oligarchs

---

[7] Robert P. Jones, "The Unmaking of the White Christian Worldview," *Time*, September 29, 2021, https://time.com/6102117/white-christian-americans-sins/.

at the apex of society. Meanwhile, the other side of the political spectrum (once it overcomes the grievous self-inflicted wounds of its own infighting) wants the wealthy to pay a bit more in taxes so that our duly elected government can afford to provide education, health care, infrastructure, and other public service for the good of everyone while also protecting the rights and freedoms of all members of society regardless of their background. The terms of the debate are just that stark, and the stakes are clearly that high.

Contemporary and forward-looking theological discourse must pay attention to the tendency to dismiss white Christian nationalism in an offhand fashion as merely a fringe or extremist modality that somehow operates within a larger framework of American religions. White Christian nationalism, in the words of twentieth-century American preacher and politician Gerald L. K. Smith, "is easy to define and simple to interpret."[8] As a political and theological movement, white Christian nationalism believes "that the destiny of America in relationship to its governing authority must be kept in the hands of [its] own people. We must never be governed by aliens. We must keep control of our own money and our own blood," Smith argued.[9] The concerns over governance, money, and blood are familiar phrases within anti-immigrant, anti-Semitic, and anti-Black rhetoric. Smith continues,

> Subversive forced, exploiting sentimental nitwits, are reading into the Constitution a code of conduct which threatens to mongrelize our race, destroy our racial self-respect and enslave the white [race].

---

[8] "Transcript: The Rachel Maddow Show, 7/25/22, Guests: Josh Shapiro, Elissa Slotkin," *MSNBC*, July 25, 2022, https://www.msnbc.com/transcripts/rachel-maddow-show/transcript-rachel-maddow-show-7-25-22-n1297593.

[9] "Transcript: The Rachel Maddow Show."

Fight mongrelization and all the attempts being made to force the intermixture of the Black and White races. Preserve America as a Christian nation, being conscious of the fact that there is a highly organized campaign to substitute Jewish tradition for Christian tradition. The most powerful Jewish organization in America is the Anti-Defamation League, which has launched a campaign to remove from all public schools any song book which contains a Christmas carol or any other hymn which mentioned the name of Jesus.[10]

Gerald L. K. Smith is but one example. Critical race theology is attentive to how white Christian nationalism both operated in the past and operates today. In its past and present forms, white Christian nationalism is not even remotely acceptable to the core teachings and practices of the religion it co-opts. Nevertheless, present-day movements in support of and explicitly embracing white Christian nationalism are growing.

Attending the 2022 Turning Point USA Student Action Summit in Florida, Rep. Marjorie Taylor Greene, of Georgia, bluntly declared, "We need to be the party of nationalism and I'm a Christian, and I say it proudly, we should be Christian Nationalists."[11] Meanwhile, after urging his followers to attend the now infamous January 6th, 2021, MAGA rally that led to riots, saying, "I'm really praying that God will pour His Spirit upon Washington, DC, like we've never seen before," Pennsylvania Republican Doug Mastriano portrayed the fight against pandemic lockdowns and Trump's electoral defeat as a fierce spiritual battle

---

[10] "Transcript: The Rachel Maddow Show."

[11] Amanda Tyler, "Opinion: Marjorie Taylor Greene's Words on Christian Nationalism Are a Wake-Up Call," *CNN*, July 27, 2022, https://www.cnn.com/2022/07/27/opinions/christian-nationalism-marjorie-taylor-greene-tyler/index.html.

against the forces of evil during his 2022 gubernatorial campaign.[12] In April 2022, Mastriano, by then the Republican Pennsylvania gubernatorial nominee, dismissed the separation of church and state as a "myth."[13] In October 2021, Josh Mandel, a candidate in Ohio's Republican primary for the state's open US Senate seat, insisted during a debate that "there's no such thing as separation of church and state."[14] Three months later, Supreme Court Associate Justice Neil Gorsuch made an offhand reference to the "so-called separation of … church and state" during oral arguments.[15] By June 2022, Colorado Rep. Lauren Boebert, speaking at a Colorado church, proclaimed, "I'm tired of the separation of church and state junk that's not in the Constitution. It was in a stinking letter, and it means nothing like what they say it does."[16]

---

[12] Eliza Griswold, "A Pennsylvania Lawmaker and the Resurgence of Christian Nationalism," *New Yorker*, May 9, 2021, https://www.newyorker.com/news/on-religion/a-pennsylvania-lawmaker-and-the-resurgence-of-christian-nationalism.

[13] Peter Smith and Deepa Bharath, "Christian Nationalism on the Rise in Some GOP Campaigns," Associated Press, May 29, 2022, https://apnews.com/article/2022-midterm-elections-pennsylvania-religion-nationalism-8bf7a6115725f508a37ef944333bc145; "Transcript: The Rachel Maddow Show."

[14] Trip Gabriel, "In Trump's Shadow, Ohio Republicans Campaign Ahead of Tuesday's Primary," *New York Times*, May 1, 2022, https://www.nytimes.com/2022/05/01/us/politics/josh-mandel-vance-ohio-senate.html.

[15] Steve Benen, "Gorsuch Derides the 'So-Called' Separation of Church And State," *MSNBC*, January 21, 2022, https://www.msnbc.com/rachel-maddow-show/maddowblog/gorsuch-derides-so-called-separation-church-state-n1287809.

[16] Jack Jenkins, "The Activist behind Opposition to the Separation of Church and State," *Religion News Service*, July 18, 2022, https://religionnews.com/2022/07/18/the-activist-behind-opposition-to-the-separation-of-church-and-state/; Cornerstone Christian Center,

When sitting members of US Congress, associate justices of the Supreme Court, and viable contenders for statewide elected offices diminish the value of church–state separation in our society, it should be a huge cause for alarm for all of us. Even with their nuanced differences, Greene, Mastriano, and others are examples of right-wing religiosity and white supremacy that has been matched by millions of other Americans under the banner of white Christian nationalism.

Formal groups and events like Pastors for Trump and the ReAwaken America tour have become leading examples of the broad networks of white Christian nationalism in the country.[17] Often, these groups use rhetorical strategies that depend on imagery of "spiritual battles" against the "evil path" on which our country journeys.[18] Some of the key figures in these organizations and events are well known beyond far-right political circles: Roger Stone and Michael Flynn.[19] Others, like Oklahoma-based pastor Jackson Lahmeyer are lesser known or unknown figures in broader US cultural conversations.[20] Though different individuals and events

---

"Cornerstone Christian Center welcomes US Congress Representative Lauren Boebert," YouTube video, June 26, 2022, https://www.youtube.com/watch?v=IWOSF3SHdUo.

[17] Peter Stone, "Pro-Trump Pastors Rebuked for 'Overt' Embrace of White Christian Nationalism," *The Guardian*, May 1, 2023, https://www.theguardian.com/us-news/2023/may/01/far-right-pastors-embracing-trump-white-christian-nationalism.

[18] Stone, "Pro-Trump Pastors Rebuked for 'Overt' Embrace of White Christian Nationalism."

[19] Richard Lardner and Michelle R. Smith, "Michael Flynn's ReAwaken Roadshow Recruits 'Army of God'," *PBS Frontline*, October 7, 2022, https://www.pbs.org/wgbh/frontline/article/michael-flynn-reawaken-america-tour/.

[20] Stone, "Pro-Trump Pastors Rebuked for 'Overt' Embrace of White Christian Nationalism."

may nuance their approach or message in different ways, they seem to share convictions that the nation has Christian roots that are deteriorating, that those roots need to be explicitly reestablished through pious patriotism and revivalist-style populist politics, and that their movement need not convince the people who are already posed against them.[21] Their adversaries are to be destroyed in the re-creation of an exclusively Christian United States.[22]

The overt embrace of white Christian nationalism poses a burgeoning threat to the witness of the church and the health of American democracy. Faith leaders, activists, journalists, scholars, and others outside of this movement have observed how the Trump campaign has tried relentlessly to woo and co-opt right-leaning

---

[21] Stone, "Pro-Trump Pastors Rebuked for 'Overt' Embrace of White Christian Nationalism"; Lardner and Smith, "Michael Flynn's ReAwaken Roadshow"; Liam Adams and Andy Humbles, "Controversial ReAwaken America Tour Brings Anxiety about Politics and Traffic," *The Tennessean* online, January 20, 2023, https://www.tennessean.com/story/news/religion/2023/01/20/reawaken-america-tour-nashville-draws-thousands-creates-traffic-woes/69818617007/; Sam Kestenbaum, "'I Think All the Christians Get Slaughtered': Inside the MAGA Road Show Barnstorming America," *Rolling Stone* online, September 17, 2022, https://www.rollingstone.com/culture/culture-features/clay-clark-reawaken-america-maga-tour-trump-1234594574/; Stella Rouse and Shibley Telhami, "Most Republicans Support Declaring the United States a Christian Nation," *Politico* online, September 21, 2022, https://www.politico.com/news/magazine/2022/09/21/most-republicans-support-declaring-the-united-states-a-christian-nation-00057736.

[22] Stone, "Pro-Trump Pastors Rebuked for 'Overt' Embrace of White Christian Nationalism"; Lardner and Smith, "Michael Flynn's ReAwaken Roadshow"; Adams and Humbles, "Controversial ReAwaken America Tour Brings Anxiety about Politics and Traffic"; Kestenbaum, "Inside the MAGA Road Show"; Rouse and Telhami, "Most Republicans Support Declaring the United States a Christian Nation."

church leaders into service of the campaign, even tempting them with greater access to the White House as well as promises to change long-standing tax law relating to financial relationships between houses of worship and political campaigns.[23] Speaking before the 2022 US House Oversight Committee's Subcommittee on Civil Rights and Civil Liberties, Amanda Tyler, executive director of the Baptist Joint Committee for Religious Liberty, stated,

> The "Christian" in Christian nationalism is more about ethno-national identity than religion. Christian nationalism is a gross distortion of the Christian faith I hold dear. Christian nationalism uses the language, symbols, and imagery of Christianity—in fact, it may look and sound like Christianity to the casual observer. However, closer examination reveals that it is using the veneer of Christianity to point not to Jesus the Christ but to a political figure, party, or ideology. Christian nationalism seeks to manipulate religious devotion into giving unquestioning moral support for its political goals.[24]

Adam Russell Taylor, president of the Christian social justice group Sojourners, has argued that these mobilization efforts "are trying to impose a Christian theocracy" and that "it's imperative that Christian leaders of all backgrounds, including conservative

---

[23] Elizabeth Dias, "'Christianity Will Have Power': Donald Trump Made a Promise to White Evangelical Christians, Whose Support Can Seem Mystifying to the Outside Observer," *New York Times*, August 9, 2020, https://www.nytimes.com/2020/08/09/us/evangelicals-trump-christianity.html?smid=tw-share.

[24] *Hearing on Confronting White Supremacy (Part 7), Before the House Oversight Committee's Subcommittee on Civil Rights and Civil Liberties*, 117th Cong. (2022) (statement of Amanda Tyler, on behalf of Baptist Joint Committee for Religious Liberty).

ones, speak out about this effort as a threat to our democracy and to the church."[25]

What exactly is white Christian nationalism and why is it on the rise now? Sociologists of religion Andrew L. Whitehead and Samuel L. Perry provided the following definition:

> Simply put, *Christian nationalism is a cultural framework—a collection of myths, traditions, symbols, narratives and value systems—that idealizes and advocates a fusion of Christianity with American civic life.*[26]

In their summation of the union between white Christian nationalism and political conservatism, Whitehead and Perry contend that this movement is significant "because calls to 'take America back for God' are not primarily mobilizing the faithful toward religious ends" but rather "they are ... seeking to retain or gain power in the public sphere—political, social, or religious."[27] Despite the strenuous claims to the contrary by its most dogged believers, there is little to nothing discernibly "Christian" in the movement's core concepts aside from terminology and imagery that has been cherry-picked from biblical texts. Whether examined on a philosophical, theological, or practical basis, Pamela Cooper-White asserts that white Christian nationalism

> is not primarily characterized by devotion to the gospel mandates of love, care, and justice as found in the teachings of Jesus but rather by a social and political goal of restoring the United States to a fictional origin as a

---

[25] Stone, "Pro-Trump Pastors Rebuked for 'Overt' Embrace of White Christian Nationalism."

[26] Andrew L. Whitehead and Samuel L. Perry, *Taking America Back for God: Christian Nationalism in the United States,* updated edition (New York: Oxford University Press, 2022), 10 [emphasis added].

[27] Whitehead and Perry, *Taking America Back for God,* 153.

"Christian nation" and a not-at-all fictional origin in white, masculinist supremacy.[28]

Even more sharply, Philip Gorski has called white Christian nationalism nothing less than "political idolatry dressed up as religious orthodoxy."[29]

Notably, there are important differences between those who emphasize the centrality of a conservative religious worldview in their personal lives and those who place a high premium on public religious expressions of white Christian nationalism. In making the distinction between conservative Christians and white Christian nationalists, American religious historian Joseph Williams explains,

> On the one hand, like many other religious conservatives, Christian nationalists typically portray abortion and same-sex marriage as a direct attack on the fundamental source of order within society: the traditional two-parent family where the mother and father fulfill gender-specific roles. On the other hand, scholars observe a significant divide between the two groups: tolerance of religious out-groups decreases specifically among those who prioritize public religiosity. For instance, Christian nationalists demonstrate a greater willingness to restrict the civil liberties of religious "others." They also frequently question the existence of unjust racial disparities in the criminal justice system and embrace nativist restrictions on immigration.[30]

---

[28] Pamela Cooper-White, *The Psychology of Christian Nationalism: Why People Are Drawn In and How to Talk Across the Divide* (Minneapolis: Fortress Press, 2022), 24.

[29] Philip Gorski, "Christianity and Democracy after Trump," *Political Theology* 19, no. 5 (2018): 3.

[30] John Chadwick, "Christian Nationalism Explained: An Interview

Simply put, white Christian nationalists discern multiple threats to American Christianity as being synonymous to dangerous risks to the nation-state. They conflate the Body of Christ with the US body politic. In this conflation, however, the white Christian nationalist imagination often views these perceived threats in highly racialized, gendered, and sexualized terms.

The Religious Right and the "culture wars" were synchronous developments within the United States in the latter half of the twentieth century. On the heels of the tumultuous upheavals of the 1960s, the emergence of the Christian Right fit neatly into a backlash narrative akin to the rise of fundamentalism in the early half of the twentieth century. Many Americans today acknowledge the robust political force that is the Religious Right because this faith-based constituency has taken aim at government policies and practices they deem controversial with an onslaught of hundreds of DC lobbyists, millions of dollars of advertising spending, and a formidable grassroots response. By understanding the history of white Evangelicals' political activity in America since the 1970s, we garner valuable information that would have otherwise eluded us. Currently, we are witnessing the coexistence of demographic animosity and democratic anxiety as increasing numbers of formerly dispossessed and disadvantaged peoples move from the margins nearer to the center of societal power and cultural possibilities. Many interpreters of contemporary American Christianity have advanced the argument that reactionary motives, either explicitly or implicitly, explain the *raison d'être* of the Religious Right. Recently, an alternate, equally compelling theory has emerged.

Simply, the Religious Right wanted to graft itself onto one of the nation's two major political parties and thus galvanize itself into a cohesive, socially relevant voting bloc that could wield its

---

with Rutgers Professor Joseph Williams," *Rutgers School of Arts and Sciences*, March 4, 2021.

discrete yet disproportionate political power as a white Christian nationalist party. According to this interpretation, this grafting is how, in the wake of the left-leaning social transformations of the 1960s, the Republican Party morphed from the "Grand Old Party" into "God's Own Party."[31] The evolution of the Republican Party

[31] D. G. Hart, *That Old-Time Religion in Modern America: Evangelical Protestantism in the Twentieth Century*, reprint ed. (Chicago: Ivan R. Dee, 2003); William Martin, *With God on Our Side: The Rise of the Religious Right in America* (New York: Broadway Books, 2005); Chris Hedges, *American Fascists: The Christian Right and the War on America* (New York: Free Press, 2008); Axel Schäfer, *Countercultural Conservatives: American Evangelicalism from the Postwar Revival to the New Christian Right* (Madison: University of Wisconsin Press, 2011); Darren Dochuk, *From Bible Belt to Sun Belt: Plain-Folk Religion, Grassroot Politics, and the Rise of Evangelical Conservatism* (New York: W. W. Norton, 2012); Daniel K. Williams, *God's Own Party: The Making of the Christian Right* (New York: Oxford University Press, 2012); Matthew Sutton, ed., *Jerry Falwell and the Rise of the Religious Right: A Brief History with Documents* (Boston: Bedford/St. Martin's Press, 2012); Michael Sean Winter, *God's Right Hand: How Jerry Falwell Made God a Republican and Baptized the American Rights* (New York: Harper One, 2012); Axel Schäfer, *American Evangelicals and the 1960s* (Madison: University of Wisconsin Press, 2013); David Swartz, *Moral Minority: The Evangelical Left in an Age of Conservatism*, reprint ed. (Philadelphia: University of Pennsylvania Press, 2014); Lisa McGirr, *Suburban Warriors: The Origins of the New American Right*, rev. ed. (Princeton, NJ: Princeton University Press, 2015); Kevin M. Kruse, *One Nation Under God: How Corporate America Invented Christian America* (New York: Basic Books, 2016); Angela Denker, *Red State Christians: Understanding the Voters Who Elected Donald Trump* (Minneapolis: Fortress Press, 2019); Ben Howe, *The Immoral Majority: Why Evangelicals Chose Political Power over Christian Values* (New York: Broadside Books, 2019); Sarah Posner, *Unholy: Why White Evangelicals Worship at the Altar of Donald Trump* (New York: Random House, 2020); Juan M. Floyd-Thomas, "The Donald Went Down to Georgia: The GOP from God's Own Party to the Party of Trump," in *Faith and Reckoning After Trump*, ed. Miguel De La Torre (Maryknoll, NY: Orbis Books, 2021), 13–24; Tim Alberta,

has been a metamorphosis based on political convenience rather than principled conviction.

Though white Christian nationalism is nothing new—it has been evident even before the nation's founding—its resurgence in recent years has been very much amplified by political figures like Jerry Falwell Sr., Paul Weyrich, Ralph Reed, James Dobson, and other key figures who sought to consolidate power by manipulating large swaths of mostly white Christians, sowing division, discontent, and disruptive violence. "A mistake a lot of people have made over the past few years," Kristin Kobes Du Mez argues, "is to suggest there is some fundamental conflict between evangelicalism and the kind of violence or threat of violence we're seeing."[32] Even though religious liberty is a fundamental American ideal enshrined in the US Constitution, its meaning routinely has been debated throughout the nation's history. Yet many conflicts that are arising from today's iteration of white Christian nationalism has been characterized by explicitly antidemocratic impulses that America is a nation of, for, and by Christians only. White Christian nationalism ideologically contributes to the Religious Right's misuse of "religious liberty" as a rationale for circumventing regulations and overturning laws aimed at safeguarding a pluralistic society that is governed by a multicultural, multiracial, and multifaith democracy. At its core, white Christian nationalism directly threatens the principle of the church–state separation, ultimately undermining the Establishment Clause of the First Amendment. Disrespect, discrimination, and, at times, violence against religious minorities and the nonreligious are the result.

The Kingdom, The Power, and The Glory: American Evangelicals in an Age of Extremism (New York: Harper, 2023).

[32] Jack Jenkins, "For Insurrectionists, a Violent Faith Brewed from Nationalism, Conspiracies and Jesus," *Religion News Service*, January 12, 2021, https://religionnews.com/2021/01/12/the-faith-of-the-insurrectionists.

Recent Supreme Court rulings have emerged as the powerfully reactionary bulwark that serve at the behest of white Christian nationalists and their right-wing political confederates within American society. Ethicist Miguel De La Torre has convincingly argued that, no matter how "genuine and sympathetic white Christians may be, the way they have been taught to read the Bible advocates classism, racism, heterosexism, and misogyny, making them heirs to those who previously used Holy Writ to persecute disenfranchised racial and ethnic groups."[33] Through legislative and executive action at various levels of government, these movements have worked zealously to overturn a century of increasing rights for people of color, the poor, workers, women, LGBTQIA+ citizens, and immigrants. They have gained their greatest foothold, however, in the nation's judicial branch of government. Legal scholar Gerald Rosenberg has argued that our nation's courts represent a "hollow hope" for those seeking substantial social reform.[34] More recently, legal scholar Keith E. Whittington contends that, in light of many of our contemporary challenges, the US Supreme Court is very likely to remain a "hollow hope" for those of us "seeking an institution that will stand up to political majorities and defend a more robust conception of limited government or individual rights."[35] This is the case because "the Court has defended these positions only when there was substantial support in the elected branches for doing so, and it has done so only in ways that were compatible with their political agendas."[36] Despite assumptions

---

[33] Miguel De La Torre, *Burying White Privilege: Resurrecting a Badass Christianity* (Grand Rapids: William B. Eerdmans, 2018), 41–42.

[34] Gerald N. Rosenberg, *The Hollow Hope: Can Courts Bring about Social Change?* 2nd ed. (Chicago: University of Chicago Press, 2008).

[35] Keith E. Whittington, "The Supreme Court as a Symbol in the Culture War," *Georgetown Journal of Law and Public Policy* 19, no. 2 (2021): 376.

[36] Whittington, "The Supreme Court as a Symbol in the Culture War," 376.

of impartiality and assertions of nonpartisan neutrality, we must have a "come to Jesus" moment in which we realize both that the nation's highest court is thoroughly tethered to politics and that that harsh truth ostensibly prevents it, at least of its own accord, from ever coming to the rescue of those who need it most.

In this observation, I am in full and steadfast agreement with Pamela Cooper-White's assessment of the first two decades of the twenty-first century. They mark "a pivotal moment in the American experiment of democracy and also in the very character of American Christianity."[37] The poisonous fervor of anti-Black racism, misogyny, anti-Semitism, Islamophobia, homophobia, transphobia, xenophobia, and other modes of oppression and exclusion remains a disturbingly persistent mainstay of right-wing extremism. Critical race theology challenges students and scholars of religion and theology alike to not imagine that the crucial insights and constructive imagination acquired in divinity schools, seminaries, and universities are simply for one's own edification. In light of the pervasive and insidious power of right-wing extremism, including white Christian nationalism, critical race theology values the study of religion and theology as vital for education of the world. The people need to know what we know.

The declaration and waging of the "culture wars" in the 1990s and 2000s is a key factor in the rise of white Christian nationalism of recent years. In his 1992 speech at the Republican National Convention (RNC), conservative writer and pundit Pat Buchanan quite literally named the so-called culture wars, emphasizing themes that still resonate today. One objective of Buchanan's message that night was to force voters to identify with one of two diametrically opposed visions, choosing "who we are" as Americans. This rhetorical maneuver of identification harkens to the Preamble of the US Constitution's opening phrase, "We the People." Centuries ago, this phrase was instrumental in establishing an "American"

---

[37] Cooper-White, *The Psychology of Christian Nationalism*, 4.

national identity in the wake of the Revolutionary War, and Buchanan sought to reignite this identification rhetorically at the outset of the culture wars.

Beyond its preamble, the US Constitution clearly identifies three populations that inhabit the United States: "people"/ "persons," "Indians" (aka Native Americans), and "other persons." Only "people" or "persons"—one might assume these to be white property-owning and privileged men—were entitled to American freedom. Those who were excluded from the Constitution-writers' definition of people/persons were African Americans, Native Americans, non-white immigrants, and women of all backgrounds. As the principles of freedom made their transition through the end of the American Revolution and into the establishment of the nation, the American Republic was marked by a growing divide between "free" Americans and those who were enslaved, oppressed, and rendered invisible by the law of the land. From the nation's start, American national identity increasingly combined racial–ethnic, civic, and even moral definitions so that the cherished phrase "we the people" eventually meant white male Protestant Americans.

Buchanan's rhetorical tactics also reflected a deliberate transition toward "identity politics," a dynamic trend for people to move away from traditional broad-based party politics and to form exclusive political agendas or alliances based on a particular racial–ethnic group, gender/sexual identity, religion, social background, etc. This trend remains a contentious concept despite its prominence in our contemporary public square. Ironically, even as he and his fellow conservatives vehemently denounced identity politics on the Left, Buchanan relentlessly championed the remaking of the Republican Party in the identity of purportedly "Judeo-Christian" values.

Early in his convention speech, Buchanan remarked, "The country-club and the establishment Republicans recoil from the social, cultural and moral issues which many conservatives and evangelicals have embraced."[38] Roots of his attention to potential political impacts of the social and moral concerns of conservative Christians can be discerned in his memoir, published four years prior to his convention address.[39] Buchanan described himself as a devout Catholic from suburban California and declared that the pro-Nazi demagogue Father Charles "The Radio Priest" Coughlin and Spanish dictator Francisco Franco were among his childhood heroes. He found common ground with his Evangelical Christian counterpart Pat Robertson in their staunch opposition to reproductive choice, feminism, immigration, affirmative action, and LGBTQIA+ rights; by endorsing "traditional" marriage and gender roles; through advocacy for Christian prayer in public schools and other hallmarks of Christian supremacy.[40]

Buchanan's address was an inhumane and insidious invective that served as the opening salvo of the "culture wars." Buchanan's political agitation was instrumental in the emergence of a new nationalist and populist right that replaced the earlier Cold War anti-communist conservative consensus, which was much more amenable to legal immigration, global trade agreements, and international military alliances than their current namesakes.[41] As Kevin Kruse and Julian

---

[38] Patrick Joseph Buchanan, "Culture War Speech: Address to the Republican National Convention" (speech, The Astrodome, Houston, TX, August 17, 1992), https://voicesofdemocracy.umd.edu/buchanan-culture-war-speech-speech-text/.

[39] Patrick J. Buchanan, *Right from the Beginning* (Lanham, MD: Regnery Gateway, 1988).

[40] Burton L. Mack, *The Myth of Christian Supremacy: Restoring Our Democratic Ideals* (Minneapolis: Fortress Press, 2022).

[41] Godfrey Hodgson, *America in Our Time: From World War II to Nixon—What Happened and Why* (New York: Doubleday, 1976); Robert Mason and Iwan Morgan, eds., *The Liberal Consensus Reconsidered: American Politics and Society in the Postwar Era* (Gainesville: University Press of Florida, 2017); Steve Kornacki, *The Red and the Blue: The 1990s and the*

Zelizer note, "Buchanan directed his red-meat remarks to not just Arkansas governor Bill Clinton, the Democratic nominee for president, but also his wife Hillary, a woman the Republican decried as a champion of a radical feminism 'that would destroy America.'"[42] More than seeing the Clintons and other Democrats as political rivals with whom they have differing policy opinions and ideological views, Buchanan framed the Democratic Party as infernal enemies in an existential struggle for dominance of their values, beliefs, and practices that dictates contemporary politics in the United States.[43] According to Buchanan,

> The agenda that Clinton & Clinton would impose on America—abortion on demand, a litmus test for the Supreme Court, homosexual rights, discrimination against religious schools, women in combat units—that's change, all right. But it is not the kind of change America needs. It is not the kind of change America wants.[44]

In his closing line, Buchanan called upon his audience to "take back our cities, and take back our culture, and take back our country."[45]

Birth of Political Tribalism (New York: Ecco, 2018); and Nicole Hemmer, *Partisans: The Conservative Revolutionaries Who Remade American Politics in the 1990s* (New York: Basic Books, 2022).

[42] Kevin M. Kruse and Julian E. Zelizer, *Fault Lines: A History of the United States Since 1974* (New York: W. W. Norton, 2019), 199.

[43] Kruse and Zelizer, *Fault Lines*, 199–200; Nic Rowan, "Don't Call It the 'Culture War Speech': Everyone in the Room in 1992 Thought Buchanan Gave an Uplifting Speech. Only Later Was It Spun as a Dark Diatribe," *American Conservative*, October 17, 2022, https://www.theamericanconservative.com/dont-call-it-the-culture-war-speech/.

[44] Buchanan, "Culture War Speech: Address to the Republican National Convention."

[45] Buchanan, "Culture War Speech: Address to the Republican National Convention."

This statement clearly draws on the white supremacist notion that America once belonged to a certain type or group of citizens— white heteronormative Christians—and that it has somehow been taken away or stolen by some group of Others. This sentiment and others have inspired many credible accusations of bigotry and racism made against Buchanan throughout his career.[46]

More than thirty years after his notorious RNC speech, Buchanan's long shadow of influence seems to be oddly ignored by mainstream media coverage of conservative political and religious influence in the country. And yet it is important to attend to his roots in conservative Catholicism, his life-long anti-Semitism and racism, and his friendliness with mainstream media elites who helped soften his image, ensuring his lasting impact on American politics.[47] In these and many other ways, Buchanan was an indispensable bridge that linked the past half-century of US conservatism from Richard Nixon to Ronald Reagan to Donald Trump. Recognizing these important links to national political power, critical race theology also calls us to attend to the ways that Buchanan's own attention to conservative Catholicism and Evangelical Protestantism brought moral and theological concerns to political dominance.

Buchanan's Evangelical counterpart, Pat Robertson, was a promethean figure in the rise of Conservative Evangelical influence

---

[46] Ta-Nehisi Coates, "The Amazing Racism of Pat Buchannan," *The Atlantic*, March 23, 2008, https://www.theatlantic.com/entertainment/archive/2008/03/the-amazing-racism-of-pat-buchannan/5350/; Anti-Defamation League, "Patrick Buchanan: Unrepentant Bigot," *ADL: Profile*, February 27, 2012, https://www.adl.org/resources/profile/patrick-buchanan-unrepentant-bigot.

[47] The Editors, "Pat Buchanan's Poison: Pat Buchanan, the Man Who Urged Ronald Reagan to Visit the Nazi Cemetery at Bitburg, Is No Stranger to Charges of Anti-Semitism," *The Nation*, October 18, 1999, https://www.thenation.com/article/archive/pat-buchanans-poison/.

in the latter half of the twentieth century. In 1960, he purchased a small TV station in Virginia Beach, saying God told him to start the Christian Broadcasting Network (CBN). For several decades, he stood as one of America's most prominent voices for the Religious Right. Through *The 700 Club*, CBN's long-running flagship television program, and his frequent interventions in national political debates, Robertson became a bigoted, sexist, homophobic, and xenophobic preacher with a nationwide audience. He founded Christian Broadcasting Network University, a private conservative Christian university known today as Regent University, and a national legal foundation in the 1970s. He doggedly worked to reshape the nation's political and legal system in the image of conservative Evangelical Christianity as he saw it.

In his retrospective essay on Robertson's life and legacy, *Rolling Stone*'s Jay Michaelson plainly stated, "More than anyone, Pat Robertson succeeded at mainstreaming the craziest fringes of Christian fundamentalism, and his descendants are, today, the base of the Republican Party: religious extremists motivated by rage, fear, and conspiracy theories."[48] After Robertson announced that he was retiring from hosting *The 700 Club* in 2021, ethicist David P. Gushee told *Religion News Service*,

> Pat Robertson contributed greatly to some of the worst trends in American Christianity over the last forty years. These included the fusion of conservative white Protestantism with the Republican Party, the use and abuse of supernaturalist Christianity to offer spurious and unhelpful interpretations of historical events, and the development of a conservative Christian media empire

---

[48] Jay Michaelson, "Pat Robertson Is Dead. His Dystopian Legacy Lives On," *Rolling Stone*, June 8, 2023, https://www.rollingstone.com/culture/culture-features/pat-robertson-dead-dystopian-legacy-1234766810/amp/.

that made money and gained power in the process of making everyday Christians less thoughtful contributors to American life.[49]

In an obituary for Robertson, the *New York Times* wrote, "Whether in the pulpit, on the stump or in front of a television camera, Mr. Robertson could exhibit the mild manner of a friendly local minister, chuckling softly and displaying an almost perpetual twinkle in his eye. But he was also given to statements that his detractors saw as outlandishly wrongheaded and dangerously incendiary."[50] Political scientist and director of the University of Virginia Center for Politics Larry Sabato remembered Robertson's influence after his death in 2023, noting that "the culture wars being waged today by just about all the national Republican candidates—that is partly a product of Robertson."[51] Robertson was undeniably indispensable to laying the ideological and religio-political groundwork for the brand of white Christian nationalism at work today.

In analyzing the culture wars that Buchanan and Robertson helped ignite and stoke, it is important to emphasize how narratives of "extremism," "hyperpartisanship," and "tribalism" have

---

[49] Mark I. Pinsky, "Pat Robertson Turned Christian TV into Political Power—And Blew It Up with Wacky Prophecy," *Religion News Service* online, October 4, 2021, https://religionnews.com/2021/10/04/pat-robertson-turned-christian-tv-into-political-power-and-blew-it-up-with-wacky-prophecy/.

[50] Douglas Martin, "Pat Robertson, Who Gave Christian Conservatives Clout, Is Dead at 93," *New York Times*, June 8, 2023, https://www.nytimes.com/2023/06/08/us/pat-robertson-dead.html?smid=url-share.

[51] Ben Finley, Peter Smith, and Deepa Bharath, "Pat Robertson United Evangelical Christians and Pushed Them into Conservative Politics," Associated Press, June 9, 2023, https://apnews.com/article/pat-robertson-evangelical-legacy-christian-broadcasting-3e42d2c44d837b1aaf61a36315dde6a1.

fostered deleterious discourses that are propelled by fantasies of false equivalency like those that bemoan the seeming loss of the "reasonable centrism" of the mythic American mainstream. As long as "both sides" can be critiqued as too polarized or too extreme for the well-being of American life, policymakers and cultural influencers alike can ruthlessly ignore the extent to which structural forces and material resources have shifted dramatically to the Right within the US political establishment. This is a clear-cut example of "polarization" that is also a narrative driven by a fantasy that ignores the very material forces that have shifted the US political establishment further to the Right. The ruling political and economic class has helped sow distrust and paranoia with decades of deadly wars, runaway and rampant inequality, lethal racism, and the failed promises of endless economic growth. For critical race theology, exposing and exploring the culture wars means exploring why such overly simplistic, narrow-minded lamentations about polarization in our divided nation are so beloved by the media and political elite.

Manifestations of white Christian nationalism have been intertwined with these notions of and narratives about polarization and partisan tribalism within the culture wars. In a fabled 1882 lecture entitled "What Is a Nation," French philosopher Ernest Renan mused about a nation as an entity based on acts of the free will of individuals forming a collective identity:

> A nation is a soul, a spiritual principle. Two things, which in truth are but one, constitute this soul or spiritual principle. One lies in the past, one in the present. One is the possession in common of a rich legacy of memories; the other is present-day consent, the desire to live together, the will to perpetuate the value of the heritage that one has received in an undivided form.[52]

---

[52] Ernest Renan and M. F. N. Giglioli, *What Is a Nation? And Other Political Writings* (1882; New York: Columbia University Press, 2018).

More recently, historian Jill Lepore has argued that "nations are made up of people but held together by history, like wattle and daub or lath and plaster or bricks and mortar. For a generation, American history has been coming undone and the nation has been coming apart, the daub cracking, the plaster buckling, the mortar crumbling."[53] Renan's ethereal considerations and Lepore's exigent concerns reflect the polar extremes of our thoughts about what makes a nation and, more importantly, what breaks it into utter ruins.

Most scholars of nationalism agree that, across various definitions of nationalism, there is a foundational belief that humankind is divisible into mutually distinct, yet discrete units or internally coherent cultural groups that are defined by shared traits like history, language, religion, ethnicity, or culture. From there, scholars say, nationalists believe that these groups should each have their own sovereign, self-determining governments that should promote and protect a nation's cultural identity as well as provide meaning and purpose for human beings. Considering this, it is important to distinguish between patriotism and nationalism. Patriotism is most often described as one's love of country, and it is quite different from nationalism, which is an intellectual understanding and ideological argument about the definition of the nation-state. When combating white Christian nationalism, critical race theology must insist that patriotism in the United States can only "love" America as a country if such an affection, appreciation, and loyalty helps us rise above and beyond our state of being within it. Patriotism that operates without any standards of true value or sense of higher purpose, besides either wielding military strength or exerting political power over others, is dangerously detached from a pure, natural vision of Christian love. "Love is never any better than the lover. Wicked people love wickedly, violent people love

---

[53] Jill Lepore, *This America: The Case for the Nation* (New York: W. W. Norton, 2019), 15.

violently, weak people love weakly, stupid people love stupidly," as Toni Morrison instructs.[54]

When viewed within the scope of Augustinian moral philosophy, the task of human morality amounts greatly to the responsibility to discern a hierarchical ordering of people, priorities, and principles and to "love" them rightly on a metaphysical level. For Augustine, rightly ordered loves were deemed righteous and virtuous while disordered loves were viewed as pure manifestations of vice.[55] Thus, patriotism as a disproportionate and disordered love of nation that fuels white Christian nationalism is sinful rather than salvific. Instead of serving as a mechanism for group hatred and collective viciousness, patriotism with a proper sense of divine purpose would help us do the good work of cultivating and improving the world as a specific part of God's creation even beyond the part of the globe we happen to inhabit. As James Baldwin has argued,

> If we—and now I mean the relatively conscious whites and the relatively conscious blacks, who must, like lovers, insist on, or create, the consciousness of the others—do not falter in our duty now, we may be able, handful that we are, to end the racial nightmare, and achieve our country, and change the history of the world.[56]

As Baldwin implies, "to achieve our country" envisions a prophetic patriotism that suggests how to "love" the United States, which also means working to improve this nation and working for justice when

---

[54] Toni Morrison, *The Bluest Eye*, Modern Critical Interpretations, edited and with an introduction by Harold Bloom (Philadelphia: Chelsea House Publishers, 1999), 2.

[55] Augustine, *City of God*, 15. 22.

[56] James Baldwin, *The Fire Next Time*, in *James Baldwin: Collected Essays*, selected by Toni Morrison (1963; New York: Literary Classics of the United States, Inc., 1998), 346–47.

it errs for the betterment of all while also holding it accountable for constructive yet compassionate critique.

In both form and function, then, white Christian nationalism is not just a misunderstanding of Christianity. It is an utter mockery of the faith. Over the course of more than four centuries—and especially its influence over the last half-century in North America, the emergence of an altogether virulent white Christian nationalism has been falsely equated with the divinely ordained right to link the very existence of the nation with a historically dominant racial–ethnic, cultural, and/or religious populace, which, in turn, has animated the rising tide of oppression, exclusion, and even genocide of minority and marginalized groups while also securing privilege for white Protestants.[57] As Cooper-White correctly states,

> Rather than faithful witness to the Christian gospel … white Christian nationalism is … a highly and often explicitly political movement that aligns itself with Conservative—mostly right-wing and racist—convictions, social attitudes, and legislative objectives. Cloaked in a

---

[57] See Cooper-White, *The Psychology of Christian Nationalism*; Whitehead and Perry, *Taking America Back for God*; Michelle Goldberg, *Kingdom Coming: The Rise of Christian Nationalism* (New York: W. W. Norton, 2007); Sarah Posner, *Unholy: How White Christian Nationalists Powered the Trump Presidency, and the Devastating Legacy They Left Behind* (New York: Random House, 2021); Katherine Stewart, *The Power Worshippers: Inside the Dangerous Rise of Religious Nationalism* (New York: Bloomsbury Publishing, 2022); Carter Heyward, *The Seven Deadly Sins of White Christian Nationalism: A Call to Action* (Lanham, MD: Rowman & Littlefield Publishing Group, 2023); Philip S. Gorski and Samuel L. Perry, *The Flag and the Cross: White Christian Nationalism and the Threat to American Democracy* (New York: Oxford University Press, 2022); Burton L. Mack and Bradley Onishi, *Preparing for War: The Extremist History of White Christian Nationalism—And What Comes Next* (Minneapolis: Broadleaf Books, 2023).

narrow interpretation of a misrepresented Bible and "Judeo-Christian" tradition … it misuses Christianity rather than being shaped by it.[58]

For critical race theology, the emphasis is to talk about this dangerously toxic complex of ideology and action within a subset of white Christians who fervently believe that the key path forward for their faith is to seek and wield maximal clout and earthly power.

In other words, critical race theology argues that white Christian nationalism has somehow understood the Gospel of Jesus to guide people toward policies and practices that enable them to alienate and abuse others at will in the vainglorious hope of trying to feel safe in dominance. Elizabeth Dias identified such a dominance-seeking approach in the white Evangelical Christian culture in Sioux Falls, Iowa, during the 2016 presidential campaign.[59] Dias recognized how then-candidate Donald Trump became a promoter and potential protector of a resurgent white Christian nationalism for these voters. Dias was not the only journalist or scholar who explored how white Evangelicals gravitated to Trump and Trumpism as they sought to feel safer and stronger amid perceived threats in the culture wars.[60] Having a bully

---

[58] Cooper-White, *The Psychology of Christian Nationalism*, 25.

[59] Elizabeth Dias, "Christianity Will Have Power," *New York Times*, August 8, 2020, https://www.nytimes.com/2020/08/09/us/evangelicals-trump-christianity.html.

[60] Dias, "Christianity Will Have Power"; Adam Russell Taylor, "It's Time to Rethink American Churches," *Sojourners*, April 8, 2021, https://sojo.net/articles/it-s-time-rethink-american-churches; Elizabeth Dias, "In Biden's Catholic Faith, an Ascendant Liberal Christianity," *New York Times*, January 23, 2021, https://www.nytimes.com/2021/01/23/us/biden-catholic-christian.html; Michael Luo, "The Wasting of the Evangelical Mind," *New Yorker*, March 4, 2021, https://www.newyorker.com/news/daily-comment/the-wasting-of-the-evangelical-mind; Chrissy Stroop, "Have White Evangelicals Finally Lost the Narrative," *Religion*

on their side, persecuting others for them, made them feel secure amid an uncertain world. Pursuing raw, vulgar power in some of its most brazen forms has made these and voters like them feel safe to practice their particular vision of a white nationalist Christianity.

Slyly, white Christian nationalism has worked to supplant the omniscience, omnipresence, and omnipotence of God with whiteness as a preeminent divine attribute. In its historical trajectory, critical race theology crucially recognizes that there is neither grace, mercy, nor love in sanctifying white racial identity as the core of one's being. Many of the most tragic episodes of modern history were made possible by powerful people who were confessing Christians seeking more earthly power. From the history of Puritan theocracy in seventeenth-century New England; through kidnapping, buying, selling, raping, torturing, and enslaving of African, Native American, and their descendant peoples; through religious and government boarding schools in the genocide of Native Americans; through Jim and Jane Crow; through the Chinese Exclusion Act and Japanese American internment camps; we must understand that neither white supremacy nor misogyny came into existence all at once, *ex nihilo* (out of nothing), or *sui generis* (of its own kind).[61] Instead, this complex has emerged as a

---

Dispatches, April 6, 2021, https://religiondispatches.org/have-white-evangelicals-finally-lost-control-of-the-narrative/; Paul Rosenberg, "The Power Worshippers: A Look inside the American Religious Right," *Al Jazeera English*, June 2, 2020, https://www.aljazeera.com/features/2020/6/2/the-power-worshippers-a-look-inside-the-american-religious-right.

[61] James D. Drake, *King Philip's War: Civil War in New England, 1675–1676* (Amherst, MA: University of Massachusetts Press, 2000); Jill Lepore, *The Name of War: King Philip's War and the Origins of American Identity* (New York: Alfred A. Knopf, 1998); James P. Byrd and James D. Hudnut-Beumler, *The Story of Religion in America: An Introduction* (Louisville, KY: Westminster John Knox Press, 2021), 42–43, 44–45; Mary Beth Norton, *In the Devil's Snare: The Salem Witchcraft Crisis of 1692* (New York:

totalizing system of being, thought, belief, and action that enabled specific groups of Europeans and their descendants to brazenly steal outsized portions of this world's labor, land, largesse, and lives from other Indigenous populations around the planet. Moreover, when whiteness is yoked to a specious notion of brilliance, beauty, belief, and belonging, it has given a pernicious sense of primacy, privilege, and power to those who identified themselves as "white." All these atrocities and more occurred and have been excused in the name of American Christianity, even though they violate the actual teachings of Jesus Christ.

In the long history of the Christian tradition, it is quite evident that every time Christians have grasped societal power in Weberian terms, they have repeatedly failed to imitate much less replicate the life, lessons, and legacy of Jesus Christ. Instead, either on an individual or collective basis, people who have power have stolen, murdered, exploited, tortured, destroyed, and have done the work of the spirit of the world's empires rather than earth's emancipator.

Vintage, 2003); Paul S. Boyer, *Salem Possessed: The Social Origins of Witchcraft* (Cambridge, MA: Harvard University Press, 1976); Frances Hill, *A Delusion of Satan: The Full Story of the Salem Witch Trials,* reprint ed. (New York: Da Capo Press, 2002); Paul Charles Hoffer, *The Salem Witchcraft Trials: A Legal History* (Lawrence: University Press of Kansas, 1997); Arthur Miller, *The Crucible—A Play in Four Acts* (New York: Penguin Books, 1976); Vine Deloria Jr., *God Is Red* (New York: The Putnam Publishing Group, 1973); George Tinker, *Missionary Conquest: The Gospel and the Native American* (Minneapolis: Fortress Press, 1992); Jace Weaver, *That the People Might Live: Native American Literatures and Native American Community* (New York: Oxford University Press, 1997); Stacey M. Floyd-Thomas and Anthony B. Pinn, eds., *Liberation Theologies in the United States* (New York: New York University Press, 2010), 149–77; and George "Tink" Tinker, "The Corons and American Indian Genocide: Weaponizing Infectious Disease as Continuation of Eurochristian Religious Project," in *Religion, Race and COVID-19: Confronting White Supremacy in the Pandemic* ed. Stacey Floyd-Thomas (New York: New York University Press, 2021), 122–41.

As easy as it would be to keep this discussion of the "culture wars" in a figurative sense, people of faith must clearly recognize that, as a fact of human history, all wars are matters of life and death with very real-world implications. The next chapter seeks to explore the conditions and explain the consequences of America's white Christian nationalism on the global stage.

3

Twilight for the Children of Light and Darkness

White Christian Nationalism in the Global Context

I initially read Reinhold Niebuhr's *The Children of Light and the Children of Darkness* (1944) almost three decades ago, as an undergraduate student. Rereading it in the wake of the rise of a new right-wing extremism has been particularly instructive. Two ongoing influences change how I read the book from then to now. First, I have sought a greater understanding of Niebuhr's intellectual and theological context in conversation with the amalgam of religion, politics, and culture in the book. As the work is quite distinct in his particular embrace of Lutheran theology, there are important influences to be understood. Second, I am concerned with how a world that was at the crossroads of the Cold War, civil rights movement, and conservatism would, in time, face the rise of radical militant populism and failed states as threats to liberal democracy worldwide.

One aspect of *The Children of Light and the Children of Darkness* is likely a virtue for the theologian but undeniably frustrating for a social scientist: the argument he poses throughout the text has no final worldly resolution. To understand why this is, and how Niebuhr can still have relevance to the question of human governance, we must first understand the Lutheran theology that influences Niebuhr, as well as the twist that his own experiences gave to his interpretation of his faith. According to William Bain, a common misperception in studies of the Lutheran tradition is seeing it as separating the spheres of religion and politics, thereby allowing politics to speak "with its own voice."[1] To the contrary, Bain argues, the secular remains both intertwined and reliant upon religion within Lutheranism. On one hand, using reason, the secular realm is needed because scripture does not tell us on its own how to govern. Moreover, because we exist in a world in which sin is present, coercion is needed to keep wickedness—both the spiritual and otherwise—in check. On the other hand, the spiritual realm is where human faith reveals divine will. Although reason in the secular world shows that earthly good must be promoted in a world rife with sin and wickedness, faith tells us the actual difference between good and evil.[2] As a result, while politics is a domain in which we apply reason to construct modes of good governance as a measure of human agency, success in this regard for most Lutherans is reliant on knowledge of the divine will through faith.

With this belief serving as Niebuhr's theological and ethical starting point, I contend that his approach was mediated through his own life's journey, including both a disillusionment with liberalism and an acceptance of the necessity of action in the service of social justice. Yet, as ethicist Gary Dorrien rightly contends, Niebuhr "got to be the leading American Christian social ethicist of the twentieth century partly by changing his politics in every decade of his career."[3] From this disposition came an

---

[1] William Bain, *Political Theology of International Order* (New York: Oxford University Press, 2020), 82.

[2] Bain, *Political Theology of International Order*, 88–99.

[3] Gary Dorrien, "Introduction," to Reinhold Niebuhr, *The Children of*

obligation to strive for an ideal. This obligation was informed by a knowledge of sin, which, in turn, prevents us from mistaking our "limited and defective accomplishments for the ideal."[4] While consistent with the Lutheran ethic of a rational political life informed by the faith of the divine, Niebuhr's interpretation of Lutheranism is influenced by a need to act against injustice. This need, in turn, is tempered by a theological caution about the hubris of human self-love that would lead our belief in the goodness of our actions into a sinful lust for power and narcissistic self-deification.

This theological and ethical approach is at the root of the tensions in *The Children of Light and the Children of Darkness* as a critical reappraisal of democracy's fate in a world at war. At times, *The Children of Light and the Children of Darkness* is a prophetic call to action that makes it feel like the same kind of quest to solve "real world" problems that we find in other contemporaneous works that sought to establish a new postwar order built on freedom, justice, equality, and dignity. However, at other times, this practical pursuit of problem-solving is hampered by a diagnosis of the human condition that is unsolvable without faith in the Divine.

In many instances, *The Children of Light and the Children of Darkness* takes us on a veritable "kitchen sink" analysis of the awful yet wondrous nature of human beings, their communities, and respective nation-states in a divided world. Instead of giving us a glimpse of this new City of Man, Niebuhr marches us to the City of God, hurling all our hopes and worries directly at the feet of the Divine. Based on his belief that "democracy has a more compelling justification and requires a more realistic vindication than is given it by the liberal culture with which it has been associated in modern

---

Light and the Children of Darkness: A Vindication of Democracy and a Critique of Its Traditional Defense (Chicago: University of Chicago Press, 2011), ix.

[4] E. D. O'Connor, "The Theology of Reinhold Niebuhr," *Review of Politics* 2, no. 3 (1961): 196.

history," Niebuhr's *The Children of Light and the Children of Darkness* offers a theological perspective on democratic governance and is deemed one of the most important volumes of his time.[5] Watching a globe torn to shreds by the overwhelming and overlapping forces of nationalism and fascism, Niebuhr turned his focus toward all historical and spiritual forces that seem to be driving us onward past imminent chaos and existential crisis. At the crossroads of humankind's final possibility and impossibility, Niebuhr wrote,

> Religious humility is in perfect accord with the presuppositions of a democratic society. Profound religion must recognize the difference between divine majesty and human creatureliness; between the unconditioned character of the divine and the conditioned character of all human enterprise. According to the Christian faith the pride, which seeks to hide the conditioned and finite character of all human endeavor, is the very quintessence of sin. Religious faith ought therefore to be a constant fount of humility; for it ought to encourage men to moderate their natural pride and to achieve some decent consciousness of the relativity of their own statement of even the most ultimate truth. It ought to teach them that their religion is most certainly true if it recognizes the element of error and sin, of finiteness and contingency which creeps into the statement of even the sublimest truth.[6]

The task of achieving the world's better, brighter future must be interpreted from the standpoint of a faith that understands the fragmentary and broken character of all historical achievements. And yet there is also an abiding confidence in the meaning of such

---

[5] Reinhold Niebuhr, *The Children of Light and the Children of Darkness: A Vindication of Democracy and A Critique of Its Traditional Defense* (New York: Charles Scribner's Sons, 1960), xii.

[6] Niebuhr, *The Children of Light and the Children of Darkness*, 135.

feats because their completion is in the hands of a Divine Power, whose resources are greater than those of mere mortals, and whose suffering love can overcome the corruption of humanity's achievements, without negating the significance of what W. E. B. Du Bois might call "our spiritual strivings."[7] Eventually, by the end of this exploration, Niebuhr leaves us with the hope of earthly solutions that may take an eternity to bring to fruition. This turn to faith and the ultimate compassion of God comes at the end of antinomies that redefine the core argument of the book from the theo-ethical to the geopolitical.

While God stands at one end of the argument as a possible resolution of these antinomies, democracy for Niebuhr stands at the other end of the book as humankind's attempt to resolve antinomies. "[Humanity's] capacity for justice," he argues in the preface, "makes democracy possible; but [humanity's] inclination to injustice makes it necessary."[8] According to Niebuhr, democracy's perceived value comes in its superiority over the unrestrained injustice of tyranny as well as its ability to deal with the plurality of human communities. However, the traditional arguments for democracy, he argues, are deeply flawed. "The social and historical optimism of democratic life represents the typical illusion of an advancing class which mistook its own progress for the progress of the world."[9]

The flaws of traditional articulations of democracy are rooted in the ways our bourgeois, liberal, and enlightened modern conceptions of democracy have confused the self-interest of a specific individual or group with an assumption for society's welfare. In his defense of democracy, Niebuhr reveals a hubris of assuming an easy harmony between differing groups in society as well as between the individual and the community. For Niebuhr,

---

[7] Niebuhr, *The Children of Light and the Children of Darkness*, 189–90.

[8] Niebuhr, *The Children of Light and the Children of Darkness*, xiii.

[9] Niebuhr, *The Children of Light and the Children of Darkness*, 2.

the constant presence of disharmony and clashing interests has marked human communities. While democracy could be used to contain—if not reconcile—those disharmonies, defending it as a means of eradicating conflicts was a dangerous illusion.[10] Niebuhr asserts that the erstwhile defenders of democracy inadvertently let democracy down through lackluster argumentation. I contend to the contrary. Democracy, both then and now, has been weakened grievously by its lax implementation.

My second concern, here, is important. At the time of its publication, the title and central metaphor for *The Children of Light and the Children of Darkness* each refer to a common trope in both early twentieth-century international relations literature and theological discourse. For Niebuhr, the Children of Light are those who have built democracy and currently defend it from doom and disaster. Furthermore, the Children of Light are problematically foolish because they assume that self-interest is easily controlled. The Children of Darkness are evil by virtue of knowing "no law beyond their [own] will and interest," yet they are also wise because they fully grasp the power of self-interest. Even as Niebuhr extols the democratic values and virtues of the Children of Light, he writes this book with the hopeful desire to arm them with the wisdom of the Children of Darkness.[11]

A key problem with Niebuhr's approach toward the dichotomy at the heart of democracy is that democracy rests on an unstable and unsavory antinomy that allegedly promotes both individual liberty and the well-being of the community. "An ideal democratic order," he argues, "seeks unity within the conditions of freedom and maintains freedom within the framework of order."[12] Arguably, the "original sin" at the center of American democracy rejects our created limits as finite and fallible human beings in our ruptured

---

[10] Niebuhr, *The Children of Light and the Children of Darkness*, 7, 60.

[11] Niebuhr, *The Children of Light and the Children of Darkness*, 9–11, 41.

[12] Niebuhr, *The Children of Light and the Children of Darkness*, 3.

relationship with God, and it also imposes the starting point for an ultimate judgment on our national history that lies above and beyond the ideas, structures, actions, and powers that make our society possible. In *The Children of Light and the Children of Darkness*, Niebuhr explicated this worldview most clearly by framing his argument as the Christian account of human beings as being both sinful yet also created in God's own image. This theological account of history wedded to human nature is the central axis for Niebuhr's perspective on theology, ethics, and political ideology, especially noteworthy in those latter works like *The Children of Light and the Children of Darkness* and *The Irony of American History* (1952) as he wrote increasingly for secular audiences. To be certain, his overt theological references to creation, sin, redemption, and judgment faded from view in his writing, but his reliance on Manichean tropes of good and evil are clearly evident.

The boundless optimism of the Children of Light had made them ignorant of the power of factional class differences and self-interests within their communities. The existence of these interests, linked to egotistical drives, introduced another antinomy: these facts of human nature made democracy simultaneously less likely and more necessary. Even as the assertion of bourgeois individuality over the community grew, this tension between individuality and community was amplified by the problem of property broadly construed.[13] Here, it is important to recognize how the book's central imagery is racially coded, softening the jagged edges between democracy and white supremacy. Most modern ideologies along the political spectrum have failed to openly acknowledge that property is power and that, on both individual and collective bases, property rights have been used as instruments of injustice against the displaced and disinherited people of the world.[14] As such, the problem of property remained

---

[13] Niebuhr, *The Children of Light and the Children of Darkness*, 54–55.

[14] Niebuhr, *The Children of Light and the Children of Darkness*, 104–110.

a foundational cause of arrogance based on societal power rooted in human difference.

In the classic article "Whiteness as Property," critical race theorist Cheryl Harris explores the extent to which white racial identity became a form of property that has been protected by juridical and legislative means in American society and culture.[15] As Harris argues, beyond serving as a racialized marker of privilege and preeminence, whiteness became valuable when people of European descent could never be relegated to property under chattel slavery. Given this realization, Harris argues it is not only the cultural legacy of enslavement that has kept Black people oppressed in the United States but a legal system that has continued to regard whiteness as normative. Therefore, we must recognize that we exist in a system that actively excludes people of color from the purview of equal rights and protections while simultaneously conferring economic advantages disproportionately to people considered "white by law."[16] As Lucian Ashworth informs us, "Since all property is power it followed that the property question, like all questions of power in society, was a perennial problem that needed constant debate and adjustment within democratic society. It could not merely be transcended by either the community or the individual."[17] Ultimately, Harris's legal argument concludes by addressing how affirmative action would challenge the injustice of whiteness as a form of property interest but only if it actively functions as a corrective to systematic bigotry and systemic bias

---

[15] Cheryl I. Harris, "Whiteness as Property," *Harvard Law Review* 106, no. 8 (1993): 1707–91.

[16] See Ian Haney Lopez, *White by Law: The Legal Construction of Race* (1996: New York: New York University Press, 2006).

[17] Lucian M. Ashworth, "Re-reading Niebuhr's *The Children of Light and the Children of Darkness*: The Crisis of Democracy in an Interdependent World Then and Now," *Journal of International Political Theory* 17, no. 2 (2021): 127.

by redistributing protection, power, and resources to those in the United States who have been historically oppressed.

Though the discourse of white racial identity as property was not at play in Niebuhr's era, racism's debilitating and inevitably destructive effect on democracy was very much on display. Niebuhr did not devote much time or space to a fulsome exploration of what many writers of the period regarded as the "race problem" in many of his writings, but I always have been particularly struck by this statement on racism he offers in *The Children of Light and the Children of Darkness*:

> Racial prejudice is indeed a form of irrationality; but it is not as capricious as modern universalists assume. Racial prejudice, the contempt of the other group, is an inevitable concomitant of racial pride; and racial pride is an inevitable concomitant of the ethnic will to live. Wherever life becomes collectively integrated, it generates a collective, as well as an individual, survival impulse. But, as previously observed in dealing with individual life, human life is never content with mere physical survival. There are spiritual elements in every human survival impulse; and the corruption of these elements is pride and the will-to-power. This corruption is deeper and more universal than is understood in our liberal culture.[18]

Later, Niebuhr turns his focus to the poisonous predicament of anti-Semitism at the molten core of Nazism's corrosion of Western democracy. He writes,

> Racial bigots bring all kinds of charges against the Jewish minority; but these charges are rationalizations of a profounder prejudice. The real sin of the Jews is twofold. They are first of all a nation scattered among the nations;

---

[18] Niebuhr, *The Children of Light and the Children of Darkness*, 139.

and therefore they cannot afford to become completely assimilated within the nations; for that would mean the sacrifice of their ethnic existence. Secondly, they are a group which affronts us by diverging doubly from the dominant type, both ethnically and culturally.[19]

Niebuhr's rather timid perspective on both "America's original sin" and "the world's oldest hatred" was written contemporaneously to that of the hateful vitriol spewed by prototypical white Christian nationalist Gerald L. K. Smith mentioned earlier. Even within Niebuhr's classical Christian realism, his approach reverberates with a racial realism, wherein all aspects of the struggle for power amongst egotistical, self-interested, and fallible humans based on human difference can barely be managed much less transcended. A sense of whiteness in relation to individual possession and communal preservation emerges from Niebuhr. Critical race theology recognizes how this dynamic of possession and preservation depends on a purportedly democratic government and a racially inscribed religious worldview that is inherently inhospitable to those perceived as Other. The whole complex of whiteness regularly shifts as it functions in an unstable state that is being constantly renegotiated to keep the power and privilege of whiteness intact.[20] "Chaos is a perennial peril of freedom," Niebuhr contends.[21] Reading this volume as a person of color who does not share the author's propensity for prolonging any preferences, privileges, or protections incumbent to whiteness, I wonder for whom this warning was written.

---

[19] Niebuhr, *The Children of Light and the Children of Darkness*, 142.

[20] David R. Roediger, *The Wages of Whiteness: Race and the Making of the American Working Class* (London: Verso, 2022); George Lipsitz, *The Possessive Investment in Whiteness: How White People Profit from Identity Politics* (Philadelphia: Temple University Press, 1998); Charles Mills, *The Racial Contract* (Ithaca, NY: Cornell University Press, 2022).

[21] Niebuhr, *The Children of Light and the Children of Darkness*, 122.

In order to function as a corrective to the American theological enterprise that understands race as a mode of human difference, critical race theology must develop an instrumental system of analysis. In *Race Rules* (1996), ethicist Michael Eric Dyson illuminates three interrelated conceptual frames by which to better discern and dissect how race and racism have affected American society and culture, namely, race as *context*, *subtext*, and *pretext*. As Dyson asserts, "Race as context helps us to understand the facts of race and racism in our society. Race as a subtext helps us to understand the forms of race and racism in our culture. And race as a pretext helps us to understand the function of race and racism in America."[22] These categories are somewhat elastic and adulterated in nature, and they often overlap with one another in confounding ways. But, according to Dyson, being aware of the existence of such distinctions (and even contradictions), we have an improved chance of reducing the anxiety and anger that surrounds a volatile and highly charged subject. "To view race as a context leads to racial clarification," Dyson asserts; "by having these facts in hand we're more likely to weave them into an accurate account of how race has shaped our culture."[23] Next, Dyson observes that race as subtext operates via racial mystification. He highlights how countless arguments in the culture wars have been used to deliberately obscure the role of race and racism in contemporary society. "Race and racism are not static forces," as Dyson notes, but rather "they mutate, grow, transform, and are redefined in complex ways. . . . Race understood as a subtext allows us to get a handle on the changing forms of racist belief and behavior in our culture."[24] Finally, race as pretext shows how arguments have been used to justify racial beliefs and to defend racial interests vis-à-vis the dual

---

[22] Michael Eric Dyson, *Race Rules: Navigating the Color Line* (Reading, MA: Addison-Wesley Publishing, 1996), 33.

[23] Dyson, *Race Rules*, 34.

[24] Dyson, *Race Rules*, 35.

scientific canards of objectivity and neutrality. If the contest of race is tied to history and the subtext to culture, then the pretext of race is linked, broadly speaking, to science by means of what Dyson terms "racial justification." The emphasis in the process of racial justification is to focus on the extent that race functions to give legitimacy to racial concepts on one hand and license to racist ideas on the other.[25]

The state of American democracy in Niebuhr's theo-ethical imagination offered the distinct possibility of a negotiated peace for groups hailing from different racial–ethnic, political, economic, regional, and religious backgrounds, if one simply overlooked the pains and problems of our actual history as a people and a nation. In this idealized sense, democracy was both a product and a producer of a pluralistic social order that allowed very different groups to coexist while also expressing themselves. But while Niebuhr viewed this conceptually as the superiority of modern liberal democracy over a creeping fog of fascism, he never demonstrated the courage of his own convictions to interrogate the extent to which America had fallen short of its own lofty goals. Indeed, while Niebuhr viewed that American democracy offered lessons for the world as human civilization faced its greatest challenge in the twentieth century, he never recognized that his desperate yearning to extend the concept of humane community on a global level was being propagated by American hegemony rather than any genuine notion of humility or honesty.

In a critical reassessment of *The Children of Light and the Children of Darkness*, Shang-Jen Chen notes, "In the West, liberal democracy is now seen as a way of life and a seemingly inevitable trend for all countries of the world."[26] Yet, despite this paradigmatic nature

---

[25] Dyson, *Race Rules*, 36.

[26] Shang-Jen Chen, "A Critical Appraisal of the *Children of Light and the Children of Darkness* in the Debate of the Necessity of Democracy in Twenty-First-Century Mainland China," *Theology Today* 77, no. 3 (2020): 286.

of the United States as a bedrock for theories of international relations and contemporary statecraft, Niebuhr refrains from any significant or stringent critique of problems and prejudices so deeply embedded in the American republic. While Niebuhr attempts to broach the subject of racism and anti-Semitism in the latter pages of *The Children of Light and the Children of Darkness,* his commentary is pretty much tone-deaf and toothless. "Concessions to the inevitability of racist resilience," according to Black feminist ethicist Traci C. West, "can diminish our ability to recognize the choices that individuals (and groups) make to perpetuate racism and undercut the impetus to develop a critique of those choices."[27] Niebuhr was a contemporary of W. E. B. Du Bois, Howard Thurman, Richard Wright, Zora Neale Hurston, James Baldwin, Gunnar Myrdal, Frantz Fanon, Ralph Ellison, Jean-Paul Sartre, and Albert Camus, among others, who could (and should) have been interlocutors during this era. His diminished response to racism was not from a lack of opportunities for engagement.

Though Niebuhr clearly wrote *The Children of Light and the Children of Darkness* cognizant of the binary antagonism at the end of the Second World War, it was becoming increasingly evident that the ideational axis in the rising world order was moving from the metaphorical to the metaphysical. The geopolitical fate of the world was represented by the United States and its allies as exemplars of liberal democracy, demographic pluralism, personal freedom, and human equality on the one side, aligned against the destructive forces of rabid nationalism, racial purity, tyranny, and global domination marked by Nazi Germany, Fascist Italy, and Imperial Japan on the opposing side. The Soviet Union, of course, would eventually emerge as the world's countervailing superpower to the United States and its allies. Niebuhr borrows

---

[27] Traci C. West, "Reinhold Niebuhr," in *Beyond the Pale: Reading Christian Ethics from the Margins,* ed. Stacey M. Floyd-Thomas, and Miguel De La Torre (Louisville, KY: Westminster John Knox, 2011), 124.

the central trope—children of light and children of darkness—to describe this geopolitical binary from the first Pauline epistle to the Thessalonians (1 Thess 5:2–8).

> For you yourselves know very well that the day of the Lord will come like a thief in the night. When they say, "There is peace and security," then sudden destruction will come upon them, as labor pains come upon a pregnant woman, and there will be no escape! But you, beloved, are not in darkness, for that day to surprise you like a thief; for you are all children of light and children of the day; we are not of the night or of darkness. So then let us not fall asleep as do others, but let us keep awake and be sober; for those who sleep sleep at night, and those who are drunk get drunk at night. But since we belong to the day, let us be sober, and put on the breastplate of faith and love, and for a helmet, the hope of salvation.

By extolling the sobriety, wisdom, and altogether virtuous nature belonging to the "children of light" in juxtaposition to the drunkenness, ignorance, and explicitly wanton behavior possessed by the "children of darkness," Paul sets forth metaphorical imagery, which, in turn, serves as an encoded paradigm that has been translated in both literal and figurative manners to be an overtly divisive outlook that fuels a toxic and bifurcated worldview over the last two millennia. Without fear of overstatement, the binary distinction reflected in this biblical passage—the so-called separation of humanity into "the children of light" and "children of darkness"—has operated as both a central rhetorical trope and theological mechanism leading to division and inequality both within and beyond the church since the dawn of the modern era. This epistle ostensibly serves the dual function of writing race in and out of the Bible.

Multilayered readings of the Bible have left a vivid imprint on modern racial theories and prejudices in both church and society alike, resulting in racism functioning as a negative mode of ecumenism. Especially within the Protestant circum-Atlantic world, racial differences and the unequal power dynamics that ensue are the conjoined products of theology, sociology, and biology, and critical race theology is deeply concerned to articulate how racial embodiment operates within the white Christian nationalist worldview. Setting aside deeply rooted problems with broad implications of Pauline theology and its impact on marginalized Christians of color, there is something both painful and poignant in the aesthetic juxtaposition that is being delineated in the aforementioned text.

Critical race theology, therefore, examines the combined theological paradoxes, sociological tensions, and biological anxieties that lurked behind the development of white supremacy as an embedded system of principles and praxis. It is acutely aware of the influence of life lived in the context of both racialist thought and racist praxis. These racialist ideas have left their mark upon new forms of religiosity and newly devised notions of modernity and humanity. Critical race theology engages this awareness as it plumbs the dynamic complex of white supremacy that has led to the emergence of empires characterized by chattel slavery and rampant capitalism.

While there have been various works that have attempted to explicate the historical and philosophical rise of race as a modern invention, such debates have not been equaled within the ranks of mainline theological discourse.[28] Contemporary works on Christian

---

[28] See Roediger, *The Wages of Whiteness*; Lipsitz, *The Possessive Investment in Whiteness*; Frantz Fanon, *Black Skin, White Masks* (London: Penguin Classics, 2021); Charles H. Long, *Significations: Signs, Symbols, and Images in the Interpretation of Religion*, 2nd ed. (1984; Boulder, CO: Davies Group Publishers, 1999); Cornel West, *Prophesy Deliverance: An Afro-American Revolutionary Christianity* (Philadelphia: Westminster Press, 1982); Nell Irvin Painter, *The History of White People* (New York: W. W. Norton, 2011); Winthrop D. Jordan, *The White Man's Burden: Historical*

theology and praxis by a majority of theologians, religious scholars, and faith leaders still find it exceedingly difficult, if not impossible, to talk about race, much less racism, in any deliberate and constructive fashion. Meanwhile, any works that truly address racial antipathy and white supremacy in any substantial and meaningful way that are authored by marginalized peoples are typically read and discussed only by marginalized peoples with little notice or impact upon normative trends in theology. For example, James Cone's essay "Theology's Great Sin" took white theologians to task for failing to tackle the matter of race and racism in their works as well as for lacking the moral insight and courage to coax the church universal toward greater levels of racial inclusion and cultural diversity.[29] Unfortunately, this problem persists virtually unabated some two decades later. As such, most faith leaders—both ordained and lay—as well as scholars of the faith rarely engage in critical conversations about racialist thought and racist praxis, presumably in the far-fetched hope that ignoring race (and quite possibly the racialized) will make such perceived "unpleasantness" miraculously go away.

The Children of Light and the Children of Darkness is a theological reflection on the possibilities and limits of political life in general and not primarily a political strategy for navigating the contours of international relations in the mid-twentieth century. Reading Niebuhr today, it is quite evident that his contemporaneous purpose was to remind white Christians in America about some of the difficulties they likely would face in the emergent global regime

---

Origins of Racism in the United States (New York: Oxford University Press, 1980); George M. Fredrickson, *White Supremacy: A Comparative Study in American and South African History* (New York: Oxford University Press, 1981); David Theo Goldberg, *Racist Culture: The Philosophy and the Politics of Meaning* (Malden, MA: Blackwell, 1993).

[29] James H. Cone, "Theology's Great Sin: Silence in the Face of White Supremacy," *Black Theology* 2, no. 2 (2004): 139–52.

that would arise after the war ended. Nevertheless, it is barely a surprise to learn roughly eight decades later that this prophetic sage neither condemned nor called out his fellow "children of light" as being responsible for many tragic events both domestically and worldwide as a result of their moral failure to confront real-world problems rooted in bigotry and bias.

The church will continue to be a faltering facsimile of its true self until it rectifies one of its most grievous concerns: the Black body as theohistorical concern. For white Christians, this issue includes the sheer process of creating and castigating the racial Other, and it is also about the ossified, albeit paradoxical, designation of all that is carnal and sinful in terms of Blackness, as suggested in the Pauline text mentioned earlier. Conversely, people of color—especially those of us who are Christian—have to profess and practice an emancipated and decolonized faith that does not frame all virtue and value in human embodiment as a great escape from what W. E. B. Du Bois once called "unforgivable blackness."[30] In either instance, the Black body enters into theological and ecclesial realities quite literally as a *problem to overcome* rather than a *presence to welcome.*

In *What's Faith Got to Do With It?* (2005), womanist theologian Kelly Brown Douglas provides a vital reassessment of the Manichean dualism embedded within early Christian thought that found its way into Pauline and Augustinian theological formulations and, eventually, made its problematic impact upon the foundations of the Black church tradition. More than anything, I have been especially persuaded by the mixed legacy of Pauline theology on the body and human sexuality woven into her argument and find myself using her keen insights to refine my own interpretive lens regarding contemporary Black Christians that actually poses a *faith-based* rather than *race-based* dilemma that the church needs to focus upon in order

---

[30] W. E. B. Du Bois, "The Prize Fighter," *The Crisis* 8, no. 4 (August 1914): 181.

to redeem its own soul.[31] One of the grand unifying concerns of the church universal has been its unwillingness—dare I say failure—to deal with exigencies of Black embodiment and existence in any benevolent or constructive fashion.

When considering the disruptive reality of a Black body within a white supremacist world, critical race theology retraces the genesis of the racist ideal of a "certain type of body" that fell beyond the scope of human compassion and concern. In *Terror and Triumph* (2003), theologian Anthony B. Pinn offers a trenchant examination of how Africans and their New World descendants became objects of human history. Toward this end, Pinn envisions this phenomenon as a twofold problem. First, he contends that white Christians during the Age of Conquest understood themselves to be part of a shared creation with Africans and yet used their reinterpretations of scripture to both account for biological and cultural diversity and make sense of a new world order that was coalescing into existence. By example, ethicist Stacey Floyd-Thomas asserts how the use of the so called Curse of Ham narrative has been used as an explanation of how Africans became a subjugated race of humans within the purview of normative standards of Western Christianity.[32] Likewise, Pinn contends, "The failure of Africans to be beautiful, Christian, and [white] or in more general terms civilized, had to be explained and this biblical story tendered an accepted explanation."[33] Pinn argues

---

[31] Kelly Brown Douglas, *What's Faith Got to Do With It?: Black Bodies/Christian Souls* (Maryknoll, NY: Orbis Books, 2005).

[32] Stacey M. Floyd-Thomas, "'I am Black and Beautiful, O Ye Daughters of Jerusalem': African American Virtue Ethics and a Womanist Hermeneutics of Redemption," in *African American Religious Life and the Story of Nimrod*, ed. Anthony B. Pinn and Allen D. Callahan (New York: Palgrave Macmillan Press, 2007), 35–51.

[33] Anthony B. Pinn, *Terror and Triumph: The Nature and Meaning of Black Religion* (Minneapolis: Fortress Press, 2003), 7.

that Black religion—a capacious term that he purposefully deploys to reference a range of religious and spiritual practices beyond Christianity—plays a key role in African Americans' struggle for what he calls complex subjectivity, a mode of being defined by ambiguity and multidimensionality. If dominant society defined Black people by their corporeality during slavery, Pinn argues Black religion is an experience mediated by and through the Black body. As such, we should understand Black flesh not only as a material reality that constitutes an important site of resistance against oppression but also as the embodiment of a performative and stylistic aesthetic that must be more prominently considered looking forward in our studies.[34]

In the second phase of this problem, he asserts that, once modernity was firmly in place, "the differentiation of black bodies, with all the implied psychosocial and cultural implications, was bolstered by theological argument and solidified by legal restrictions."[35] Following this logic, although the Protestant Reformation, the Renaissance, and the Enlightenment were discretely different epochs in terms of the means of their particular reordering of human experience, they all coincided with the emergence and evolution of the Middle Passage. In that vein, womanist theologian M. Shawn Copeland demonstrates how these epochal hallmarks of modernity ultimately found commonalty with one end, namely, the translation of racial Otherness vis-à-vis the dehumanization of Black bodies from divinely inspired to socially inscribed. The rise of modernity for Black people meant a shift over the span of several centuries away from theological beliefs of Black women, men, and children as lesser beings created by the One True God to the supposedly "enlightened" rationale that

---

[34] Anthony B. Pinn, "Black Bodies in Pain and Ecstasy: Terror, Subjectivity, and the Nature of Black Religion." *Nova Religio: The Journal of Alternative and Emergent Religions* 7, no. 1 (2003): 76–89.

[35] Pinn, "Black Bodies in Pain and Ecstasy," 11.

Blacks represented beings who could not have been created by a logical and loving God in the first place.[36]

In comparable fashion, Colin Kidd complicates this matter even further by exploring how the Bible and its later interpretations have been integral to modern racial theories and prejudices. Viewing the Bible as the central text of modern culture, Kidd's examination of race and Christian scripture is interesting because, unlike many projects that emphasize the encounters white Christians have had with people of color—both Christian and non-Christian alike—his efforts focus more intently upon the impulses and imperatives that compelled the interpreters and even the original scribes of scripture to frame the sacred text in terms of varying narratives and schemas of race. He pursues this task because

> the Bible tells us very little about the racial appearance of the figures who feature within it.... Just as the Bible says nothing about race, and functions, in this respect, merely as a screen on to which its so-called interpreters project their racial attitudes, fears, and fantasies, so race itself is a construct, an interpretation of nature rather than an unambiguous marker of basic natural differences within humankind.[37]

Though the claims about the absolute colorblindness of the sacred text could be disputed, Kidd's larger argument still holds merit worthy of attention. Kidd calls our attention to the many ways that scripture has been reinterpreted over the centuries and has led to race *qua* physical identity, cultural heritage, and biopolitical hierarchy in a continual reinvention. Kidd reveals how Anglophone Protestant Christianity of the nineteenth century contributed to

---

[36] M. Shawn Copeland, *Enfleshing Freedom: Body, Race, and Being* (Minneapolis: Fortress Press, 2009).

[37] Colin Kidd, *The Forging of Races: Race and Scripture in the Protestant Atlantic World, 1600–2000* (New York: Cambridge University Press, 2006), 3.

racialized discourses by employing biblical narratives to differentiate European peoples as superior to Jews and other races.[38] As a result, Kidd poses the crucial assertion that

> All theories of race ... are examples of cultural construction superimposed upon arbitrarily selected features of human variation. All racial taxonomies ... are the product not of nature but of the imagination combined with inherited cultural stereotyping as well ... as the empirical observation of genuine (though superficial, trivial, and inconsequential) biological differences.[39]

Does the fact that race is a social construction make it any less real than a table, chair, building, or bomb? Even if we consider ourselves as spirits in a material world, how can we continue to avoid looking at the body as a material reality, a sociocultural metaphor, and, most significantly for our purposes, a theological concern? Most importantly, how do we grapple with the notion of race as social construct without coming to terms with the socially constructed nature of our scripture, our theology, and even our vision of God? Can our churches ever truly transcend the flawed and fragile essence of the people who create and populate them?

Toward this end, womanist ethicist Katie G. Cannon explained white Christianity's complicity with chattel slavery:

> Not surprisingly, [mainline] denominations sprang officially to the defense of slave trading, slaveholding, and the Christianization of Africans with ingenious economic arguments. Wealthy slaveholders transmuted a portion of their disproportionate economic profit into modes of social control by public gestures that passed as generous voluntary acts of charity. They used revenue from

---

[38] Kidd, *The Forging of Races*, 168–202.

[39] Kidd, *The Forging of Races*, 8–9.

slave labor to pay pastors, maintain church properties, support seminaries, and sustain overseas missionaries. Seduced by privilege and profit, White Christians of all economic strata were made, in effect, coconspirators in the victimization of Black people. In other words, slave apologists were successful in convincing at least five generations of White citizens that slavery, an essential and constitutionally protected institution, was consistent with the impulse of Christian charity.[40]

When thinking about a way forward beyond this current situation, I wonder whether the ways in which many of the theological frameworks to which we are currently attached—doctrines of God, Creation, Salvation, and Sin chief amongst them—are so intrinsically flawed by stark binary opposition of spirit and flesh that Christians of color will forever be viewed as the misbegotten products of a lesser creation.

In the hope of overcoming this problem, I often toy with the thought of reframing the classic refrain about the prospects of his young children's future in a postsegregated American society raised within Rev. Dr. Martin Luther King Jr.'s legendary "I Have a Dream" speech. What if we focus on the work of redeeming the precious as well as precarious nature of Black humanity by practicing a loving embrace of both "the color of their skin" and "the content of their character"? Rather than seeing these two dimensions of Black humanity—the material and the ethereal—as bitter enemies to one another, there needs to be a concerted effort to envision a *new theohistorical sensibility* that can bring these two ostensibly broken halves into a better, more beloved whole. In turn, this quest for wholeness and human flourishing might find its resolution in the

---

[40] Katie G. Cannon, "Slave Ideology and Biblical Interpretation," in *The Black Studies Reader*, ed. Jacqueline Bobo, Cynthia Hudley, and Claudine Michel (New York: Routledge, 2004), 46.

realization that we are all always already children of both light and darkness whose humanity hinges upon being able to recognize the humanity in others to restore the divinity in ourselves.

In *The Children of Light and the Children of Darkness,* however, Niebuhr's foremost concern is not to focus on the terrible decisions and tragic actions by those who have used the rhetoric of freedom, justice, equality, and democracy by twisting it to their own purposes and become agents of oppression. To the contrary, his concentration on the children of light remains steadfast in the presumption that they and everything about them represents the greater good, even as they have a willful myopia regarding the limits of their own thoughts and praxis in terms of subtle complicity and structural commitments with racism, misogyny, elitism, homophobia, transphobia, and xenophobia. While Niebuhr assesses the dynamics of human belief and behavior in a rational manner, history is filled with circumstances where the ambitions and aspirations end with one side holding power over another. This dialectic arguably reflects an intrinsic naiveté at the core of Niebuhr's theo-ethical worldview in a situation wherein it is difficult to distinguish a victory for the children of light as opposed to the children of darkness. This result is unsurprising because, for Niebuhr, the sheer mechanics of human nature is more basically enduring than the ideas that shape the contours and conditions of modern politics.

In Luke 16:1–9, Jesus shares a parable in which a dishonest steward turns his master's generosity and forgiveness to his own benefit. Jesus ends the narrative by remarking that "the children of this age are more shrewd in dealing with their own generation than are the children of light" (Luke 16:8). And herein lies the problem for Niebuhr: the inherent foolishness of the children of light envisions a social order that surpasses all of our contemporary expectations for peace, prosperity, pluralism, and principled action but, with this goal within their view, they misjudge their capability to reach and accomplish it. His unconditional justification of

American democracy in *The Children of Light and the Children of Darkness* makes a political case for religious freedom that our system of democratic governance may be relevant even in societies around the globe that lack many of the institutions, traditions, and cultural ethos of liberal democracy. At the same time, his insistence on developing "religious humility" within US political culture becomes even more important under conditions of religious and political pluralism.[41]

For Niebuhr, the most fundamental tragedy of our extant political culture is that the children of light might potentially *become* children of darkness. The greatest perceived threat to American political experiment in democratic self-governance is a denigration—literally a *blackening*—of our politics both in form and function. The founding rhetoric at the heart of the American republic about freedom, justice, and equality was beautiful in its abstract idealism, but the white supremacist bent of that soaring language served as an essential tool for asserting the corruptibility of their own authority and exercising control over their opponents both foreign and domestic. This possibility is an inherent facet of human nature, which is always capable both of subordinating other persons and interests to its own struggle for survival. A transcendence of an individual's or group's own interests toward more universal goals, namely, the search for a set of ideals and ideas that cannot be exploited in this way, is futile as is the effort to cultivate a will so pure that it would not be subject to this temptation. That is why political chaos and corruption are so widespread, even in movements for genuine political change. Moreover, Niebuhr believed this theological and ethical truth was confirmed by both an honest embrace of history intertwined with an abiding recognition of human behavior. As ethicist Robin Lovin notes, Niebuhr's views "would be rejected ... both by those

---

[41] Robin Lovin, "Reinhold Niebuhr's Realistic Pluralism," *Theology Today* 77, no. 3 (2020): 300.

who considered that they were in possession of a set of ideas that could transform history from within and by theologians who believed that the mysteries of God's judgment could not so easily be captured by human observation."[42] Niebuhr's worldview actually conformed itself to the perspectives and purposes of the American empire rather than transforming the world.

Much like Niebuhr before him, Francis Fukuyama presents a rather morally lopsided portrait of the United States as a global superpower that is propped up by a somewhat murky historical narrative delivered in relatively florid and boilerplate prose in *The End of History and the Last Man* (1992). There were other noteworthy contemporaneous texts within international relations literature that echoed several key concerns in the perceived conflicts and crises emerging in the premillennial era illuminated in Fukuyama's book—Samuel Huntington's *The Clash of Civilizations* (1993), Robert Kaplan's *The Coming Anarchy* (1994), Benjamin Barber's *Jihad vs. McWorld* (1995), and Thomas Friedman's *The Lexus and the Olive Tree* (1997) foremost among them. It is noteworthy, though, that none of those books strove to be an exercise in *soulcraft*, an activity that is nourishing or fulfilling to the soul as something that shapes and modifies the core being of an individual or community. Throughout the twentieth century, economist Amartya Sen argues, democracy has been recognized as "the 'normal' form of government to which any nation is entitled—whether in Europe, America, Asia, or Africa."[43] Furthermore, as Jared Hickman observes, "Increasingly, 'democracy' is presumed to be both a 'universal value' and a portable practice devoid of specific content."[44] Oddly enough, although more stridently secular its

---

[42] Robin Lovin, "Reinhold Niebuhr's Realistic Pluralism," 300.

[43] Amartya Sen, "Democracy as a Universal Value," *Journal of Democracy* 10, no. 3 (1999): 3–4.

[44] Jared Hickman, "The Theology of Democracy." *New England Quarterly* 81, no. 2 (2008): 177.

outlook, Fukuyama's *The End of History* was akin to Niebuhr's work from decades earlier by striving to formulate a political philosophy of democratization as a palatable and pragmatic prophecy in perilous and precarious times. While embracing much of the argument in *The End of History,* philosopher John W. de Gruchy addresses Fukuyama's myopia toward overlooking the role that Christian churches have had in the development of civil society and liberal democracy within European history.[45] Here, Fukuyama is not alone as, too often, political analysts ignore this role because of a persistent antireligious bias that thinks that Christianity has a dampening effect on democratic struggle and social transformation. To the contrary, the central premise of John W. de Gruchy's book *Christianity and Democracy* is that "democracy cannot survive without the spiritual basis which gives meaning to life."[46]

Fukuyama has been deeply uncertain about the liberalism he supposedly champions in his landmark book. Historian Daniel Bessner argues there was good reason for Fukuyama's breakthrough text to not be entirely sure about what the end of the Cold War would usher forth on the world stage. This growing indecision is because, as Bessner contends,

> The Soviet Union provided Fukuyama with a calling—his professional specialty was Soviet behavior in the Third World—and it also gave him ideological perspective.... When it went away, he lost far more than a worthy adversary; he lost the object against which he'd defined his own moral and political compass.[47]

---

[45] John W. de Gruchy, *Christianity and Democracy: A Theology for a Just World Order* (Cambridge: Cambridge University Press, 1995), 10.

[46] De Gruchy, *Christianity and Democracy*, 247.

[47] Daniel Bessner, "A Bad Breakup: The Discontents of Francis Fukuyama," *The Nation*, April 17, 2023, https://www.thenation.com/article/society/francis-fukuyama-liberalism-discontents/.

Unlike communism and socialism, full-blown liberalism does not seem to inspire breathtaking acts of rebellious solidarity nor any international movements rife with heroic everyday people. In its purest, most unsullied form, liberalism focuses on the individual, isolated and self-interested. Yet, in most of Fukuyama's writings, this abiding ambivalence toward liberalism and whether it should wither comes through loud and clear. While he has derided both the Left and Right in efforts toward philosophical evenhandedness— often drawing false equivalences between the sides—Fukuyama fails to muster much of a rousing vindication of liberalism. His failure, in large part, is because he does not seem to think that he needs to bother making such an effort in the first place. Fukuyama's work suggests that liberalism may not be the best ideational system that humanity can offer the world, but it appears to be the only one that is currently being offered. The core of his argument is that liberalism has not won because of its legitimacy, but rather because of its longevity, supported on the global stage by the vast wealth and military might of the United States.

Bessner notes that this is a truly shaky foundation upon which to build any political vision. Yet, he also feels there is some genuine truth in this canny realization. Perhaps the "tragedy of our times," Bessner writes, is that Fukuyama believes "he doesn't really need to [defend liberalism], because the argument he proffered in *The End of History* has proved correct. No ideology has arisen to challenge liberalism, whether in the United States or elsewhere."[48]

As a Reagan–Bush era conservative, Fukuyama was able to harness the power of centrism as a persuasive enough force to convince devotees from both sides of the political and ideological divide that they no longer needed to fear the rest of the world. As much as Fukuyama's musings are steeped in political philosophy at first glance, the cold hard truth remains that his prose does

---

[48] Bessner, "A Bad Breakup."

not amount so much as a definitive ideology as it offers an ambient mood. Fukuyama—like Niebuhr before him—inscribed a convenient and comfortable narrative about the alleged victories of democratic governments and capitalist economies across the globe that, in turn, serves as the solid bedrock from which both neoconservativism and neoliberalism drew a shared common sense of their respective visions of the global future being both intertwined and inevitable. Those who adhere to it take it so for granted that they do not even feel the need to defend it.[49]

The 2022 Russian invasion of Ukraine has spiraled into an interminably bloody war of attrition and stands as a tragic example of this concern. The North Atlantic Treaty Organization (NATO),

---

[49] Francis Fukuyama, "Reflections on the End of History, Five Years Later," *History and Theory* 34, no. 2 (May 1995): 27–43; Francis Fukuyama, "More Proof That This Really Is the End of History," *The Atlantic*, October 17, 2022, https://www.theatlantic.com/ideas/archive/2022/10/francis-fukuyama-still-end-history/671761/; Louis Menand, "Francis Fukuyama Postpones the End of History," *New Yorker*, August 27, 2018, https://www.newyorker.com/magazine/2018/09/03/francis-fukuyama-postpones-the-end-of-history; Paul Hirst, "Endism: Why 1989 Was Not the 'End Of History'," *OpenDemocracy*, November 20, 2019, https://www.opendemocracy.net/en/endism/; Maximillian Alvarez, "The End of the End of History," *Boston Review*, March 25, 2019, https://www.bostonreview.net/articles/maximillian-alvarez-end-end-history/; Timothy Stanley and Alexander Lee, "It's Still Not the End of History," *The Atlantic*, September 1, 2014, https://www.theatlantic.com/politics/archive/2014/09/its-still-not-the-end-of-history-francis-fukuyama/379394/; Eliane Glaser, "Bring Back Ideology: Fukuyama's 'End of History' 25 Years On," *The Guardian*, March 21, 2014, https://www.theguardian.com/books/2014/mar/21/bring-back-ideology-fukuyama-end-history-25-years-on; Alan Wolfe, "Francis Fukuyama's Shrinking Idea," *New Republic*, January 16, 2019, https://newrepublic.com/article/152668/francis-fukuyama-identity-review-collapse-theory-liberal-democracy.

an expanding instrument of US global military prowess adorned in the lofty rhetoric of multilateral security cooperation, stood idly by and witnessed Vladimir Putin's Russia engage in a criminal invasion and inhumane occupation of Ukraine.[50] Even as the consequences of the war cascade onward, political attention to the conflict has waned. Let us not be fooled: for all the scary saber rattling happening among the heads of state, military brass, and press corps, there are valid fears that this proxy war between the crumbling Russian Federation and the late-stage American Empire could ignite World War III. We must stop the war and war crimes and embark on strategic measures and diplomacy that should lead to a just peace.

Watching how quickly after the invasion the US and European Union (EU) began shipping high-priced, insanely lethal weapon systems to Ukraine, I cannot help but remember 2Pac's insight: "They Have Money For War / But Can't Feed The Poor."[51] Decades later, his words still ring true. Furthermore, a chief part of the US and NATO's inability to adequately deal with Vladimir Putin is the West's failure to unmask and uproot white supremacy's impulse to either dominate or destroy those deemed "weaker." As Frantz Fanon notes, "Imperialism, which today is waging war against a genuine struggle for human liberation, sows seeds of decay here and there that must be mercilessly rooted out from our land and from our minds."[52] The "might makes right" logic that propels Western culture has left most news outlets ill equipped to fully process how Ukraine as underdog has withstood Russia's terrible onslaught thus far. As the Religious Right in the United States

---

[50] David Gress, *From Plato to NATO: The Idea of the West and Its Opponents* (New York: Free Press, 2004).

[51] Tupac Shakur, "Keep Ya Head Up," *Strictly 4 My N.I.G.G.A.Z.* (1993).

[52] Frantz Fanon, *The Wretched of the Earth*, trans. Richard Philcox (New York: Grove Press, 2004), 181.

has condemned reproductive choice as murder of innocent babies, condemned Black Lives Matters protesters and other "woke" allies for not caring about "all lives," and made queer folks' lives utterly hellish to allegedly protect children, it has remained largely silent on Putin's unjust and inhumane war of choice. Where are all the white Evangelical preachers and pastors condemning Putin and Russia for their unrepentant warring ways? Do All Lives *not* Matter if those lives are Ukrainian? Where is the putatively reflective "What Would Jesus Do"?

Political theorist Yascha Mounk has identified an equally challenging trend emerging in the politics of modern nation-states that he calls "undemocratic liberalism."[53] Mounk is observing how severe damage to public trust in traditional politics over the past twenty years due to stagnating social mobility, staggering shifts in social demographics, and the skyrocketing rise of unaccountable social media has impacted some key social debates. Mounk argues that the usual political factions are not sites for public contest of these debates, thereby creating a system of rights without democracy.[54] As absurd as it may sound, many of the most notable modern-day dictators—China's Xi Jinping, Hungary's Viktor Orbán, Turkey's Recep Erdogan, the Philippines' Rodrigo Duterte, India's Narendra Modi, and Russia's Vladimir Putin—have attempted to keep up populist and democratic appearances during their early years in office even as their nations spiraled into what journalist and global affairs analyst Fareed Zakaria famously called "illiberal democracies."[55] Zakaria observes that

---

[53] Yascha Mounk, "The Undemocratic Dilemma," *Journal of Democracy* 29, no. 2 (April 2018): 98–112, https://www.journalofdemocracy.org/articles/the-undemocratic-dilemma/.

[54] Mounk, "The Undemocratic Dilemma"; Yascha Mounk, *The People vs. Democracy: Why Our Freedom Is in Danger and How to Save It* (Cambridge, MA: Harvard University Press, 2020).

[55] Fareed Zakaria, "The Rise of Illiberal Democracy," *Foreign Affairs* 76, no. 6 (November/December 1997), https://www.foreignaffairs.com/

"across the globe, democratically elected regimes, often ones that have been reelected or reaffirmed through referenda, are routinely ignoring constitutional limits on their power and depriving their citizens of basic rights and freedoms" in direct opposition to the expansion of constitutional rights and privileges ensured in a liberal democratic republic such as ours.[56] Aside from securing the full functioning of rule of law and free markets in our society, a democratic republic in the Western imagination is also supposed to guarantee the promise of liberty for all people.

The Russian invasion of Ukraine and the ensuing war present real dilemmas for the mainstream media as well as the international relations establishment, especially on the question of how to balance the need to thwart a brutal violation of international norms with the equally urgent necessity of bringing an end to the conflict. Many on the Left remain divided on the proper balance to strike regarding how to react and respond to the nakedly brutal aggressions of a tyrant and war criminal such as Putin.[57] Meanwhile, as the Russian Federation seems to be charting its fate as a failed state, many observers are wondering for better or worse what a world without Putin could possibly look like.[58]

---

world/rise-illiberal-democracy; Fareed Zakaria, *The Future of Freedom: Illiberal Democracy at Home and Abroad*, rev. ed. (New York: W. W. Norton, 2007); Marc F. Plattner, "Illiberal Democracy and the Struggle on the Right," *Journal of Democracy* 30, no. 1 (January 2019): 5–19, https://www.journalofdemocracy.org/articles/illiberal-democracy-and-the-struggle-on-the-right/; Jorgen Moller, "A Critical Note on 'The Rise of Illiberal Democracy'," *Australian Journal of Political Science* 43, no. 3 (2008): 555–61.

[56] Fareed Zakaria, "The Rise of Illiberal Democracy." *Foreign Affairs* 76, no. 6 (1997): 22.

[57] Matthew Duss, "Why Ukraine Matters for the Left," *New Republic*, June 1, 2022, https://newrepublic.com/article/166649/ukraine-matters-american-progressives.

[58] The Economist, "Russia's Elite Begins to Ponder a Putinless

More than a decade after the Arab Spring was supposed to unleash democratic possibilities throughout its region, the modern nation-state of Israel continues to violate international norms and laws with its occupation of Palestine. Responding to a ghastly terrorist act of October 7, 2023, Israeli military strategy and action have ignored the human costs in its assault on the Palestinians of Gaza. Since October 8, 2023, however, tens of thousands of innocent Palestinians have been killed in the carpet bombing of Gaza, many of them women and children. Hundreds of thousands have been displaced and forced from their homes. The Israeli government's decision to cut off food, water, electricity, and humanitarian aid to a captive civilian population threatens to worsen a growing humanitarian crisis. These decisions could further harden Palestinian attitudes for future generations, erode global support for Israel, openly play into the hands of Israel's enemies, and undermine long-term efforts to achieve peace and stability in the region.

In his reflection on the harsh history of anti-Semitism rooted in the Holy Land under imperial Roman rule, Howard Thurman wrote,

> There is one overmastering problem that the socially and politically disinherited always face: Under what terms is survival possible? In the case of the Jewish people in the Greco-Roman world the problem was even more acute than under ordinary circumstances, because it had to do

Future," *The Economist*, October 26, 2022, https://www.economist.com/europe/2022/10/26/russias-elite-begins-to-ponder-a-putinless-future; The Editorial Board, "A Brutal New Phase of Putin's Terrible War in Ukraine," *New York Times*, January 21, 2023, https://www.nytimes.com/2023/01/21/opinion/russia-ukraine.html?smtyp=cur&smid=tw-nytimes; Arkady Ostrovsky, "Russia Risks Becoming Ungovernable and Descending into Chaos," *The Economist*, November 18, 2022, https://www.economist.com/the-world-ahead/2022/11/18/russia-risks-becoming-ungovernable-and-descending-into-chaos.

not only with physical survival in terms of life and limb but also with the actual survival of a culture and a faith. Judaism was a culture, a civilization, and a religion—a total world view in which there was no provision for any form of thoroughgoing dualism. The crucial problem of Judaism was to exist as an isolated, autonomous, cultural, religious, and political unit in the midst of the hostile Hellenic world.[59]

Several years later, Howard Thurman and his wife Sue Thurman arrived in Israel on December 2, 1963. They were hosted by several Jewish colleagues and had a brief visit to Jerusalem and its outskirts. While Thurman was in sympathy with the idea of a Jewish return to Palestine, he was immediately "puzzled" in his first visit to the modern nation-state Israel.[60] The modern state of Israel was born in the crucible of war. To Thurman, this Jewish return appeared to be as "a political and nationalistic fulfillment rather than merely a spiritual returning or homecoming to a soil made sacred by divine encounter."[61]

In 1947, the year before the founding of the modern state of Israel in 1948, the United Nations produced a partition plan that proposed to carve and craft the narrow stretch of land from the Jordan River to the Mediterranean Sea into two states, one Arab and one Jewish. The surrounding Arab countries rejected the plan, as did Palestinians living on the land. On May 15, 1948, a day after Israel declared itself a state, four Arab countries attacked. Jewish Israelis saw the ensuing war, which they won, as an existential fight for survival.

---

[59] Howard Thurman, *Jesus and the Disinherited* (Nashville: Abingdon Press, 1949), 20.

[60] Howard Thurman as cited in Peter Eisenstadt, "Howard Thurman in Israel," *Israel Horizons* (April 2021): 11.

[61] Thurman in Eisenstadt, "Howard Thurman in Israel," 11.

This war came just a few years after the Holocaust, and Israel calls it a "War of Liberation." For Palestinians, the aftermath of 1948 marked the *Nakba*—Arabic for "disaster" or "catastrophe"—in which 700,000 people fled or were forcibly expelled from their homes. Many displaced people either went to the West Bank, where Jordan took control, or the Gaza Strip, which Egypt occupied at the time. Through implementation of Plan Dalet, the WEIRD (Western, Educated, Industrialized, Rich, and Democratic) nations of the world stood by and watched as "more than half of Palestine's native population, close to 800,000 people, had been uprooted, 531 villages had been destroyed, and eleven urban neighbourhoods emptied of their inhabitants."[62]

Decades later, Rabbi Abraham Joshua Heschel wrote, "In regard to cruelties committed in the name of a free society, some are guilty, while all are responsible."[63] Engaging questions of democracy today, a critical race theology insists that we not remain fearful and silent about horrible behavior or hateful attitudes regardless of who is on either side of the dilemma. Historically abused and perennially aggrieved peoples should never forget or make themselves immune to the reality that situational ethics and selective outrage are twisted siblings.[64]

Palestinian Arab Christian and pioneering postcolonial scholar Edward Said recognized in his work on orientalism that he was "writing the history of a strange secret sharer of western anti-Semitism. That anti-Semitism and, as I have discussed in its Islamic branch, Orientalism resemble each other very closely is a historical, cultural, and political truth."[65] To some extent,

---

[62] Ilan Pappé, *The Ethnic Cleansing of Palestine* (Oxford: Oneworld, 2023), xiii.

[63] Abraham Joshua Heschel, *Moral Grandeur and Spiritual Audacity: Essays* (New York: Farrar, Straus & Giroux, 1996), 225.

[64] Pappé, *The Ethnic Cleansing of Palestine*, 225–34.

[65] Edward W. Said, *Orientalism: Western Conceptions of the Orient* (New York: Penguin, 1978), 27–28.

Said's "secret sharer" anticipated the subsequent trajectories of scholarship tracing the historical connections between race and religion vis-à-vis approaches to international relations that are inundated with anti-Semitism and Islamophobia.[66] Such an inundation deeply complicates the binary narratives of white vs. non-white, Christian vs. non-Christian, and colonizer vs. colonized. For Said, "The conflict [between Israel and Palestine] appears intractable because it is a contest over the same land by two peoples who always believed they had valid title to it and who hoped that the other side would in time give up or go away."[67] While his statement might have seemed like overblown paranoia in 1999, it has now become an inconvenient yet obvious truth.

Now serving his sixth term as Israel's prime minister, Benjamin Netanyahu remains as staunchly attached now as ever to the 1977 Likud Party platform's genocidal delusion for the Jewish Israeli population's control of this contested territory. They insist that they can exercise unilateral and unquestioned sovereignty over "a land without people" (i.e., Palestinians).[68] In the wake of the events of October 7, 2023, this geopolitical vision appears to serve as the grand unifying principle of Netanyahu's premiership.

---

[66] Yolande Jansen and Nasar Meer, "Genealogies of 'Jews' and 'Muslims': Social Imaginaries in the Race–Religion Nexus," *Patterns of Prejudice* 54, no. 1–2 (2020): 1–14.

[67] Edward Said, "The One-State Solution," *New York Times*, January 10, 1999, https://www.nytimes.com/1999/01/10/magazine/the-one-state-solution.html?smid=url-share.

[68] D. D. Guttenplan, "To Stop the Slaughter in Gaza, We Need the Broadest Coalition Possible," *The Nation*, March 7, 2024, https://www.thenation.com/article/world/israel-gaza-ceasefire-genocide-language/; "Likud Party: Original Party Platform (1977)," in *The Israel-Arab Reader: A Documentary History of the Middle East Conflict*, 6th ed., ed. Walter Laqueur and Barry Rubin (New York: Penguin Books, 2001); *Jewish Virtual Library: A Project of AICE*, https://www.jewishvirtuallibrary.org/original-party-platform-of-the-likud-party.

It is virtually unaltered or revised from its original orientation in the 1990s.[69]

Arguably, Michel Foucault's articulation of biopower as "power's hold over life" or that power which promotes life or permits death for specific peoples, is crucial for understanding the present genocide.[70] With this insight, it becomes easy to draw connections between biopower and divine power. If it is the case that power over life and the power to create life has been traditionally presented as power that only the divine has, the function of the state becomes eerily close to that of the Divine. This issue is compounded when it is overlaid with other extremities of power, particularly power within societal institutions and knowledge. Ultimately, the complexity of biopower illuminates the horrific picture of the conflict between Israel and Hamas in Gaza, wherein nation-states (Israel) and quasi-states (Hamas) attempt to function as God by repressing the cries of the oppressed underfoot.

To be anti-state violence, then, is not the same as promoting anti-Semitism, and the work of uprooting the terrorist mind-set of Hamas must distinguish between innocent Palestinians and deadly quasi-state terrorists. Likewise, one can be in favor of saving Palestinian lives while also honestly despising and wholeheartedly detesting the terrorism of Hamas. Failing to attend to these complexities will only fuel mass violence and sacred hatred in the public sphere. Avraham Burg, an Israeli-born son of Holocaust survivors and former Speaker of the Israeli Knesset, writes,

---

[69] Joshua Leifer, "The Netanyahu Doctrine: How Israel's Longest-Serving Leader Reshaped the Country in His Image," *The Guardian*, November 21, 2023, https://www.theguardian.com/world/2023/nov/21/the-netanyahu-doctrine-how-israels-longest-serving-leader-reshaped-the-country-in-his-image.

[70] Michel Foucault, *"Society Must Be Defended": Lectures at the Collège de France, 1975–1976* (Michel Foucault Lectures at the Collège de France, vol. 5), 1st ed. (London: Picador, 2003).

We fight to break the vicious cycle, which was our portion since Esau, Pharaoh, Goliath, Adrian, Vespasian, Khmelnytsky, Hitler, and the rest of the supervillains. But the more we fight them, the more we feel heavy handed, like them, like Esau. We have forgotten the obligations that our earlier generations took upon themselves. We treat "them" as if we have never vowed in Hillel the Elder's brilliant summation of the Torah: Do not do onto others what is hateful to you. We hated it, and we are doing it, sometimes much too joyously. Is it any wonder no one wants to be our friend anymore when we practice expropriations, injustice in military courts, abuse, roadblocks, food shortages, and worst of all, contempt for Arab life.[71]

Burg both addresses the phenomenon of his fellow citizens reviling Palestinians as "Others" and summarizes the psychologically and morally precarious position of modern Israel as the Jewish State today. For "just peace" to become real in the region, his critique can be instructive and transformative.[72]

Critical race theology proposes a solution to such problems: "prophetic patriotism." Rev. Dr. Martin Luther King Jr. offers considerable guidance to my thinking in this regard. Toward the end of King's life, as he condemned America's military conflict in Vietnam, he declared, "In the days ahead, we must not consider it unpatriotic to raise certain basic questions about our national character."[73] "In the best sense of the word," Michael Eric Dyson says, "King was an American patriot. His was a complex

---

[71] Avraham Burg, *The Holocaust Is Over; We Must Rise from Its Ashes* (New York: St. Martin's Griffin, 2008), 89.

[72] Glen Stassen, *Just Peacemaking: Transforming Initiatives for Justice and Peace* (Louisville, KY: Westminster John Knox Press, 1992).

[73] Martin Luther King Jr., *Where Do We Go From Here: Chaos or Community?* (Boston: Beacon Press, 2010).

and vigorous patriotism—one of the head and heart ... King profoundly loved a country that despite his unerring fidelity, denied him and millions of other loyal blacks the right to exist on the same terms as white Americans."[74] The courage and confidence of King to demand, as he did in his "I Have A Dream" speech, that the United States must "be true to what [it] said on paper" reflects the conviction of one who wants to love as well as trust the nation. King strove to hold society accountable for both its problems and promises alike with no greater interest than the betterment of living conditions for all who live within it. For critical race theology, such striving should be the gold standard for understanding prophetic patriotism moving forward.

The overarching objective for critical race theology is to dismantle white Christian nationalism and supplant it with this vision of prophetic patriotism. We must assert our collective will toward the creation of a just democratic world order that extends beyond our own selfish, shallow quest for white supremacy's survival and toward a vast redefinition of our political and religious culture both domestically and globally. This requires that we look beyond the immediate and intense tribal interests that animate our culture wars and demands that, instead, we engage in an out-and-out battle for better ideas for a shared future. When so much of what passes for Christian virtue has been reduced and recruited for sociopolitical power and economic motives in a fashion that is irreverent and illegitimate in nature, critical race theology is poised to critique traditions of domination and aim us toward the better way of justice that is possible. The reduction and recruitment of Christian virtue within the Western historical tradition leads to the hijacking of religious faith until we can no longer see the transcendent and transformative spiritual ideals that remind us that human beings are complex and sacred. Historian

---

[74] Michael Eric Dyson, *I May Not Get There with You: The True Martin Luther King, Jr.* (New York: Free Press, 1999), 246–47.

of religion Charles H. Long observes that "every adequate hermeneutic is at heart an essay in self-understanding. It is the effort to understand the self through the mediation of the other."[75] Greatly informed by Long's definition of hermeneutic, critical race theology must redefine the hermeneutic of harm that lives in the molten hot core of white Christian nationalism beyond something that threatens only physical safety. Critical race theology must articulate how those who have been grievously injured by white Christian nationalism and its weaponized whiteness have had their emotional, mental, and spiritual well-being threatened.

Millennials and members of Generation Z are far more attuned to calling out and addressing potential impacts of harm than previous generations. Expanding a definition of harm means acknowledging a greater expectation that all communities—most especially those based on shared confession of faith—protect their members from threats to their physical safety and psychological well-being. The use of critical race theology to disentangle whiteness as a linchpin of modern Western Christian identity equally requires decentering white supremacy to restore the vision of grace, mercy, and love that makes possible reconciliation of all people with God that resides at the heart of remaking American Christianity more squarely in accordance with the life, lessons, and legacy of Jesus Christ. For those individuals identified as white within the church, part of constructing a critical race theology can be accomplished by interrogating patterns of disdain, discrimination, and dehumanization regarding human difference. Every form of Othering—racism, sexism, elitism, ageism, ableism, homophobia, transphobia, and xenophobia—is desecration of the wondrous children of God. The goal of such Othering behavior is nothing less than the perversion of the gospel to bolster prejudice, public ridicule, torture, and even death to all people.

---

[75] Long, *Significations*, 51.

Critical race theology is a means to openly and actively counter white supremacist ideas, images, and impulses within our most cherished sacred and secular discourses. It is not enough to be coincidentally nonoppressive in one's beliefs, being, and behavior. We must be explicitly humane in discourse, dogma, doxology, and daily praxis toward those deemed as outcasts, outsiders, outliers, and unholy Others. Although all white Christians ought to address the problem of oppression, exclusion, and dehumanization, the necessity of decentering white Christian identity in political and religious spheres resonates with recent scholarship and activism on antiracism.

In *How To Be an Anti-Racist*, historian Ibram X. Kendi argues that whiteness and white supremacist ideologies are best resisted by engaging in intentional practices of antiracist thinking and reframing society in that fashion. Racism functions in part as a set of practices and epistemologies that seeks the conformity of racialized bodies to dominant white norms. Following this logic, Kendi and others suggest that an antiracist framework is necessary because it centers the mutual flourishing of all people.[76]

The Christianity emanating from a WEIRD interpretation of the religion continuously provides a vast web of references, imagery, and metaphor. This web of concepts is ever relevant, particularly at this juncture, when so much of what passes for Christian sentiment is bullying, reductive, and illegitimately recruited for political and economic motives. Such forces risk hijacking religious conversation so that we can no longer see ideals that might remind us that human beings are capacious and sacred and that our dealings with one another ought to reflect as much. In his essay "The White Man's Guilt," James Baldwin observes this situation as follows:

---

[76] Ibram X. Kendi, *How To Be an Anti-Racist* (New York: OneWorld, 2019), 18–21, 31–34.

People who imagine that history flatters them (as it does, indeed, since they wrote it) are impaled on their history like a butterfly on a pin and become incapable of seeing or changing themselves, or the world. This is the place in which it seems to me, most white Americans find themselves. Impaled. They are dimly, or vividly, aware that the history they have fed themselves is mainly a lie, but they do not know how to release themselves from it and they suffer enormously from the resulting personal incoherence.[77]

As I understand Baldwin, the key problem of whiteness and all it entails is not merely an identity per se. The problem of whiteness as an ideology is that it perpetuates both white privilege and white supremacy by means of the minimization and Othering of non-white people in their own native land and also in their own worldviews.

"Almost all Christians," Eugene Rogers writes, "need to learn that life with God is not their due reward, not their natural possession, not theirs to demand or extort."[78] Worst of all, submitting to white Christian nationalism rather than a living, loving, and liberating God as a governing set of ideals has wrought profound damage and devastation on white-identified people. Critical race theology offers each of us a life-giving chance to build a world without the rupture between them, the Divine, and the diverse plethora of humanity that constitutes God's creation. Critical race theology reframes racial embodiment for the flourishing of each and every one of us, together.

---

[77] James Baldwin, *James Baldwin: Collected Essays*, selected by Toni Morrison (1963; New York: Literary Classics of the United States, Inc., 1998), 723.

[78] Eugene F. Rogers Jr., "Supplementing Barth on Jews and Gender: Identifying God by Anagogy and the Spirit," *Modern Theology* 14 (1998): 66.

4

"With Their Backs against the Wall"

Theologizing Black Lives Matter in the Era of the Religious "Nones"

In December 2014, tens of thousands of protesters crowded onto the streets of US cities to challenge the rising tide of police brutality in the nation. This mass mobilization of activists and concerned citizens became known as the Black Lives Matter (or BLM) movement and gained worldwide attention following the deaths of Michael Brown and Eric Garner. Demonstrators marched in Ferguson, New York City, Baltimore, Los Angeles, Nashville, Philadelphia, Atlanta, and countless other cities, filling the night sky with a now familiar repertoire of chants: "No justice, no peace"; "Hands up, don't shoot"; "I can't breathe." As a sad testament to that particularly turbulent year, "I can't breathe"—Eric Garner's last words as police officer Daniel Pantaleo choked him to death on a Staten Island sidewalk—topped the *Yale Book of Quotations* list of the most notable words of 2014.[1] These mobilizations coalesced around

---

[1] Elahe Izadi, "'I Can't Breathe.' Eric Garner's Last Words Are 2014's Most Notable Quote, according to a Yale Librarian," *Washington Post,* December 9, 2014, https://www.washingtonpost.com/news/post-nation/wp/2014/12/09/i-cant-breathe-eric-garners-last-words-are-2014s-most-notable-quote-according-to-yale-librarian/?utm_term=.a379860ca434.

the slogan "Black lives matter." These three words will probably be the most remembered phrase emerging from this troubled and perplexing era. For critical race theology, it is important to understand why that is the case.

The original hashtag #BlackLivesMatter was created in 2012 by Alicia Garza, Patrisse Cullors, and Opal Tometi, after George Zimmerman, the murderer of seventeen-year-old Trayvon Martin, was acquitted for his crime. Rooted in the world of grassroots activism, these three women recognized and channeled the energy and imagination of a broad range of people, especially queer and gender-nonconforming individuals, immigrants, and criminalized youths. #BlackLivesMatter expressed their ire succinctly and successfully while also igniting the online social media landscape in ways that largely circumvented the mainstream media, surprised academics, and supplanted the activist leadership usually associated with religious organizations. Since the 2010s, #BlackLivesMatter has evolved beyond denunciation of extrajudicial killings of Black people by police officers and vigilantes to a movement of political importance in ways that expose the political and moral bankruptcy of the contemporary church regardless of race. As the media, the academy, and the church cannot claim credit for either creating or controlling the movement, implicit recognition of #BlackLivesMatter's disruptive potential within the body politic arguably threatens their perceived authority as agents of social transformation moving forward.

Even more unsettling for these more traditional institutions may very well be the multiple layers of meaning and possibility invoked by the very phrase "Black Lives Matter." #BlackLivesMatter is both transforming and transcending the established norms of new social movement theory by establishing a new paradigm of protest that is more fluidly dynamic and multivalent in nature, offering us an effective glimpse of a social metamovement. #BlackLivesMatter can conjure an array of different yet equally salient dimensions of the movement's significance to the broader context of liberationist struggles: BLM as a shorthand reference to the original brainchild of Opal Tometi, Patrisse Cullors, and Alicia Garza; BLM as the localized groups of protesters engaged in nonviolent civil disobedience via various mass-mobilization efforts; #BLM as the decentralized, global organizational network of grassroots activists and allies; #BLM as the viral social media hashtag; and #BLM as the most recognized and iconic slogan of this historical era. Unlike the media, the academy, the church, and even the more established civil rights organizations, #BlackLivesMatter has been able to make an almost seamless integration of the virtual realm and the real world without missing a step. In August 2016, nearly sixty organizations associated with the Black Lives Matter movement released a series of six demands in the hopes of taking their goals beyond local protests into the formal arena of national electoral politics.[2] Taken as a whole, the dynamism of #BlackLivesMatter might appear to defenders of the status quo as the movement's most threatening and disruptive potential.

Between #BlackLivesMatter and #MakeAmericaGreatAgain, the work of combating the systematic dehumanization of Black bodies and the destruction of Black lives has particular significance in our time. The polar extremes of the transcendent and the tragic realities of Blackness provide the key context for understanding the intergenerational poverty, *de facto* hypersegregation, and widespread oppression that still largely define Black life today. In his acclaimed book *Between the World and Me*, Ta-Nehisi Coates captures much of this sentiment when he argues,

> In accepting both the chaos of history and the fact of my total end, I was freed to truly consider how I wished to

---

[2] For more details, see The Movement for Black Lives, "A Vision for Black Lives: Policy Demands for Black Power, Freedom, & Justice," https://archive.org/details/20160726M4blVisionBookletV3/mode/2up.

live—specifically, how do I live free in this black body? It is a profound question because America understands itself as God's handiwork, but the black body is the clearest evidence that America is the work of [humans].[3]

The #BlackLivesMatter protests that riveted the world's attention in recent years seem to have their immediate roots in the civil rights and Black power eras, yet the movement's origins are rooted in the rise of modernity itself. On this score, perhaps no worldview is as important, yet drastically underestimated, as Black humanism in the modern world.

This chapter attends to Black humanism as a vital expression of Black liberation in the face of insidious and death-dealing movements in the United States. Critical race theology emphasizes Black humanism's importance as a legitimate system of thought and praxis. Historically, this humanism has placed an emphasis on human possibility that demands an end to racism, misogyny, homophobia, and poverty as well as staunch opposition to imperialism, heterosexism, religious fundamentalism, xenophobia, ecological degradation, and violence. In turn, the articulation of Black humanism in its various forms throughout history illustrates a richer, more complex understanding of the ongoing struggle for human rights in the United States. Our discourse and our disciplines are riddled with insidious bigotry and implicit bias, positing that Blackness *qua* race is a degrading, distracting, and potentially destructive and superadded element to any system of thought and belief that humans can devise. Faced with this tension, critical race theology insists that emergent forms of humanist thought and praxis, such as the Black Lives Matter movement, must be taken seriously.

---

[3] Ta-Nehisi Coates, *Between the World and Me* (New York: Spiegel and Grau, 2015), 12.

Sometimes the greatest scholarly contribution anyone can make is to ask a timely question in the face of a timeless problem. Howard Thurman wrote in the pivotal moments in the aftermath of a global struggle against totalitarian dictatorships, militarized bloodshed, and godless genocide and on the verge of a rising tide of oppressed peoples fomenting social justice and anticolonial movements in latter half of the twentieth century. In the preface of his classic text *Jesus and the Disinherited* (1949), Thurman articulates his concerns:

> The significance of the religion of Jesus to people who stand with their backs against the wall has always seemed to me to be crucial ... This is the question which individuals and groups who live in our land always under the threat of profound social and psychological displacement face: Why is it that Christianity seems impotent to deal radically, and therefore effectively, with the issues of discrimination and injustice on the basis of race, religion, and national origin? Is this impotency due to a betrayal of the genius of the religion or is it due to a basic weakness in the religion itself?[4]

Whether one is a confessing Christian or not, how we answer this potent question speaks volumes about the efficacy and even the exigency of our faith. As Thurman himself proclaims, "There must be the clearest possible understanding of the anatomy of the issues facing" those with their backs against the wall.[5] Critical race theology strives to understand this anatomy in solidarity with Keeanga-Yamahtta Taylor's reflections on our current historical moment by "also looking at whether the Black Lives Matter

---

[4] Howard Thurman, *Jesus and the Disinherited* (Nashville: Abingdon Press, 1949), 7.

[5] Thurman, *Jesus and the Disinherited*, 108.

movement opens a broader opportunity to explore what black liberation looks like in the United States. Can this movement that's narrowly fixated on police brutality become a much broader interrogation of American society?"[6]

As we address this crisis anew in the twenty-first century, our houses of worship and faith communities must be places to ask deeper, more probing questions of ourselves, of our nation, of our world, and even of our faith traditions, especially in times of local, national, and global crises. Today, we navigate war and rumors of war, domestic and international terrorism, and acts of violence beyond comprehension. Thurman reminds us that our work and witness calls us to reflect on critical theological questions and to find the courage to embrace difficult, desperate answers.

What do the words of sacred scripture and the work of social witness mean for a hurting humanity who are brutalized, beleaguered, and burdened on this all too bitter earth? What does Jesus have to say to the walking wounded and the openly outcast people of our world? For those who perennially rank amongst the "least of these" of this world, what hope or help can a feckless faith provide? To paraphrase the incisive insights of Janet Jackson, "I know your religion used to do nice stuff for you, but what has it done for you lately?"

It is neither apostasy nor apathy to ask legitimate questions about whether the current religion is sufficient as a remedy for those who have their backs against the wall. How can we harness our belief, being, and behavior to serve as instruments of social justice to achieve divine peace in a world that's quite literally on fire?

---

[6] Ansel Herz, "From Hashtag to Movement: Author Keeanga-Yamahtta Taylor on Black Lives Matter and Police Reform," *The Stranger*, April 27, 2016, https://www.thestranger.com/crime/2016/04/27/24006958/from-hashtag-to-movement-author-keeanga-yamahtta-taylor-on-black-lives-matter-and-police-reform.

In the best merger between faith, intellect, and action, we must dare to ask the questions that probe, challenge, and push, affirming that, only by reasoning together, with respect and charity, can we propose solutions to the question of how to serve those whose backs are against the wall. Such religious reflection demands of us that, while confronting widespread indiscriminate loss of life, we recognize that, and how, this carnage is fueled by wholesale indifference toward the value of human life in our society and culture.

As a theologian, pastor, and mystic, Thurman served as a spiritual muse and mentor to Rev. Dr. Martin Luther King Jr. and the civil rights movement. Following Thurman, critical race theology insists that a real Christian and a compelling preacher of the gospel must ask, "What, then, is the word of the religion of Jesus to those who stand with their backs against the wall?" [7] The value of one's faith is inextricably linked with ethical material reality, liberating the oppressed and righting what is wrong. When one has wronged an innocent person, one has violated the inherent worth and dignity of that person and the divinity within them as well.

A person's worth and dignity, though inherent and woven with divinity, is vulnerable. More than a century ago, pioneering historian and sociologist W. E. B. Du Bois discussed this dilemma of criminalization in his seminal work, *The Souls of Black Folk* (1903). By discussing the early phase of the racialization of the prison industrial complex, Du Bois recognizes that

> daily the Negro is coming more and more to look upon law and justice, not as protecting safeguards, but as sources of humiliation and oppression. The laws are made by men who have little interest in him; they are executed by men who have absolutely no motive for treating the black

---

[7] Thurman, *Jesus and the Disinherited*, 29.

people with courtesy or consideration; and, finally, the accused law-breaker is tried, not by his peers, but too often by men who would rather punish ten innocent Negroes than let one guilty one escape.[8]

Paying strict attention to this sordid history of anti-Blackness and structural bias within law enforcement, Michael Eric Dyson explores how use of lethal violence by police officers against Black people demonstrates how systemic racism has operated in an uninterrupted and unreasonable fashion since the founding of the American republic:

> The history of race would yet again be condensed into an interaction between the cops and a young Black anybody from Black anywhere doing Black anything on any given Black night. Yes, it was random, you were to that degree random, but it was a randomness that exists within a universe of perverse predictability that means any Black person can be targeted anywhere at any time. This reinforces the vulnerability that all of us Black folk share.[9]

How can we even strive to remedy the ingrained brutality and unfairness of the American criminal justice system when it is becoming public knowledge that the largely white police force and increasingly white vigilantes are functioning as self-styled judges, juries, and executioners? In her pathbreaking text *Stand Your Ground: Black Bodies and the Justice of God* (2015), Kelly Brown Douglas writes,

> The seeds of "Stand Your Ground" law were planted well before the founding of America. These seeds produced a

---

[8] W. E. B. Du Bois, *The Souls of Black Folk* (New York: St. Martin's Press, 1997), 140.

[9] Michael Eric Dyson, *Long Time Coming: Reckoning with Race in America* (New York: St. Martin's Press, 2020), 2.

myth of racial superiority that both determined America's founding and defined its identity. This myth then gave way to America's grand narrative of exceptionalism. This narrative, replete with its own sacred canopy, in turn constructed cherished property and generated a culture to shelter that property, thus insuring that America remain "exceptional." I identify this culture as "stand-your-ground culture." This culture itself is generative. It has spawned various social-cultural devices—legal and extralegal, theoretical and ideological, political and theological—to preserve America's primordial exceptional identity.[10]

As Douglas correctly indicates, the collapse of the Reconstruction era's radical reforms led directly to the deliberate and decisive criminalization of the newly emancipated Black populace of the postbellum American South. She asserts that

the various Black Codes and Jim Crow laws in particular served to plant the image of the black body as a criminal body deep within America's collective consciousness. Essentially, these legal productions criminalized black people. Just as black people became trapped in the chattel cycle, they became trapped in the criminal cycle. This occurred through the judicious implementation of racially biased laws.[11]

Rather than imagine that the implicit bias at the heart of our legal system is somehow a matter of haphazard chance and circumstance, Douglas makes abundantly clear there were conscious choices by law enforcement agents and legislators alike so that "these laws assured that the black body would be viewed as a criminal body

---

[10] Kelly Brown Douglas, *Stand Your Ground: Black Bodies and the Justice of God* (Maryknoll, NY: Orbis Books, 2015), 4.

[11] Douglas, *Stand Your Ground*, 77–78.

within the collective imagination. They literally made a criminal of black people. All the black people had to do was be black."[12]

Michelle Alexander's acclaimed text *The New Jim Crow* (2010) shifted a great deal of public attention to the crisis of mass incarceration and its role in fomenting the prison industrial complex as a mainstay of modern American life. In the opening pages of the book, Alexander states, "I was careful to define 'mass incarceration' to include those who were subject to state control outside of prison walls, as well as those who were locked in literal cages."[13] Because of the nature of contemporary life and culture, the scale and scope of Alexander's concept of "incarceration" includes people who have been arrested (but not yet tried), people on parole, and people who have been released but are still labeled as "criminals" and "offenders." Hence, Alexander's definition is intentionally much broader than simply indicating those individuals currently imprisoned in some form of physical detention.

When Alexander's work debuted, it began to reframe the public discourse about the interplay of race, class, and mass incarceration. Many Black Christian clergy were still largely reluctant to mobilize in sizable and sustained numbers against the American legal system writ large. In the early 2000s, with the notable exception of the Samuel Dewitt Proctor Conference and their collective engagement with Alexander's text, there was a small contingent of prophetic people who were ready, willing, and able to openly address the looming crisis that the prison industrial complex represented for Black, Latinx, and working poor communities nationwide.[14] With

---

[12] Douglas, *Stand Your Ground*, 79; see also Khalil Gibran Muhammad, *The Condemnation of Blackness: Race, Crime, and the Making of Modern Urban America* (Cambridge, MA: Harvard University Press, 2010).

[13] Michelle Alexander, *The New Jim Crow: Mass Incarceration in the Age of Colorblindness* (New York: New Press, 2010), xxvi.

[14] Shawn Bell, "The New Jim Crow Study Guide," Samuel DeWitt Proctor Conference, March 2, 2022, https://sdpconference.

the ascendancy of the nation's first Black president, who also happened to be both a grassroots community organizer and an Ivy League–educated lawyer, the brewing debates about systemic racism and its impact on public policy, policing, and prisons were perfectly timed but poorly engaged by even the most ardent advocates. The cruelest irony of the Obama era might have been the realization that even as conversations about prison sentencing reforms began to gain traction, public attention sadly shifted to police officers and vigilantes wantonly killing Black and Latinx people at will.

In thinking about Black Lives Matter in its most recent iteration, it is useful to make direct comparisons between two of the most notable police murders of recent years: Breonna Taylor and George Floyd. For critical race theology, such comparisons can demonstrate the key tensions that BLM has forced American society and culture to confront in a forthright manner. While there are a great deal of similarities surrounding these two highly publicized cases, I draw greater attention to and emphasize the disparities between them.

At midnight on March 13, 2020, four police officers arrived at the home of Breonna Taylor, a young Black emergency room technician in Louisville, Kentucky. Much earlier, these police officers had obtained a "no-knock" warrant based on dubious information, claiming that the state had reason to believe that her former boyfriend, a suspected drug dealer, had been using Taylor's apartment to receive and hide his contraband. The actual suspect they were pursuing lived more than ten miles away from Taylor's home, yet the police successfully obtained the no-knock warrant. The warrant empowered them to forcefully break into her residence with a battering ram without previously identifying themselves as police, as witnessed by Kenneth Walker, Taylor's boyfriend.

---

info/2022/03/the-new-jim-crow-study-guide/.

At midnight, Taylor and Walker were awakened when they heard many loud strikes at the door. According to Walker's testimony, when they asked who was outside their door, no one responded, and Walker stated he was afraid that it was Taylor's ex-boyfriend attempting to break in and harm them. According to reporting from the *New York Times*, "After the police broke the door off its hinges, Mr. Walker fired his gun once, striking Sgt. Jonathan Mattingly in the thigh. The police responded by firing several shots, striking Ms. Taylor five times. Mr. Hankison shot 10 rounds blindly into the apartment."[15]

Local emergency medical services were notified by the police one hour before the raid to prepare to dispatch an ambulance close to Taylor's apartment. When the ambulance arrived at the scene, a paramedic tried her best to treat wounds of the police officers while giving no medical care to Taylor before Walker called 911 for help. Moreover, in the confusing aftermath of the botched police raid, Walker told the police officers that Ms. Taylor struggled to breathe for at least five minutes while waiting for medical assistance. The Jefferson County coroner's office alleged that, given the severity of her injuries, Taylor could not have survived for more than one minute after so many wounds.

It was later revealed that the no-knock warrant had been altered *ex post facto* to a "knock and announce warrant" before the break-in took place; the police then asserted that they had identified themselves several times as police officers and showed their identification, which contradicted the testimony of Walker.[16]

---

[15] Richard A. Oppel, Derrick Bryson Taylor, and Nicholas Bogel-Burroughs, "What to Know about Breonna Taylor's Death," *New York Times*, May 30, 2020.

[16] Richard A. Oppel Jr., and Derrick Bryson Taylor, "Here's What You Need to Know About Breonna Taylor's Death," *New York Times*, September 1, 2020, https://www.nytimes.com/article/

Although this tragedy led to the death of Taylor, none of the police officers were accused of any wrongdoing in her death. After roughly five months, the Justice Department charged those four officers with civil rights violations and lying to obtain the no-knock warrant to Taylor's home. Subsequently, Hankison, one of the police officers in the raid, was the only one accused of wanton endangerment of neighbors and was described as "manifesting extreme indifference to the value of human life."[17] However, he pleaded not guilty and was acquitted. The other two policemen that participated in the raid were fired by the police department of Louisville five months after the raid, but none of them faced prison consequences or legal sentencing. On August 27, 2020, Jamarcus Glover, Ms. Taylor's ex-boyfriend, was arrested for drug trafficking.[18] He said that Ms. Taylor was not involved in such activities. No drugs were found in Ms. Taylor's house.

In March of 2023, the US Department of Justice (DOJ) investigation revealed Louisville's city government and police department conducted practices that violated the US Constitution. The investigation was launched after Louisville officers shot and killed Breonna Taylor. The DOJ report states, "Officers' forcible and violent entry into a person's home strikes at the heart of the constitutional protection against unreasonable government intrusion.... But Louisville Metro's and LMPD's unlawful conduct did not start in 2020."[19] Some of Louisville PD's unconstitutional

---

breonna-taylor-police.html.

[17] Nicholas Bogel-Burroughs, "What Is 'Wanton Endangerment,' the Charge in the Breonna Taylor Case?" *New York Times*, September 5, 2023, https://www.nytimes.com/2020/09/23/us/wanton-endangerment.html.

[18] Elizabeth Joseph and Dakin Andone, "Breonna Taylor's Ex-Boyfriend Has Been Arrested and Says She Had Nothing to Do with Alleged Drug Trade," CNN.com, August 28, 2020, https://www.cnn.com/2020/08/27/us/breonna-taylor-jamarcus-glover-arrest.

[19] Mia McCarthy, "Louisville Police Department Practices Violated

patterns included unjustified neck restraints, unreasonable dog and taser use, unlawful searches and traffic stop practices, discrimination against Black people and those with behavioral health disabilities, deficiencies in response to sexual assault and domestic violence allegations against officers, use of racist and ableist slurs by officers, and videotaped evidence of officers throwing drinks at people from their cars.[20]

On May 25, 2020, a shop clerk reported that George Floyd had purchased cigarettes with fake twenty-dollar bills. In response, a cohort of four police officers stopped Floyd as he was driving his car on the street. The policemen later said that Floyd seemed to be under the influence of an illegal substance. After several seconds, Mr. Floyd opened his car door while simultaneously apologizing for opening it late. After being dragged out of his car by the police, Floyd refused to sit in the back of their vehicle, claiming that he was claustrophobic. He pulled himself out of the police car, saying that he was just going to lie on the ground, and the interaction turned fatal.

> Three officers pin Mr. Floyd facedown—Mr. Chauvin kneeling on his neck, Mr. Kueng kneeling on his upper legs and holding his wrist, and Mr. Lane holding Mr. Floyd's legs. (Mr. Thao was keeping bystanders away.) Mr. Floyd began saying repeatedly that he could not breathe. Mr. Chauvin kept his knee on Mr. Floyd's neck for nine and a half minutes.[21]

Constitution, DOJ Finds," *Politico* (March 8, 2023), https://www.politico.com/news/2023/03/08/louisville-police-violated-constitution-doj-00086081.

[20] McCarthy, "Louisville Police Department Practices Violated Constitution, DOJ Finds."

[21] "How George Floyd Died, and What Happened Next." *New York Times*, September 8, 2020.

After six minutes of Floyd being held down on the street, bystanders shouted to the policemen to check his condition. One of the policemen, J. Alexander Kueng, checked his breathing and pulse and said that he could not detect any signs of life. Nevertheless, these policemen held Floyd down on the ground for an additional two and a half minutes until the emergency responders arrived and loaded him into an ambulance. He was officially declared dead later that night.

Our society was already crushing the life out of George Floyd as he struggled to make his constantly frustrated dreams of a successful and sustainable future a reality. The structural inequality of this lopsided economy was choking him, for allegedly passing a counterfeit $20 bill is not a crime worthy of death. The failure of our society to live with grace and mercy toward those who have been imprisoned was crushing George Floyd as a formerly incarcerated man. His autopsy revealed that George Floyd was positive for COVID-19 at the time of his death. Under threats to well-being in the coronavirus pandemic, economic panic, and political pandemonium, he ultimately fell victim to the more lethal and loathsome "policemandemic."[22]

Compared to the killing of Breonna Taylor, the aftermath of this instance was far more pronounced. The day after the killing, large-scale protests erupted in Minneapolis, and Mayor Jacob Frey announced that the four officers involved in the death of George Floyd had been fired. Derek Chauvin, the most senior of the policemen involved in the incident, was the main person culpable in the murder because he had kept his knee firmly on Floyd's neck for more than nine minutes. As a result, Chauvin was arrested on May 29, 2020, and initially charged with third-degree murder.

---

[22] Juan M. Floyd-Thomas, "Deep in the Heart of Texas: Race, Religion, and Rights in the COVID-19 Era," in *Religion, Race and COVID-19: Confronting White Supremacy in the Pandemic,* ed. Stacey Floyd-Thomas (New York: New York University Press, 2021), 190–92.

William P. Barr, then–US Attorney General, intervened to reject the agreement, which also included a guarantee Chauvin would not be charged with violating federal civil rights laws. According to a February 2021 *New York Times* article, Chauvin purportedly agreed to plead guilty within days of Floyd's death.[23] However, during the trial, Chauvin had asserted through his attorney that the way he handled Floyd's arrest constituted a legal and appropriate use of force. It was found during the proceedings that Chauvin had received at least twenty-two complaints or internal inquiries over the course of his nearly twenty years of service with the department, one of which resulted in disciplinary action.

On April 20, 2021, Chauvin was convicted of second-degree murder, third-degree murder, and second-degree manslaughter after a lengthy trial. Toward the end of the trial, Carolyn Pawlenty, Chauvin's mother, offered testimony in court as a character witness for her son's defense. As one might expect, she pled for clemency on behalf of Chauvin because, as she told the court "my son is a good man" who "never did anything wrong" and, in her estimation, he was not a racist. "I believe a long sentence will not serve Derek well," she said. Pawlenty noted that she and Chauvin's father will likely not be alive when he is released from prison. In a particularly striking moment during Chauvin's murder trial, Pawlenty directly addressed her son in court and told him that he is her "favorite son" amid her sworn remarks. Although relatively short in duration, Pawlenty's testimony illustrated the familial milieu that could have given rise to moral ambivalence demonstrated by Chauvin the fateful day he encountered George Floyd. In contrast to Chauvin's attorneys' request for probation and time-served credit, Chauvin was given a sentence of twenty-two and a half years in prison in June of that same year.

---

[23] Tim Arango, "Why William Barr Rejected a Plea Deal in the George Floyd Killing," *New York Times*, March 29, 2021, https://www.nytimes.com/2021/02/10/us/george-floyd-death.html.

The punishment was less than the thirty years that the prosecution requested. With his combined state and federal sentence, Chauvin's potential release date is likely to be in 2038.[24]

Breonna Taylor's and George Floyd's murders happened in 2020, and both cases demonstrate an overpolicing problem, where police officers exerted an unwarranted use of force in their interactions with citizens. One involved a team of police officers forcefully breaking into a private home without identifying themselves and then discharging their weapons indiscriminately in her apartment building. This incident finally led to Taylor's death after sustaining multiple gunshot wounds while lying asleep in her bed. The other incident involved only $20, but the police suffocated Floyd to death because he refused to get in a police car due to being claustrophobic.

These two murders indicate how the government often sanctions recklessly violent acts by police officers and other authorities toward Black people. The ambulance that arrived in front of Taylor's house did not realize the dire condition of Taylor, attending the scene at the request of police. The policemen who restricted Floyd's ability to breathe did not even notice that he was dying and, therefore, did not even consider administering any first aid until it was too late.

Though the dates, actions, and results of these two cases were similar, the aftermath of each case was dramatically different. While the Louisville Metropolitan police department did many things wrong, none of the police officers in Breonna Taylor's case faced legal responsibility for her death—none faced charges for murder or even manslaughter. By contrast, the four policemen in the case

---

[24] William Bornhoft, "Federal Sentence Likely Extends Chauvin's Prison Stay by about 3 Years." *Saint Paul, MN Patch*, July 8, 2022, https://patch.com/minnesota/saintpaul/federal-sentence-likely-extends-chauvins-prison-stay-3-years.

of Floyd were fired and sentenced, with the longest sentence being twenty-two and a half years. Five months passed before state and federal investigations even began grappling with Taylor's case. Floyd's case was resolved in two weeks.

This difference in time for the legal process shows a difference in attention from the public and the intensity of social judgment as well as a tangled metanarrative of racism and sexism in our broader media culture. Taylor's death happened in the middle of the night, with no video footage documenting the event, and Floyd's death was chronicled on video and posted on social media, eventually seen by millions of viewers globally. There is a stark contrast between the hypervisibility of Black men and the corresponding invisibility of Black women as targets of police violence.

Adding more complications, the lack of public attention to Taylor's case compared to Floyd's might also be due to a combination of race, gender, and partisan politics. In an exceedingly rare coincidence, the state attorneys general who would oversee the investigation and possible prosecution of these cases were both African American men: Daniel Cameron was attorney general for the Commonwealth of Kentucky at the time of Taylor's death, while Keith Ellison was attorney general for the state of Minnesota when Floyd was murdered. For Cameron, as a Black conservative Republican, if he participated heavily in the case of Taylor, he might be seen as dishonoring the police or intentionally helping Black women, which might affect his future political ambitions. For Ellison, as a Black progressive Democrat, it was easier for him to say that the killing of George Floyd was wrong and should be criticized because there was an outburst of national anger toward the policemen. Moreover, the invisibility of Taylor's death to the public reduced the extent of its influence. In this way, Cameron could more easily sit back and pretend nothing had happened.

While many of us were left too emotionally exhausted and mentally overwhelmed to even look at the viral video of Floyd's murder on that Memorial Day, a brave and bold seventeen-year-old young woman never weakened and wavered in recording the moments that left the entire world breathless. There was a breathlessness for many of us as we wondered what to do next. The next day, a stream of protesters, activists, and people of good faith and conscience grew. By the hundreds, then the thousands, then the millions worldwide, folks from Atlanta to Australia, Ghana to the Gaza Strip, Berlin to Baltimore, Los Angeles to London flooded the streets, proclaiming "Black Lives Matter!" We witnessed rare actions to hold those killer cops accountable in Minneapolis pair with the emergence of a silent, submerged multitude, who finally said, "Enough is enough." People stayed marching all the while demanding a better world for us, our family, friends, neighbors, and even strangers. In the face of these largely peaceful and positive acts of civil disobedience, too many police departments around the nation have responded to talks of de-escalation, defunding, and possibly dismantling the police force with clenched fists rather than open hands.

There are many moments that leave us both literally and figuratively breathless. As mighty and miraculous as the human body is, the spark of life within each one of us must also be regarded as precious and precarious in nature. Losing access to simple things like food, sleep, water, and air brings us to the brink of death. On average, a human can go without food for about three weeks, without sleep for about twelve days, and without water for about three days. The average human takes about 23,000 breaths a day. We cannot survive more than three minutes without oxygen. Holding on for the nine-minute and twenty-nine-second ordeal in which former officer Derek Chauvin and his accomplices choked the life from him, George Floyd did something superhuman.

Watching George Floyd's dying breath triggered my experiences of seeing my late mother fighting for her last gasp of air as she succumbed to a misdiagnosed case of metastatic lung cancer in 2017, crying, "I can't breathe." This flood of memories and emotions made me even more mindful of the Hebrew concept of *Ru' ach*, that divine spirit-wind-breath as a gift that only originally comes from God. I was and am taken aback by how much we take breath for granted until it is finally gone.

I think of my early upbringing in the Catholic Church and the Latin language. Respiration, inspiration, and conspiracy share a common linguistic root in the word *spire*, meaning "to breathe." Conspire, quite literally meaning "to breathe together," in and of itself does not have wicked or evil connotations. Yet, conspirators have hijacked the relationality of the word with the most wretched of intentions. For far too long in human history, we have witnessed conspiracies of hatred that are cruel, chaotic, corrupt, and criminally minded. Political and corporate leaders who presently rule the land try to crush the very life from every one of us because they do not want to see any changes in the status quo. Yet we have also witnessed a growing conspiracy of helplessness pervading our culture and society. In courthouses, statehouses, church houses, and creeping into newsrooms, hospital rooms, classrooms, and even our bedrooms, it is becoming more acceptable that some of us must die grim, grisly, and needless deaths without ever knowing a safe or sacred space to call our own.

Recognizing these conspiracies of hatred, critical race theology's turn to Black humanism becomes vital. "Beyond the loss of our bodies," as Michael Eric Dyson reminds, "we faced metaphysical death, too, since the nation cruelly imagined the nonbeing of Black folk."[25] This created a paradox wherein, according to Dyson, "whiteness had inherent value" while conversely "Black life was morally and culturally deficient."[26] The wholesale arrest and imprisonment of Black people in both literal

---

[25] Dyson, *Long Time Coming*, 17–18.
[26] Dyson, *Long Time Coming*, 17–18.

and figurative senses serves as the imposition of government power and the rationalization of our nation's quintessential obsession with "law and order."

> It is no accident that stand-your-ground culture has been most aggressively if not fatally executed after every period in which certain "rights" are extended to black people, ostensibly bringing them closer to enjoying the "inalienable rights of life, liberty, and the pursuit of happiness." This pattern of "white backlash" began with the emancipation. After emancipation, Black Codes, Jim Crow laws, and the heinous "punishment" of lynching was enforced. The "law and order" mandates of the post-civil rights era continued this pattern. White backlash surely is reflected in the virulent stand-your-ground reality that has followed the election of the first black president. In each instance, stand-your-ground culture has asserted itself in an effort to "seize" the rights of whiteness and to return the black body to its chattel space.[27]

In his 1927 work, *The Public and Its Problems*, philosopher and educator John Dewey made clear that democracy involves treating the negotiation of citizens in public life as an open network of sorts across which their multiple and often competing problems and concerns get communicated by different groups. In this perpetual process, our coordinated effort to address such concerns leads us as a people and a nation to build a shared life together grounded in the principle of equality as mutual regard.

The distinction between why people *ought* to comply with authority and why people actually *do* comply with authority, though, is critically important for wrestling with present relations between white Americans, the state, and people of color in the United

---

[27] Dyson, *Long Time Coming*, 117.

States. Describing it as a "legitimation crisis," Jürgen Habermas argues that this distinction between philosophical and sociological observations is a crisis that is marked by the increasing inability of the state to securely fulfill its designated governing functions in administrative and even moral terms. In turn, the public's trust in institutions declines, leading to heightened levels of despair that eventually destroy faith that the citizenry would otherwise place in those previously cherished institutions.[28] In our current decline, we have witnessed a virulent strain of white supremacy that is advanced by the alt-Right and involves a perversion of democratic empathy by treating the concerns of white Americans as the only true and legitimate concerns of the body politic. Whiteness, therefore, prompts the only concerns in need of remedy or redress.

Following Charles Blow's observation that "'Make America Great Again' is in fact an inverted admission of loss—lost primacy, lost privilege, lost prestige"—critical race theology critiques the white supremacist insistence that the interests of people of color are either less important or unworthy of any consideration if attending to these interests in our democratic society involves even the slightest devaluation of whiteness.[29] Because perceptions—even false or misguided ones—can be stronger than reality itself, these losses have become magnified and take on added force among many voters, supporters, and enablers of Donald Trump because they generate a perception of uncertainty regarding one's status. This uncertainty corresponds to a fear of falling to a level that would make white Americans *merely equal* to their non-white counterparts. The most rudimentary definition of legitimacy within the body politic depends on a reservoir of good will and trust that

---

[28] Jürgen Habermas, *Legitimation Crisis* (Boston: Beacon Press, 1973).

[29] Charles M. Blow, "Trump Reflects White Male Fragility," *New York Times*, August 4, 2016, https://www.nytimes.com/2016/08/04/opinion/trump-reflects-white-male-fragility.html.

allows the institutions of government to go against what people may want sometimes without suffering debilitating consequences of perceived unreliability.

While we often question the loss of confidence and the struggle to retain legitimate authority for leadership of secular institutions, I assert that an equal, if not greater, scrutiny of our collective relationship with sacred institutions is necessary. Eddie Glaude Jr.'s article "The Black Church Is Dead" is a useful source for critical race theology's attention on our relationship with faith communities and institutions.[30] First, Black churches have always been much more complicated spaces than was presumed by the conventional wisdom of mainstream society. Contrary to what has become the normative narrative on African American Christianity, the Black church is not simply the NAACP with more biblical verses and gospel choirs. It is a truly sophisticated social and spiritual space. Second, African American communities are much more differentiated than stereotypes and the status quo would suggest. Ironically, even as so much civil rights activism hinged on extolling the great values of diversity in society, to speak of internal divisions and dynamism within the communities and cultures of African-descended peoples often has been minimized for the sake of not diluting the impact of group identity and progress. Third and most importantly, his assertion that we have witnessed the routinization of Black prophetic witness arguably presaged the motivating force for the Movement for Black Lives in our current era. The weighty force of nostalgia about the moral actions and accomplishments of the historic civil rights movement has lulled too many Black churches and their leadership with the seductive allure of past-reflected glory. To be clear, the challenges provided by Glaude's writings were supposed to prompt

---

[30] Eddie Glaude Jr., "The Black Church Is Dead," *HuffPost: The Blog* (August 23, 2012), https://www.huffpost.com/entry/the-black-church-is-dead_b_473815.

significant changes within the Black church's public witness. The challenge is to encourage this sacred institution to remain hallowed, but not hollowed out, in its truest nature.[31]

Too often, thousands of American houses of worship have sanctioned silence about police brutality because it is deemed "too political." This silence is also political. Ultimately, this silence opposes the Gospel of Jesus Christ.

Examples of courageous clergy—Rev. Al Sharpton, Rev. Traci D. Blackmon, Rev. Michael McBride, Rev. Osagyefo Sekou, Rev. Dr. William J. Barber II, and Rev. Dr. Frederick Douglass Haynes III have embraced BLM even at supreme risk to themselves, their ministries, and missions—are, sadly, too few and far between. Christians must always remember that, as a key part of the Passion narrative, Jesus was brutally tortured, beaten, and mocked by prison guards and Roman sentries. Preaching against and protesting police brutality is well within the scope of the gospel. While most ecclesial institutions have not-for-profit status for tax purposes, unfortunately far too many churches in our society are "not-for-prophet" institutions.[32]

This deafening and enduring silence is also political. Audre Lorde warned us many years ago that "your silence will not protect you."[33] While no one can or should bind the pulpit to their own

---

[31] Sandra L. Barnes, "The Black Church Revisited: Toward a New Millennium DuBoisian Mode of Inquiry," *Sociology of Religion* 75, no. 4 (2014): 607–21, http://www.jstor.org/stable/24580110.

[32] Jessica Grose, "Christianity's Got a Branding Problem," *New York Times* (May 10, 2023), https://www.nytimes.com/2023/05/10/opinion/christian-religion-brand-nones.html.

[33] Audre Lorde, "The Transformation of Silence into Language and Action," paper delivered at the Modern Language Association's "Lesbian and Literature Panel," Chicago, Illinois, December 28, 1977. First published in *Sinister Wisdom* 6 (1978) and *The Cancer Journals* (Spinsters, Ink, San Francisco, 1980).

political calculus or preferences, the silence that pervades pulpits actively betrays the gospel because it seeks only to preserve a feeble peace and false piety under the influence and illusion of a selfish and shallow vision of American Christianity. Critical race theology cannot abide the misunderstanding that American Christianity is somehow apathetic and apolitical in the face of injustice. Meanwhile, the most disinherited and disrespected members of our society must continually negotiate and navigate the realities of a harsh world wherein, as the poet Lucille Clifton reminds us, "everyday something has tried to kill me and has failed."[34]

Given my research, teaching, and conversations for over twenty years about crime and policing, most concerns hover around an assumed discourse of "lack" that is too often aimed at people and communities of color: lack of jobs, opportunities, resources, mutual respect or self-respect, role models and positive influences, trust, moral values, and even a shared vision of humanity. As Rossana Rodriguez and Eric Reinhart recognize:

> When police take a life, a public-relations machine whirrs into motion. The goal of the subsequent press releases and media interviews is to cast whoever has been killed by a police bullet, car, or baton in an unsympathetic light. She may have been using drugs. He had an aggressive face. She was experiencing a mental health crisis. He had a gun. He ran. He had been arrested before. He was in a gang. Such well-worn lines serve a purpose: to keep the public from seeing the person and their family as victims deserving of rights, care, or mourning.[35]

---

[34] Lucille Clifton, "won't you celebrate with me," *Book of Light* (Port Townsend, WA: Copper Canyon Press, 1993).

[35] Rossana Rodriguez and Eric Reinhart, "After Another Police Killing in Chicago, We Need to Focus on Care, Not Cops," *The Nation*, February 17, 2023, http://www.thenation.com/article/politics/chicago-police-isidro-valverde/.

The reluctance of churches to directly challenge, much less change, unequal social relations and unjust conditions likely contributes to the lack of interest in and eventual rejection of traditional religions and their institutions for many millennials and members of Generation Z. In the tension between US cultural white supremacy and the #BlackLivesMatter protest campaign's desired goals of securing freedom, justice, equality, and human dignity for people of African descent in the United States, #BlackLivesMatter and the broader movement is both a theological critique and challenge.

The *sui generis* origin and evolution of Black Lives Matter took place outside and beyond any identifiable Black religious institution. Historian Robin D. G. Kelley reminds us that "insisting that we are human and productive members of [American] society has been a first principle of Black abolitionist politics since at least the eighteenth century."[36] Thus, it is important to recognize the contemporary significance of #BlackLivesMatter by placing it within a broader historical context of Black humanism, resonating with many tenets of the traditional Black freedom struggle while yet charting future directions, including nontheistic thought and praxis, such as atheism, agnosticism, humanism, and other expressions of unbelief, as part of the broader African American experience.

The demographic growth of the "nones" within the US population has been dramatic. In 1972, just 5 percent of Americans claimed "no religion" on the General Social Survey. In 2018, that portion of the American populace increased to roughly 23.7 percent. The latest Pew Research Center survey of the religious composition of the United States finds the religiously unaffiliated share of the public is six percentage points higher than it was five years ago and ten points higher than a decade ago. Currently,

---

[36] Robin D. G. Kelley, "Beyond Black Lives Matter," *Kalfou* 2, no. 2 (2015): 331.

when asked about their religious identity, an estimated three-in-ten US adults (29 percent) are religious "nones"—people who described themselves as atheists, agnostics, skeptics, or "nothing in particular."[37] Although many scholars of religion and theology tend to ignore this trend, this expansion makes the religiously unaffiliated as numerically significant a segment of American society as both Evangelical Protestants and Roman Catholics.

In 2009, Pew Research Center data on religious pluralism in the United States revealed that more than 12 percent of African Americans nationwide readily self-identified as being unaffiliated with any religion.[38] This group of Black nonbelievers constitutes the third largest cohort within African American religious life—a major development in the history of African American faith and culture that ought to be more fully explored and explained. Scholars have discussed the origins and varied nature of Black humanism at considerable length. The argument in this chapter builds upon that existing research by examining the origins and nature of Black humanism within the history of the Black freedom struggle.[39]

---

[37] Gregory A. Smith, "About Three-in-Ten U.S. Adults Are Now Religiously Unaffiliated," Pew Research Center, December 14, 2021, https://www.pewresearch.org/religion/2021/12/14/about-three-in-ten-u-s-adults-are-now-religiously-unaffiliated/.

[38] Neha Sahgal and Greg Smith, "A Religious Portrait of African-Americans," Pew Research Center's Forum on Religion & Public Life, January 30, 2009, http://pewrsr.ch/14gjBl9.

[39] Anthony B. Pinn, ed., *By These Hands: A Documentary History of African American Humanism* (New York: New York University Press, 2001), 1–21; Anthony B. Pinn, *African American Humanist Principles: Living and Thinking Like the Children of Nimrod* (New York: Palgrave, 2004), 1–40; Norm R. Allen Jr., *African American Humanism: An Anthology* (New York: Prometheus, 1991); Mark D. Morrison-Reed, *Black Pioneers in a White Denomination* (Boston: Skinner House Books, 1984); Juan M. Floyd-Thomas, *The Origins of Black Humanism in America: Reverend Ethelred Brown and the Unitarian Church* (New York: Palgrave Macmillan, 2008); Melanie L. Harris,

The secularizing shifts evident in American society so far in the twenty-first century show no signs of slowing down. Every indication is that the "nones" will be the largest religious group in the United States in the next decade. They represent a seismic shift in the understanding of American religion and the Christian church. Sociologists of religion have long analyzed the theory of secularization: moving away from religious faith corresponds with a society's advance in terms of educational achievement and prosperity. The trajectory in many of the world's WEIRD (Western, Educated, Industrialized, Rich, and Democratic) nations, particularly throughout Europe following World War II, seems to confirm this theory. Yet the United States remained a persistently stubborn outlier to this trend throughout much of the twentieth century.[40]

The rapid growth in the percentage of Americans claiming no religious affiliation is drastically reshaping the country's religious and cultural landscape. Generally, religiously unaffiliated people are increasingly concentrated among young adults—35 percent of Millennials (those born 1981–1996) are self-identified as "nones." In addition, the unaffiliated are presently getting even younger. The median age of unaffiliated adults is currently thirty-six years old, down from thirty-eight in 2007, and significantly younger than the overall median age of US adults was in 2014.[41] Addressing this matter more broadly, ethicist Miguel De La Torre insists,

---

"Womanist Humanism: A New Hermeneutic," in *Deeper Shades of Purple: Womanism in Religion and Society*, ed. Stacey M. Floyd-Thomas (New York: New York University Press, 2006), 211–25.

[40] William H. Swatos and Kevin J. Christiano, "Secularization Theory: The Course of a Concept," *Sociology of Religion* 60, no. 3 (1999): 209–28; Charles Taylor, *A Secular Age* (Cambridge, MA: Belknap Press, 2007).

[41] Michael Lipka, "A Closer Look at America's Rapidly Growing Religious 'Nones'," Pew Research Center, May 13, 2015, https://www.pewresearch.org/short-reads/2015/05/13/a-closer-look-at-americas-rapidly-growing-religious-nones/.

"Lacking vision, churches perish."[42] Moreover, De La Torre notes, "Millennials [and Generation Z] are abandoning the church in droves, not because they lack spirituality but because the church has failed them."[43]

As both a sociologist of religion and a Baptist pastor, Ryan Burge examines the macrolevel forces that are shaping churches across the nation; mostly in mainline Protestant denominations. The data Burge studies does not show a surge of people coming back to mainline religious institutions. What does that mean for churches? For instance, just 5 percent of Black people said they were unaffiliated with a religious group in 1980. However, the percentage rose to an estimated 20.8 percent by 2018.[44] Ryan Burge argues that no segment of the American population is immune to the rising tide of religious disaffiliation, but he stops short of diagnosing why this widespread crisis of faith is occurring in the first place.[45]

William R. Jones's *Is God a White Racist?: A Preamble to Black Theology* (1973) remains a landmark critique of the Black church's treatment of evil and the nature of suffering in the face of white supremacy. In his powerful and provocative examination of the early liberationist frameworks of James Cone, J. Deotis Roberts, and Joseph Washington, among others, Jones questions whether their foundation for Black Christian theism—the belief in an omniscient, omnipotent, and omnipresent God who is benevolent and has dominion over the totality of human history and current

---

[42] Miguel A. De La Torre, *Burying White Privilege: Resurrecting a Badass Christianity* (Grand Rapids: William B. Eerdmans, 2019), 1–2.

[43] De La Torre, *Burying White Privilege*, 1–2.

[44] Ann A. Michel, "Understanding the Nones—Lewis Center for Church Leadership," Lewis Center for Church Leadership—Advancing the Knowledge and Practice of Church Leadership, April 20, 2021, https://www.churchleadership.com/leading-ideas/understanding-the-nones/.

[45] Ryan P. Burge, *The Nones: Where They Came from, Who They Are, and Where They Are Going* (Minneapolis: Fortress Press, 2021).

reality—can provide an adequate theological foundation to effectively dismantle the economic, social, and political framework of oppression.

According to Jones, liberation theology, by its very nature, should be committed to the end of oppression and suffering at the core of unjust and unbearable existential realities. Following this logic, Jones contends that engagement with the concept of theodicy must be central to the work of anyone focused upon the annihilation of oppression. Ultimately, this work must be done with the objective "to eliminate the suffering that is the heart of oppression ... The theologian or philosopher of liberation, in short, *must* engage in the enterprise of theodicy if he is to accomplish his task."[46]

Elsewhere, I have argued that Black humanism is radically different from its white counterpart because of the divisive history of race and the insidious permanence of racism in the Western world.[47] Although humanist traditions across racial lines are definitely connected to one another in certain ways, Black humanism functions in ways that are vastly divergent from those of its white counterpart because it has different obstacles to overcome and different objectives to attain. As William R. Jones asserts, we must acknowledge the different origins of Black and white humanism because "though black humanism and those humanists who trace their lineage to the enlightenment [*sic*] or the scientific revolution are akin in attacking the superstructure of theism, their criticisms develop from radically different socio-economic contexts."[48] Regardless of how a white person defines their embrace of humanism,

---

[46] William R. Jones, *Is God a White Racist?: A Preamble to Black Theology* (Garden City, NY: Anchor Press, 1973), xxv–xxvi.

[47] Floyd-Thomas, *The Origins of Black Humanism in America.*

[48] William R. Jones, "Religious Humanism: Its Problems and Prospects in Black Religion and Culture," *Journal of the Interdenominational Theological Center* 7, no. 2 (1980): 180.

white humanists operate in a realm governed by several key presuppositions, namely that people of European descent are human beings upon birth; people of European descent have their personal freedom as both natural birthright and normative existential expectation; people of European descent are always already recognized as thinking, feeling creatures and deserved to be acknowledged as such; and people of European descent can be considered fully functioning, holistic, and independent moral actors free to choose isolation or community.[49]

However, the same is not true for Black humanists. Whereas white humanists often trace their intellectual genealogy to the rising tide of modernity that culminated with the Enlightenment, the roots of Black humanism can be found within the ferment of New World enslavement.

The humanity of Black people has always been challenged, questioned, and denied. In *Prophesy Deliverance!*, Cornel West declares boldly, "The notion that black people are human beings is a relatively new discovery in the modern West."[50] Modern liberal Western democracies—those WEIRD societies and cultures described earlier in this book—have often ignored and even abnegated their responsibilities to Black people when advancing human rights, failing to recognize our full humanity in legalistic and sometimes literal terms. Richard Rorty echoes this critique by observing that violations of human rights are often not recognized as such by the violators because they never regard their victims as rational and normative human beings in the first place. The victimized must be viewed as insufferable children, demonic beasts, or anything subhuman to allow such abuse and atrocities to happen.[51]

---

[49] Floyd-Thomas, *The Origins of Black Humanism in America*, 5.

[50] Cornel West, *Prophesy Deliverance! An Afro-American Revolutionary Christianity* (Philadelphia: Westminster Press, 1982), 47.

[51] Richard Rorty, "Human Rights, Rationality, and Sentimentality,"

When set against the backdrop of both West's and Rorty's reflections, Black humanism and other modes of unbelief exist as a direct refutation to the presumptive belief in modern Western thought regarding the intrinsic respect for human life espoused in Immanuel Kant's categorical imperative. In his classic text, *Groundwork of the Metaphysics of Morals*, Immanuel Kant describes this concept as follows: "There is … only a single categorical imperative and it is this: Act only on that maxim through which you can at the same time will that it should become universal law."[52] For Kant, all human beings ought to conduct themselves in accordance to ethical principles that would be unconditionally shared by everyone without any exception or question as a matter of moral duty. However, Black bodies, being denied any irrevocable claim to humanity, are perennially deprived of sympathy, love, solidarity, and the whole host of moral sentiments that serve not only as the foundation of Kantian notions of respect but also as the underpinnings of modern doctrines of universal human rights.[53]

Unable to uncritically *adopt* dominant Western ideas, Black people had to *adapt* them to match our own needs and concerns. Theologian Adam Kotsko contends,

> We often hear from politicians that slavery is "America's original sin." This phrase has become a cliché, thoughtlessly intoned mostly by Democrats, though occasionally also deployed by Republicans in a bid to look like they are taking racism seriously. In most cases, it seems like little more than a way of gesturing at the

---

in *On Human Rights: The Oxford Amnesty Lectures, 1993*, ed. Stephen Shute and Susan Hurley (New York: Basic Books, 1993), 111–34.

[52] Immanuel Kant, *Groundwork for the Metaphysics of Morals*, trans. H. J. Paton (1785; repr. New York: Harper Torchbooks, 1964), 22.

[53] Kant, *Groundwork for the Metaphysics of Morals*, 28–29; Michael J. Sandel, *Justice: What's the Right Thing to Do?* (New York: Farrar, Straus, and Giroux, 2009), 116–23.

unique gravity of racism. Nevertheless, if we take this bromide at its word—that grappling with racial oppression is not just a social or political problem, but also downright theological—it reveals the inherent deadlocks in liberal anti-racism.[54]

Philosopher George Yancy argues, "Religion becomes an empty theological exercise if it does not address human suffering—and this includes the anguish wrought by systems of mass incarceration and policing."[55] More recently, Mariame Kaba and Andrea J. Ritchie have written that reform measures that leave policing's core functions intact ultimately will not prevent persistent lethal state violence against Black, Latinx, and Indigenous people. To build a more just and equal society for the good of all, they argue that we as a people and nation must abolish policing altogether.[56]

Though the debate about policing is not new, the Black Lives Matter movement has given a new life to the discussion. Crafted following a global groundswell of Black Lives Matter protests in 2020, the "George Floyd Justice in Policing" Act was intended to address structural racism, racial profiling, pervasively aggressive paramilitary police culture, and the excessive use of deadly force in law enforcement in the United States. More than three years

---

[54] Adam Kotsko, "Liberal Anti-Racism Is Fixated on Symbolic Gestures. We Need Concrete Action." *Truthout*, October 27, 2021, https://truthout.org/articles/liberal-anti-racism-is-fixated-on-symbolic-gestures-we-need-concrete-action/.

[55] George Yancy, "Christianity Is Empty if It Doesn't Address the Racist Carceral State," *Truthout*, September 26, 2021, https://truthout.org/articles/christianity-is-empty-if-it-doesnt-address-the-racist-carceral-state/.

[56] Mariame Kaba and Andrea J. Ritchie, "Why We Don't Say 'Reform the Police'," *The Nation*, September 2, 2022, https://www.thenation.com/article/society/no-more-police-excerpt/.

later, the bill still has not been passed into law by the US Congress, and it is unclear if it ever will become law. Progress has often been stymied by conflicting ideas across the political spectrum about the prospects for policing reforms.

Republican politicians and broader right-wing rhetoric have effectively used the presence of crime in the United States and a perceived rise in violent incidents to mobilize their electorate through their fear of lawlessness. In the 2022 midterm elections, Republicans spent about $50 million on crime-related ads in the final two months of the campaign.[57] This sort of political fearmongering vis-à-vis "tough-on-crime" political ads and messaging in campaign speeches continues to saturate our media ecosystem, dominating public discourse. It will further exacerbate the nation's conjoined policing and mass incarceration problems in advance of upcoming elections.[58]

Since the Black Lives Matter movement originally surfaced as a visible and vibrant mass mobilization of protesters in 2014, it has been quite credibly compared to the US civil rights movement

---

[57] Adam Gabbatt, "Stark Warning over Republicans' 'Dehumanizing' Rhetoric on Crime," *The Guardian*, May 14, 2023, https://www. theguardian.com/us-news/2023/may/14/republican-tough-on-crime-us-elections-2010#.

[58] The US Crisis Monitor, a joint project between the Armed Conflict Location and Event Data Project (ACLED) and the Bridging Divides Initiative (BDI) at Princeton University, collects real-time data on these trends to provide timely analysis and resources to support civil society efforts to track, prevent, and mitigate the risk of political violence in America. With supplemental data collection extending coverage back to the week of Floyd's killing in late May 2020, the data set now encompasses the latest phase of the Black Lives Matter movement, growing unrest related to the health crisis, and politically motivated violence ahead of the November 2020 general election, https://acleddata.com/special-projects/us-crisis-monitor/.

of the 1950s and 1960s.[59] BLM advocates and allies have argued that this movement is clearly a continuation of previous efforts to advance social justice within a contemporary context, but the movement's critics have argued that the BLM movement has lacked the US civil rights movement's dogged emphasis on nonviolence *qua* Kingian pacifism as its central organizing principle. Critics accused 2020 BLM protesters for being pale imitations of the protest marches at the peak of the civil rights movement in the 1960s. During and since 2020's so-called summer of racial reckoning, conservative media outlets have condemned BLM-inspired protests for "tearing apart our cities."

Contrary to such negative claims, recent research has found that the 2020 BLM-related protests were overwhelmingly peaceful.[60] Political scientists Erica Chenoweth and Jeremy Pressman reported that their Crowd Counting Consortium (CCC) found that less than 4 percent of the BLM protests involved property damage while 1 percent involved police injuries.[61] Other

---

[59] Juan M. Floyd-Thomas, "'A Relatively New Discovery in the Modern West': #BlackLivesMatter and the Evolution of Black Humanism," *Kalfou: A Journal of Comparative and Relational Ethnic Studies* 4, no. 1 (2017): 30–39; Christopher Cameron and Phillip Luke Sinitiere, eds., *Race, Religion, and Black Lives Matter: Essays on a Moment and a Movement* (Nashville: Vanderbilt University Press, 2021); Christophe D. Ringer, Teresa L. Smallwood, and Emilie M. Townes, eds., *Moved by the Spirit: Religion and the Movement for Black Lives* (Lanham, MD: Lexington Books, 2023).

[60] Erica Chenoweth and Jeremy Pressman, "This Summer's Black Lives Matter Protesters Were Overwhelmingly Peaceful, Our Research Finds," *Washington Post: Monkey Cage*, October 16, 2020, www.washingtonpost.com/politics/2020/10/16/this-summers-black-lives-matter-protesters-were-overwhelming-peaceful-our-research-finds/?itid=lk_inline_manual_4.

[61] Kerby Goff and John D. McCarthy, "Critics Claim BLM Protests Were More Violent Than 1960s Civil Rights Ones. That's Just Not True." *Washington Post: Monkey Cage*, October 12, 2021, https://www.

data collections similarly found that 95 percent of the protest marches were peaceful.[62] When compared to the civil rights era protests in the 1960s, their research revealed that, on every available metric, the 2020 BLM protests were more peaceful and less confrontational.[63] Martin Luther King Jr. and other leaders of the earlier movement argued that protesters' nonviolence would contrast with their opponents' violence, providing tremendous moral authority. In their day, critics blamed the protesters for instigating the violence that was being inflicted on them.

Regarding property destruction, the CCC's findings indicate that 11 percent of the civil rights era's 2,681 events contained property damage over eight years of actions while only 4 percent of the 12,839 protests in 2020 involved property damage.[64] In the civil rights era, police officers were injured in 6 percent of the protests.[65] Injuries to police officers were reported in only 2 percent of the 2020 protests.[66] Conversely, police officers were also more openly "aggressive during the civil rights movement. Police arrested some protesters in 36 percent of all civil rights movement events," Goff and McCarthy report.[67] Arrests in the

---

washingtonpost.com/politics/2021/10/12/critics-claim-blm-was-more-violent-than-1960s-civil-rights-protests-thats-just-not-true/.

[62] Goff and McCarthy, "Critics Claim BLM Protests Were More Violent."

[63] Goff and McCarthy, "Critics Claim BLM Protests Were More Violent."

[64] Goff and McCarthy, "Critics Claim BLM Protests Were More Violent."

[65] Goff and McCarthy, "Critics Claim BLM Protests Were More Violent."

[66] Goff and McCarthy, "Critics Claim BLM Protests Were More Violent."

[67] Goff and McCarthy, "Critics Claim BLM Protests Were More Violent."

recent Black Lives Matter protests occurred "in just 7 percent" of the events.[68] From high-profile events like 1965's Bloody Sunday attack in Selma, Alabama, to less-known events across the nation, "civil rights era protests were more dangerous for protesters than the 2020 protests," Goff and McCarthy write.[69] Finally, the CCC report found that there were crowd injuries in 12 percent of all civil rights movement protests, compared with only 3 percent of the 2020 protests.[70] By and large, the accusations of the violence and lawlessness associated with the 2020 BLM protests were grossly overexaggerated.

Explicit acts of violence and direct engagement with police officers is only one aspect of policing that concerns the kind of Black humanism that shapes critical race theology. The legal pattern of "qualified immunity" is another policing issue that is important in large part because of its impact on the lives of many Americans. "Qualified immunity" is a legal doctrine that

> provides that a police officer cannot be put on trial for unlawful conduct, including the use of excessive or deadly force, unless the person suing proves that: 1. the evidence shows that the conduct was unlawful; and 2. the officers should have known they were violating "clearly established" law, because a prior court case had already deemed similar police actions to be illegal.[71]

---

[68] Goff and McCarthy, "Critics Claim BLM Protests Were More Violent."

[69] Goff and McCarthy, "Critics Claim BLM Protests Were More Violent."

[70] Goff and McCarthy, "Critics Claim BLM Protests Were More Violent."

[71] "Qualified Immunity," Equal Justice Initiative, 2024, https://act. moveon.org/go/170527?t=6&akid=345915%2E26336651%2EwaTegI.

US Supreme Court Justice Sonia Sotomayor said qualified immunity "tells officers that they can shoot first and think later."[72] As both aspects of the doctrine must be satisfied in order for a police officer to be considered liable in a case, qualified immunity reduces law enforcement's accountability even when someone is able to prove that an officer acted unlawfully.[73] Qualified immunity has granted the worst elements of American policing to operate with horrifying impunity toward those most often deemed as the "least of these" in our world.

Qualified immunity originated in a 1967 US Supreme Court decision, *Pierson v. Ray*, which stated that an officer "who arrests someone with probable cause is not liable for false arrest simply because the innocence of the suspect is later proved.... The same consideration would seem to require excusing him from liability for acting under a statute that he reasonably believed to be valid, but that was later held unconstitutional, on its face or as applied."[74] In the intervening years, qualified immunity, law professor Joanna Schwartz asserts, "has come to represent all that is wrong with police accountability."[75] For Schwartz, it has become one of multiple barriers erected by the courts and legislatures to make justice through civil rights lawsuits practically unattainable. Qualified immunity insulates police officers from the professional consequences and economic repercussions of excessive or lethal force, and it also preempts the victims of police brutality and

---

[72] Andrew Kisela v. Amy Hughes, 584 U.S. (2018) (Sotomayor dissenting opinion).

[73] "Qualified Immunity," Equal Justice Initiative.

[74] Pierson v. Ray, 386 U.S. 555 (1967).

[75] Mina Kim, "Why Qualified Immunity Makes Police 'Untouchable,'" *KQED*, March 14, 2023, https://www.kqed.org/forum/2010101892477/why-qualified-immunity-makes-police-untouchable; Joanna Schwartz, *Shielded: How the Police Became Untouchable* (New York: Viking, 2023).

their loved ones from seeking justice in court. As long as qualified immunity remains intact, police officers who are prone to abuse their authority will continue to wield their power in an unchecked fashion against other people as long as they believe themselves to be above the law. The struggle to dismantle the doctrine of qualified immunity is as complex and multifaceted as the doctrine itself, but it can be dismantled. It must be.

Aggressive policing practices that have been, at least implicitly, encouraged by legal doctrines like qualified immunity and economic shifts toward paramilitary gear and strategy in municipal settings further complicate the trauma and anguish regarding efforts to change the very nature of policing in this nation. On January 7, 2023, Tyre Nichols, a twenty-nine-year-old Black man who lived in Memphis, Tennessee, was involved in a traffic stop by five Memphis police officers. Mr. Nichols was violently beaten by these Black police officers, sustaining severe injuries, eventually dying in a local hospital on January 10, 2023.

Sadly, this exchange reveals that, contrary to general assumption, Black police officers are not necessarily more benevolent when patrolling communities of color than their white counterparts. Video footage from the police body cams revealed that the five officers—Tadarrius Bean, Demetrius Haley, Desmond Mills Jr., Emmitt Martin III, and Justin Smith—swarmed and pummeled Tyre Nichols to death in cold blood.[76] These police officers were part of the SCORPION unit, a special police task force of the Memphis Police Department. Their full title, "Street Crimes Operation to Restore Peace in Our Neighborhoods," reveals their aim and intent: strike quickly and dominate

---

[76] "What We Know about the Criminal, Administrative Cases Surrounding Tyre Nichols' Death," *Memphis Commercial Appeal*, February 21, 2023, https://act.moveon.org/go/170536?t=8&akid=345915%2E2 6336651%2EwaTegI.

forcefully any individual in their path, regardless of whether they are criminal or civilian, to "restore" the neighborhood.[77] James Baldwin's observation in *The Evidence of Things Not Seen* describes this complexity:

> Black policemen were another matter. We used to say, "If you must call a policeman"—for we hardly ever did—"for God's sake, try to make sure it's a White one." A Black policeman could completely demolish you. He knew far more about you than a White policeman could and you were without defenses before this Black brother in uniform whose entire reason for breathing seemed to be his hope to offer proof that, though he was Black, he was not Black like you.[78]

This terrible incident illustrates how Black police officers might incite greater terror among Black communities because they have to "prove themselves" through the fear and power that a badge and gun garner when policing in a white supremacist culture.

Tyre Nichols, tragically, was not the only Black person killed by police in January 2023. Keenan Anderson, a thirty-one-year-old English teacher and a cousin of Patrisse Cullors, one of the co-founders of #BlackLivesMatter and the broader Movement for Black Lives, was killed on January 3, 2023. Responding to a hit-and-run accident, the Los Angeles Police Department detained Anderson due to his suspected involvement in the traffic incident and tasered him six times in a span of forty-two seconds while

---

[77] Ivan Pereira and Meredith Deliso, "What Was the SCORPION Unit, the Now-Deactivated Police Task Force at The Center pf Tyre Nichols' Death?," January 28, 2023, *ABC News*, https://abcnews. go.com/US/scorpion-unit-memphis-police-task-force-center-tyre/ story?id=96720313.

[78] James Baldwin, *The Evidence of Things Not Seen* (New York: Holt, Rinehart and Winston, 1985), 66.

trying to gain control of the unarmed man.[79] "About four and a half hours later," Zak Cheney-Rice writes, "Anderson became the third person to die in LAPD custody" in 2023.[80] Separated by only a few days at the start of a brand-new year, the police officers involved in both Keenan Anderson's and Tyre Nichols's deaths moved decidedly from legal authority to lethal activity in response to a traffic incident. According to the Mapping Police Violence project, during most of the Black Lives Matter era, the rate of police killings averaged almost 1,090 people a year but, in 2020, the number of such incidents topped 1,100, and by 2022 it was up to 1,201.[81]

While there might be those who cannot abide calls for abolitionism because they still believe that police serve a vital albeit regrettable function in our society, hopefully reasonable people can agree to the need to end police brutality and extrajudicial killings. A considerable step forward toward achieving this objective could be accomplished by taking up the following concerns: ending the overcriminalization of communities of color, bringing the war on drugs to a halt, suspending the use of "broken window" (known more commonly as "stop-and-frisk") policing, ending "no-knock" warrants, and demilitarizating urban police

---

[79] Richard Winton, "LAPD Offciers Tased Keenan Anderson 6 Times in 42 Seconds," *Los Angeles Times* (January 19, 2023), https://www.latimes.com/california/story/2023-01-18/lapd-tasing-of-keenan-anderson-brings-scrutiny-to-police-policy.

[80] Zak Cheney-Rice, "The Uprising That Ran Out: The Death of Keenan Anderson Marks the End of an Era," *New York: Intelligencer*, January 30, 2023, https://nymag.com/intelligencer/2023/01/lapd-keenan-anderson-death-black-lives-matter-racial-justice-protests.html.

[81] Mapping Police Violence, "2020 Police Violence Report," https://policeviolencereport.org/2020/; Mapping Police Violence, "2022 Police Violence Report," https://policeviolencereport.org/2022/.

departments. Reimagining a more humane approach to policing requires ceasing arrest quotas and mandatory minimums in the upper echelons of police departments and other branches of the criminal justice system as these approaches seem to have done more to escalate incarceration than to deter criminality. Ultimately, critical race theology values the rigorous debate and comprehensive rethinking of what "police work" means in American society on a daily, grounded basis. As these discussions have shown in different contexts, as we rethink policing, we can recognize that we need to stop using police officers as EMTs, mental health care specialists, marriage counselors, and municipally funded concierge services. Historically and today, policing focuses on property crimes and other crimes that ostensibly threaten an economically secure class's security. Policing should place the primacy of personhood above the protection of property if we are truly to be the people and nation that we imagine ourselves to be.

Among #BlackLivesMatter's many significant critiques of policing and other legal structures in this country, realizing that practices and patterns of dehumanization of, divestment from, and devaluation of Black communities and other communities of color are a *feature* rather than a *failure* of our current system may be the most revolutionary. Calls for police reform—ending civil asset forfeiture and cash bail systems are some of the simplest proposals—as well as for the dismantling of qualified immunity as part of defunding or even abolishing police forces in this country emerge through an intentional humanist concern. Far too many municipal governments allow overly aggressive policing tactics to occur in economically distressed communities as a way to augment a lagging tax base and refill coffers that are in desperate need of a cash infusion. Prioritizing financial gain over human well-being is a well-noted pattern of white supremacy throughout our country's history.

The phrase "defund the police" has ebbed and flowed within public discourse since it entered mainstream consciousness. During the historic 2020 global protests, this expression became a slogan for the marchers and a genuine call for political action. It has been an urgent demand to shift taxpayers' funding away from the skyrocketing budgets for police and toward social service providers. The movement for such a debate has spurred grassroots efforts nationwide in countless cities that were seeking to change the balance sheets of city budgets away from police.

The very suggestion of a national debate about possible alternatives to, if not outright abolition of, the modern police force in US society quickly prompted a highly defensive, pro-police backlash among many politicians and media pundits. They argued strenuously that we must "Back the Blue" in order to have any semblance of a civilized society. With familiar fearmongering, they have argued that altering *any* aspect of policing would plummet US society into a quagmire of unstopped and unsolved murders, rapes, robberies, and more. In their argument, however, they often fail to address the present statistics on these criminal offenses, statistics that show that our current mode of policing has done horribly in terms of solving, much less preventing, these cases and cases like them.

As pro-policing rhetoric and policy has come from both Republicans and Democrats, a critical race theology must reassert its humanist analysis of how issues of class, race, and gender always weave through policing and legislative patterns in a white supremacist society. Unsurprisingly, then, criminal justice reform has been met with swift and vicious reactions from many directions. Police unions, sleazy politicians, right-wing think tanks, and conservative and liberal media alike prey on propagandized public fears, attacking reforms as ushering in a new era of dystopian lawlessness. They demagogue anecdotal examples, often using racist tropes and exploiting the media feedback loop to push back against and curtail movements for reform. Pondering this situation, James Baldwin says,

The prison is overcrowded, the calendars full, the judges busy, the lawyers ambitious, and the cops zealous. What does it matter if someone gets trapped here for a year or two, gets ruined here, goes mad here, commits murder or suicide here? It's too bad, but that's the way the cookie crumbles sometimes. I do not claim that everyone in prison here is innocent, but I do claim that the law, as it operates, is guilty, and that the prisoners, therefore, are all unjustly imprisoned. Is it conceivable, after all, that any middle-class white boy—or, indeed, almost any white boy—would have been arrested on so grave a charge as murder, with such flimsy substantiation, and forced to spend, as of this writing, three years in prison? Does the law exist for the purpose of furthering the ambitions of those who have sworn to uphold the law, or is it seriously to be considered as a moral, unifying force, the health and strength of a nation?[82]

And yet, here we are in a historic moment. We stand in desperate need of restorative justice and the fire this time. Pairing James Baldwin's profound warning with the insights of what eluded John Rawls in his famous work, *A Theory of Justice* (1971), I think this discussion leaves room to open discussions at various levels for deeper, more meaningful debates at the local, state, and national levels that render the autobiographical and anecdotal as a prime mode of analysis.[83] Just how deeply rooted is our white supremacist

---

[82] James Baldwin, *No Name in the Street* (1972), in *James Baldwin: Collected Essays the Library of America*, ed. Toni Morrison (New York: Random House, 1998), 445.

[83] Jedediah Britton-Purdy, "What John Rawls Missed: Are His Principles for a Just Society Enough Today?" *New Republic*, October 29, 2019, https://newrepublic.com/article/155294/john-rawls-missed-create-just-society.

cultural ethos that keeps the status quo of community policing and mass incarceration so firmly intact?

When religious ministries and the communities they serve are ready, willing, and able to shape and challenge our country's public policy and private corporate action in and beyond criminal justice systems, how can a critical race theology empower their shaping and challenging? "The degree of civilization in a society can be judged," as John Herbert may have attributed to Fyodor Dostoevsky, "by entering its prisons."[84] A critical race theology must wrestle with what it means for our society to continually treat so many of our fellow human beings as deficient, defective, and disposable. The severity and savagery of our system of policing and mass incarceration is truly brutalizing people on both sides of jailhouse doors and barbed wire fences. We must seek how we can redeem and reclaim those millions of broken bodies and stolen souls that our society has created yet has never found the wherewithal to begin concrete plans to restore and renew to some semblance of hope and healing.

In his denunciation of a liberal intelligentsia that was able but not willing to raise its voice against the sheer brutality of state-sanctioned belligerence and violence in an earlier era, George Orwell wrote, "We have now sunk to a depth at which the restatement of the obvious is the first duty of intelligent [people]."[85] This dreadful duty is even further heightened in our contemporary fast-paced world. We are so inundated with increasingly worse news on a daily basis that it is difficult for many of us to recall the names and faces of those who were taken away far too soon.

---

[84] Ilya Vinitsky, "Dostoyevsky Misprisioned: 'The House of the Dead' and American Prison Literature," *Los Angeles Review of Books*, December 23, 2019. https://lareviewofbooks.org/article/dostoyevsky-misprisioned-the-house-of-the-dead-and-american-prison-literature/.

[85] George Orwell, "Review of *Power: A New Social Analysis* by Bertrand Russell," *The Adelphi* (January 1939).

The murders of Trayvon Martin, Tamir Rice, Walter Scott, Eric Garner, Rekia Boyd, John Crawford III, Ezell Ford, Dante Parker, Michelle Cusseaux, Tanisha Anderson, Akai Gurley, Rumain Brisbon, Jerame Reid, George Mann, Mathew Ajibade, Frank Smart, Natasha McKenna, Tony Robinson, Anthony Hill, Mya Hall, Phillip White, Eric Harris, William Chapman II, Alexia Christian, Brendon Glenn, Victor Manuel Larosa, Jonathan Sanders, Michael Brown, Freddie Gray, Freddie Blue, Joseph Mann, Salvado Ellswood, Sandra Bland, Danroy Henry, Albert Joseph Davis, Philando Castile, Alton Sterling, Darrius Stewart, Bill Ray Davis, Samuel Dubose, Michael Sabbie, Brian Keith Day, Christian Taylor, Troy Robinson, Asshams Pharoah Manley, Felix Kumi, Keith Harrison McLeod, Junior Prosper, Lamontez Jones, Paterson Brown, Dominic Hutchinson, Anthony Ashford, Alonzo Smith, Tyree Crawford, India Kager, La'Vante Biggs, Michael Lee Marshall, Jamar Clark, Richard Perkins, Nathaniel Harris Pickett, Bennie Lee Tignor, Miguel Espinal, Michael Noel, Kevin Matthews, Bettie Jones, Quintonio Legrier, Keith Childress Jr., Janet Wilson, Randy Nelson, Antronie Scott, Wendell Celestine, David Joseph. Calin Roquemore, Dyzhawn Perkins, Christopher Davis, Marco Loud, Peter Gaines, Torrey Robinson, Darius Robinson, Kevin Hicks, Mary Truxillo, DeMarcus Semer, Willie Tillman, Terrill Thomas, Sylville Smith, Terence Crutcher, Paul O'Neal, Alteria Woods, Jordan Edwards, Aaron Bailey, Ronell Foster, Stephon Clark, Laquan McDonald, Antwon Rose II, Botham Jean, Pamela Turner, Dominique Clayton, Atatiana Jefferson, Elijah McClain, Christopher Whitfield, Christopher McCorvey, Eric Reason, Michael Lorenzo Dean, Ahmaud Arbery, Breonna Taylor, George Floyd, Rayshard Brooks, Keenan Anderson, Tyre Nichols, and far too many others in recent years illustrate the painfully obvious: the #BlackLivesMatter movement serves as a vitally necessary humanist intervention for those of us working to achieve a world in which Black people are no longer systematically and intentionally targeted for death and destruction.

More than a decade after its emergence, the movement illustrates a new, inchoate phase coming into existence: *commonsense humanism.* As a commonsense humanistic enterprise, #BlackLivesMatter by its very design affirms the lives of all humanity, including queer and transgender folks, disabled and disadvantaged folks, folks with criminal records as well as those with undocumented immigration status, and all folks barely surviving along the spectrum of poverty and wealth inequality.[86]

To comprehend how Black humanism currently functions in this turn to commonsense humanism, critical race theology calls us to acknowledge its historic roots and broad contours. For Anthony Pinn, Black humanism describes "Black self-control, self-assertion, and concern for the human family . . . Humanism is a statement of humanity's connectedness/oneness and need for self-determination, without a conscious discussion of this assertion's impact on traditional conceptions of divinity or ultimate reality."[87] Norm Allen Jr. suggests that Black humanism "is a rational, human-centered life stance that is primarily concerned with life in the here and now."[88]

Pinn's foundational model presents Black humanism as a static system of thought and experience defined by the diametrical extremes of "weak" and "strong" humanism. Yet Black humanism needs to be examined dynamically. Allen's definition lives in the perpetual "now" of contemporary life.[89] We

---

[86] Alicia Garza, "A Herstory of the #BlackLivesMatter Movement," *Feminist Wire,* October 7, 2014, http://www.thefeministwire.com/2014/10/blacklivesmatter-2/.

[87] Anthony B. Pinn, *Why, Lord? Suffering and Evil in Black Theology* (New York: Continuum, 1995), 139.

[88] Norm R. Allen Jr., *The Black Humanist Experience: An Alternative to Religion* (Buffalo, NY: Prometheus Books, 2002), 9.

[89] In *Why, Lord?,* Pinn offers a binary model of strong versus weak humanism as a means of describing the level of a person's demonstrable

must extend Allen's definition and address the *longue durée* of life.

I intend this discussion to expand the meaning of the phrase so that "Black humanism" more comprehensively encompasses social justice struggles. I have introduced a third definition of humanism for people of African descent, arguing that "instead of viewing Black humanism as a *repudiation* of faith, it could actually be considered as a *redirection* of faith in the work of human heads, hearts, and hands rather than heavenly help to resolve the problems of the world."[90] I am concerned to highlight the developmental phases of nontheism in Black religion, which I have named *contextual humanism*, *contractual humanism*, and *constitutive humanism*.[91]

Most clearly evident in the global epoch defined by the forcible extraction, enslavement, and exploitation of African peoples in the Western Hemisphere for roughly a half millennium, contextual humanism refers to external circumstances and imposed conditions that place questions of theism (belief in God) and theodicy (critical examination of divine role in human suffering) more centrally in the lives of Black women, men, and children striving to survive in an antagonistic world. In the latter half of the nineteenth century and the beginning of the twentieth century—an era that historian Rayford Logan called the "nadir of American race relations"—contractual humanism emerged wherein people of African descent were directly targeted and victimized by overt white supremacy in attempts to abolish racial segregation and terroristic hate crimes in the United States as well as imperial domination across the Caribbean archipelago, Central and South America, and the African continent. Witnessing the

---

application of humanist traits and values. While this mechanism is suitable in a biographical or theological sense, it is arguably insufficient in a grand historical sense. To put it another way, the framework of strong/weak humanism is not *incorrect* so much as it seems *incomplete*.

[90] Floyd-Thomas, *The Origins of Black Humanism in America*, 4.

[91] Floyd-Thomas, *The Origins of Black Humanism in America*, 6.

questionable lack of institutional means or ideological resources within contemporaneous Black faith communities to immediately counteract such negative forces, a proportionately small number of Black people gravitated toward philosophical and ideological systems—including Marxism, literary modernism, existentialism, Black nationalism, pan-Africanism, and radical feminism—in order to resist the creeping fog of racial injustice and other modes of inhuman oppression. Though divergent in many of their key ideals, many of these systems frequently shared an outright repudiation of Christian theism as a central factor of their affiliation. Finally, in tandem with the various Black liberation struggles that have taken place since the end of the Second World War, constitutive humanism reflects the premise that an explicitly nontheistic perspective is neither accidental nor anomalous to the Black religious experience. Rather, it is an intrinsic dimension of the worldviews of African descended peoples that requires equal consideration alongside theistic traditions and cultural expressions of Black religiosity worldwide.[92] Looking beyond the individual to focus on matters of communal concern, aggregate action, and collective culpability helps explain how demonstrations of unbelief—nontheistic thought and practice—function as organic components of African American life and culture.

Given the unspeakable conditions, mass suffering and death, and traumatic reverberations of the Middle Passage, some of the enslaved Africans surely must have questioned the existence or benevolence of a divine creator. This suffering produced what Charles Long describes as a metaphysical rupture, one that provoked African people in the American continent to develop a religion that was less a cultural system, a theological language, or a corpus of rituals and performances than what he terms "an orientation, a basic turning of the soul toward another defining

---

[92] Floyd-Thomas, *The Origins of Black Humanism in America*, 3–20.

reality."[93] More importantly, Michael Eric Dyson illuminates the recurrent and persistent nature of transhistorical trauma wrought by the Middle Passage when he writes,

> Black death has hounded us from 1619 to this day. The theft of our bodies and is, and our culture too, has offered the country unimaginable wealth, stability, and enjoyment. The plague has descended on our communities, police bringing us terror from the plantation to the pavement. The wiles of white supremacy have seduced us, teaching us to hate and despise each other, and to take a cheap discount on justice, in ways that dishonor our best traditions. Black bodies have been killed and progress has been stalled to provide white comfort. But still, despite everything, we have continued, must continue, to hope.[94]

The supposed cultural and intellectual apex of white humanist accomplishment—the Renaissance and the Enlightenment—took place while Europeans were engaging in the trafficking of human beings with reckless abandon. In their refusal to reckon with the hell on earth endured by enslaved Africans, European civilizations unwittingly called into being the irrepressible hunger for liberation at the core of the Black freedom struggle. In his first slave narrative, Frederick Douglass offers his reflections on the utter hypocrisy of US Christianity:

> Indeed, I can see no reason, but the most deceitful one, for calling the religion of this land Christianity. I look upon it as the climax of all misnomers, the boldest of all frauds,

---

[93] Charles H. Long, "Passage and Prayer: The Origin of Religion in the Atlantic World," in *The Courage to Hope: From Black Suffering to Human Redemption*, ed. Quinton Hosford Dixie and Cornel West (Boston: Beacon Press, 1999), 14.

[94] Dyson, *Long Time Coming*, 7–8.

and the grossest of all libels. Never was there a clearer case of "stealing the livery of the court of heaven to serve the devil in." I am filled with unutterable loathing when I contemplate the religious pomp and show, together with the horrible inconsistencies, which everywhere surround me. We have men-stealers for ministers, women-whippers for missionaries, and cradle-plunderers for church members. The man who wields the blood-clotted cowskin during the week fills the pulpit on Sunday, and claims to be a minister of the meek and lowly Jesus.[95]

Similarly, Harriet Jacobs argues in her slave narrative: "There is a great difference between Christianity and religion at the south [*sic*]."[96] Jacobs and Douglass outline the preconditions for nontheism as a logical response to white Christian hypocrisy unwaveringly yoked to white supremacy. This rejection of organized religion has not meant resignation and despair. It has led to an embrace of a passionate and egalitarian humanism that manifests in many ways in African American life and culture, including the Black Lives Matter movement. Instead of questioning and quarreling about how contemporary generations are rejecting the faith of their ancestors, it would be more worthwhile to consider how too many historic Black churches are complacent with and complicit in a status quo that has failed to advance the freedom, fullness, and flourishing of Black humanity.

The most remarkable fact about the humanistic vision of #BlackLivesMatter as a burgeoning movement is that it was not spawned from self-defense or self-interest but from self-love

---

[95] Frederick Douglass, *Narrative of the Life of Frederick Douglass, an American Slave, Written by Himself*, ed. David W. Blight, 2nd ed. (Boston: Bedford-St. Martin's Press, 2007), 119–20.

[96] Harriet Jacobs, *Incidents in the Life of a Slave Girl*, ed. Nellie McKay and Frances Smith Foster (New York: W. W. Norton, 2001), 62–63.

and self-respect. Boldly challenging the horrific notion that dark-skinned humanity is disposable is a revolutionary act of love for oneself and the larger society.

While #BlackLivesMatter arose amid acts of fear, hatred, and murder, the movement has resisted these dread forces through its dogged embrace of hope, love, and life in even greater measure. When conservative politicians and reactionary critics of #BlackLivesMatter respond in cries of "All Lives Matter," their attempts at deflection serve only to highlight the hypocrisy at the heart of the matter. If all human lives truly were held in full and equal regard, then people of color would not be murdered routinely by rogue police officers and random vigilantes.

In the final analysis, the humanist appeal at the core of #BlackLivesMatter hinges on a love of Black life and culture amid the reality of an ongoing existential struggle against a rising tide of dehumanization, despair, and death that makes our survival as human beings not just possible but worthwhile. When reflecting on the life, lessons, and legacy of Ivory Perry, an exemplar of an earlier generation of the Black freedom struggle, George Lipsitz makes a statement that I would also apply to those who have taken up the cause of #BlackLivesMatter today:

> The meaning of life is in living, that love and struggle go together, that there can be no peace without justice, and no justice without struggle. [They] drew from the deep rivers of resistance running through the African American past for moral visions and direct actions that helped people from all groups.[97]

A critical race theology that is attentive to the necessity of reflection and remembrance within this commonsense humanism

---

[97] George Lipsitz, *A Life in the Struggle: Ivory Perry and the Culture of Opposition*, rev. ed. (Philadelphia: Temple University Press, 1988), 268.

demonstrates a pragmatic approach to rebuilding notions of liberationist and social justice movements today. These movements, then, can become the fulfillment of our contemporary national potential as a multiracial, multiethnic, multicultural, and multifaith democratic society in the truest sense.

Considering the real meaning of "Black liberation" that lies at the heart of Black Lives Matter, Keeanga-Yamahtta Taylor asserts,

> The struggle for Black liberation requires going beyond the standard narrative that Black people have come a long way but have a long way to go—which, of course, says nothing about where it is that we are actually trying to get to. It requires understanding the origins and nature of Black oppression and racism more generally. Most importantly, it requires a strategy, some sense of how we get from the current situation to the future. Perhaps at its most basic level, Black liberation implies a world where Black people can live in peace, without the constant threat of the social, economic, and political woes of a society that places almost no value on the vast majority of Black lives. It would mean living in a world where Black lives matter. While it is true that when Black people get free, everyone gets free, Black people in America cannot "get free" alone. In that sense, Black liberation is bound up with the project of human liberation and social transformation.[98]

Sadly, making these painfully obvious observations in today's world is still a relatively new discovery. Despite the wrongheaded criticism of conservatives and reactionaries, the call for Black lives to matter is a rallying cry for the protection and preservation of *all*

---

[98] Keeanga-Yamahtta Taylor, *From #BlackLivesMatters to Black Liberation* (Chicago: Haymarket Books, 2016), 194.

human lives who strive to be defined by freedom, justice, equality, and dignity. Toward this end, if religious institutions and their related communities of faith seriously desire to be in constructive relationships with society in this world, Charles Long suggests that finding beauty amid the ashes means developing a true theology of freedom:

> But what would be a history stemming from the oppressed? Are they destined to initiate and repeat a destructive cycle of events? The appearance of theologies of the opaque might promise another alternative of a structural sort, but only if these theologies move beyond the structural power of theology as the normative mode of discourse and contemplate a narrative of meaning that is commensurate with the quality of beauty that was fired in the crucible of oppression. Those who have lived in the cultures of the oppressed know something about freedom that the oppressors will never know.[99]

Critical race theology advances a counternarrative of a struggle for human freedom that, while far from being perfect, strives toward life and liberation. Critical race theology is, then, both an academic and an activist concern that links divine justice to social justice so that *all* people, in every part of God's dream of creation, can enjoy freedom, justice, and equality with dignity and decency. Critical race theology recognizes that Black religion works best and is at its fullest when it merges orthodoxy—right thinking—with orthopraxis—right action. It is perfectly fine for folks to engage Black religion to understand how we preach, pray, sing, and minister, but this engagement must also recognize

---

[99] Charles H. Long, *Significations: Signs, Symbols, and Images in the Interpretation of Religion*, 2nd ed. (1984; Boulder, CO: The Davies Group Publishers, 1999), 210.

how we plan, protest, strategize, and mobilize. For critical race theology, we must guarantee that the prophetic and the pastoral dimensions of Black faith are never encountered as enemies or strangers to one another, but rather are experienced as coexisting in seamless harmony.

5

"To Hell and Back"

Sanctified Violence, American Democracy's Identity Crisis, and the Need for Hope in Monstrous Times

On July 27, 2021, Officer Michael Fanone of the District of Columbia Metropolitan Police Department testified before the House Select Committee to Investigate the January 6th Attack on the US Capitol.[1] During his testimony, Officer Fanone described in graphic detail how the insurrectionists beat him mercilessly and even threatened to "kill him with his own gun."[2] The officer squarely condemned "those elected Members of our government who continue to deny the events of that day."[3] Even with such a condemnation, Fanone insisted that the investigative response to the insurrection should not "have anything to do with political parties," for it should "make sure this institution of our democracy

---

[1] *The Law Enforcement Experience on January 6th, Before the House Select Committee to Investigate the January 6th Attack on the United States Capitol*, 117th Cong. (2021) (statement of Michael Fanone, Officer of the District of Columbia Metropolitan Police Department).

[2] Fanone, *The Law Enforcement Experience on January 6th*, 2.

[3] Fanone, *The Law Enforcement Experience on January 6th*, 5.

never again falls into the hands of a violent and angry mob."[4] Having suffered a heart attack as well as a traumatic brain injury resulting from being attacked by insurrectionists, Fanone barely survived the devastating events of that fateful day.[5] "I feel like I went to Hell and back to protect the people in this room. But too many are now telling me that Hell doesn't even exist—or that Hell actually wasn't all *that* bad," Fanone testified, furiously banging his fist on the table.[6]

Rather than seeing the January 6, 2021, insurrection as an unfortunate anomaly within American political experiment, a critical race theology insists that we must address how America has embraced *sanctified violence* as a machinery of social death and civic despair to chill any vestige of a rich and robust grassroots democracy. The misguided notion of sanctified violence runs deep in contemporary American society and culture. Unlike the state-sanctioned violence addressed in the previous chapter pertaining to the issues of Black Lives Matter and community policing, sanctified violence has been an insidious yet instrumental dimension of US political culture. This final chapter charts the various ways in which the sociopolitical, economic, cultural, intellectual, and spiritual forces that dominate American society embrace death-dealing institutions as nothing more than the will of the Divine. This vast matrix of death includes but is not limited to a wildly bloated military-national security industrial complex; the punitive antiwelfare bureaucratic state; a dysfunctional electoral process; predatory and pernicious modes of late-stage capitalism; and a growing set of amoral, authoritarian, death-driven far-right political and thought leaders who sanction mass shootings, torture, targeted assassinations, police lethality, perpetual war psychology, and other forms of nihilism.

---

[4] Fanone, *The Law Enforcement Experience on January 6th*, 6.

[5] Fanone, *The Law Enforcement Experience on January 6th*, 5.

[6] Fanone, *The Law Enforcement Experience on January 6th*, 5.

Although she was writing during a somewhat different cultural moment, Susan Sontag once observed that there was a willful ignorance of how an emerging marker of governance and power "dissolves politics into pathology."[7] Nevertheless, as David Gushee reminds us, democracy, "while flawed, still appears to be the best available political ordering of human community," and it "is still worth our support."[8] Over the nearly two and a half centuries of the American experiment, it has been generally held as conventional wisdom that our existence as a democratic republic relied on power being in the hands of the people, and the *telos* of our values and ideals as a nation has been resilient enough to prevent democracy from being undermined or lost forever. And yet there was a misguided and malicious contingent of Americans who participated in the insurrection on January 6, 2021, with the belief that anyone can learn to love their bitterness and barbarity, if they believe that outrage is their only birthright and inheritance. To quote the amazing young poet Amanda Gorman, we are now at pivotal moment when "we've seen a force that would shatter our nation rather than share it / Would destroy our country if it meant delaying democracy."[9] Our nation has either forgotten—or maybe never learned in the first place—some of the most earnest, essential lessons about how to envision a more humane future together.

A distinctly militant type of white Christian nationalism thoroughly infused with white supremacy was on display for the whole world to see on January 6, 2021. When throngs of Trump supporters stormed the Capitol that day, there were, undoubtedly,

---

[7] Susan Sontag, "Mind as Passion," *New York Review of Books,* September 25, 1980.

[8] David P. Gushee, *Defending Democracy from Its Christian Enemies* (Grand Rapids: William B. Eerdmans, 2023), 191.

[9] Amanda Gorman, *The Hill We Climb: An Inaugural Poem for the Country* (New York: Viking, 2021), 20.

countless white Christian nationalists in their midst. While some might argue that these otherwise innocuous churchgoers were not part of any white power militia or organized hate group *per se*, Kobes Du Mez has rightly observed that their theological worldview and personal beliefs about religion and violence seemed to align quite seamlessly with many or all of those involved in the attempted insurrection against the US government on that fateful day.[10]

Jacob Chansley—known more commonly as the "QAnon Shaman"—was among the angry mob of Trump supporters involved in the infamous assault on the US Capitol. In a widely circulated online video, Chansley stood in the well of the US Senate chamber and summoned the horde of invaders together for a moment of worship using a megaphone.[11] Chansley prayed,

> Thank you heavenly father for gracing us with this opportunity to stand up for our God-given unalienable rights. Thank you heavenly father for being the inspiration needed to these police officers to allow us into the building, to all us to exercise our rights, to allow us to send a message to all the tyrants, the communists, and the globalists, that this is our nation, not theirs, that we will not all the America, the American way of the United States of America to go down. Thank you divine, omniscient, omnipotent, and omnipresent creator God for filling this

---

[10] Laura Barrón-López, "Concerns Grow over the Increasing Ties between Christianity and Right-Wing Nationalism." *PBS NewHour*, October 11, 2022, https://www.pbs.org/newshour/show/concerns-grow-over-the-increasing-ties-between-christianity-and-right-wing-nationalism.

[11] Luke Mogelson, "A Reporter's Footage from inside the Capitol Siege: The New Yorker." YouTube video, 12:32, January 17, 2021, Beginning about 8:00, https://youtu.be/270F8s5TEKY.

chamber with your white light and love, with your white light of harmony. Thank you for filling this chamber with patriots that love you and that love Christ.[12]

While there is plenty to unpack within both the content of Chansley's prayer, the context of the prayer speaks to Chansley's self-perception as one who was tearing down the wall of separation between church and state, reclaiming Christianity's place in the rightful heart of government. He was confident that he was helping to restore the proper order alongside "patriots that love [God]," driving out those who have no right to claim the nation as "theirs." Months later, Chansley was arrested, tried, and sentenced to forty-one months in prison for his active involvement in the attack on the US Capitol with the intention to derail the peaceful transfer of political power.[13]

Rather than seeing Chansley and other insurrectionists as God's chosen warriors and holy "patriots," FBI Director Christopher Wray testified to the US Congress a few months later that the FBI sees these individuals as "domestic violent extremists" (DVEs). Wray further elaborated that DVEs pose terroristic threats to the national security of the United States, and "commit violent criminal acts in furtherance of social or political goals stemming from domestic influences—some of which include racial or ethnic bias, or anti-government or anti-authority sentiments."[14] As the seat of power in our nation's government was transformed into

---

[12] Mogelson, "A Reporter's Footage," 8:00–8:52.

[13] Hannah Rabinowitz and Katelyn Polantz, "'QAnon Shaman' Jacob Chansley Sentenced to 41 Months in Prison for Role in US Capitol Riot | CNN Politics." CNN.com, November 17, 2021, https://www.cnn.com/2021/11/17/politics/jacob-chansley-qanon-shaman-january-6-sentencing/index.html.

[14] *Examining the January 6 Attack on the U.S. Capitol, Before the House Oversight and Reform Committee*, 117th Cong. (2021) (statement of Christopher Wray, Director, Federal Bureau of Investigation).

one massive crime scene, numerous groups were there, including the Proud Boys, Three Percenters, the Oath Keepers, neo-Nazis, and QAnon adherents. Many other people who were not part of any specific white supremacist group, but whose political views and personal beliefs most certainly aligned with any or all of those, were involved in the insurrection. Having survived the insurgent attack on January 6, 2021, DC police officer Daniel Hodges later observed, "It was clear the terrorists perceived themselves to be Christians. I saw the Christian flag directly to my front, another 'Jesus is my savior.' 'Trump is my president.' Another 'Jesus is king.'"[15]

In 2011, Charlotte Ward and David Voas coined the term *conspirituality*.[16] "Conspirituality," they wrote, "is a rapidly growing web movement expressing an ideology fueled by political disillusionment and the popularity of alternative worldviews."[17] QAnon, one of the more influential movements on the events of January 6, 2021, is one expression of conspirituality. The Southern Poverty Law Center describes QAnon as

> the umbrella term for a sprawling spiderweb of right-wing internet conspiracy theories with anti-Semitic and anti-LGBTQIA+ elements that falsely claim the world is run by a secret cabal of pedophiles who worship Satan and are plotting against President Trump.... QAnon believers falsely claim the cabal is abducting children to kill them and harvest their blood for a chemical known as adrenochrome, which is used to extend their lives.[18]

---

[15] John Wagner, Kim Bellware, Karoun Demirjian, et al., "Police Officers Deliver Emotional Testimony about Violent Day at Capitol: Live Coverage," *Washington Post*, July 27, 2021, https://www.washingtonpost.com/politics/2021/07/27/jan-6-commission-hearing-live-updates/.

[16] Charlotte Ward and David Voas, "The Emergence of Conspirituality," *Journal of Contemporary Religion* 26, no. 1 (January 2011), 103–21.

[17] Ward and Voas, "The Emergence of Conspirituality," 103.

[18] Hatewatch Staff, "What You Need to Know About QAnon,"

On October 28, 2017, "Q" emerged from the 4chan online message board before entering online wellness communities, where it initially found a following largely among women, who continue to share phrases like "Save the Children." The phrase was first used by eventual QAnon believers who spread the false claim that 2016 presidential candidate Hillary Clinton abused children and drank their blood. With various subcultures, including some for people who approach studying online posts from "Q" in a manner akin to a Bible study, QAnon followers come to QAnon from New Age spiritual movements, more traditional conspiracy theory communities, the far right, and Evangelical Christian communities. Many QAnon followers appear to be older Republican voters, signaling the shift in the party's base that was briefly tracked earlier in this book through Pat Buchanan's call to culture war. Today, "Save the Children" and other Q-related phrases are just as likely to be seen on social media posts by paramilitary militia members, conspiracy theorists, and far-right extremists as by yoga teachers, soccer moms, and wellness influencers.

In his keynote speech to the 2023 Conservative Political Action Committee Conference, Donald Trump issued a clarion call that captured prominent themes in the Q narrative and other conspirituality movements for those white Americans who believed they have been wronged and betrayed by the status quo of American politics and culture. "For those who have been wronged and betrayed," Donald Trump proclaimed, "I am your retribution."[19] The vitality and vibrancy of the actual system of governance (derisively called the "deep state" by its critics) is better

---

Southern Poverty Law Center: Hatewatch, October 27, 2020, https://www.splcenter.org/hatewatch/2020/10/27/what-you-need-know-about-qanon.

[19] Isabella Murray, Soo Rin Kim, and Adam Carlson, "Trump, Who Told Supporters 'I Am Your Retribution,' Now Says, 'I'm Being Indicted for You,'" *ABC News* online, June 26, 2023. https://abcnews.go.com/Politics/trump-told-supporters-retribution-now-im-indicted/story?id=100386551.

defined by those who inhabit it rather than those who try to inhibit it because the latter group cannot take responsibility for the little they have accomplished despite the privileges they have been given. Calling himself the human incarnation of "retribution" is the entire Trumpian worldview in a rarely succinct sales pitch from Trump himself.

Presently, US conservatism has become completely out of step with the broad swath of Americans because it has morphed from a governing philosophy to a bullying posture. This is, sadly, why politicized violence and insurrection have more sway among the GOP than policy visions and ideas. While some far-right figures have tried to suggest Trump's faux grandeur and fictitious accomplishments are an iconic paragon of latter-day conservatism, scores of publications, including books, multimedia documentaries, and long-form journalism have documented the innumerable acts of personal criminality, governmental incompetence, and general catastrophe that culminated in his tumultuous tenure in the Oval Office. Despite such monstrous acts and the thoughts that fuel them, there has been little room in the collective theological imagination to entertain what was once deemed unthinkable in public, namely, that *sanctified violence* in service of establishing anger, aggression, and authoritarianism is within the providential scheme of the Divine.[20]

---

[20] Sanctified violence has never been confined exclusively to one religion, culture, or populace or to one set of religious practices and beliefs. This view of the concept lies squarely at the heart of Alfred J. Andrea and Andrew Holt's definition of sanctified violence. Throughout at least five thousand years of human history, sanctified violence has been regarded in terms of "holy wars" purportedly fought by rival combatants in service to a deity, a spirit, or a religious ideology ranging from animism to Zoroastrianism and everything in between. Over those five millennia, violent conflict as an outgrowth of religious differences not only has been part of the human experience from nearly every religious tradition and

The preponderance of the media coverage and critical discourse surrounding sanctified violence in recent memory has focused overwhelmingly on the topic of jihads and "radical Islamic terrorism" almost to the exclusion of other religions. The contemporary challenges we face dictate that we shift our perspectives away from the lofty labels of "holy war" and reframe our consideration of sanctified violence in a manner that underscores the mundane pervasiveness of these conflicts beyond the traditionalist elements of the model. A perennial paradox sits at the crux of critical reflection on the reality of sanctified violence. Why have many violent conflicts been fought in the name of religion when so many of the world's great religious traditions advocate peace?[21]

Philosophers and social theorists, including Thomas Hobbes, Jean-Paul Sartre, René Girard, and others, consider religion as a key mode of human difference within the collective violence of

---

religious expression, but it also has been a global and transcultural extent. Through their in-depth historical studies of holy wars, crusades, jihads, and other types of divinely identified conflicts from antiquity to the cusp of modernity, Andrea and Holt have crafted a prolegomenon to inspire further debate and deeper research for how we consider the conjoined issues of religion, culture, and violence throughout human history. Alfred J. Andrea and Andrew Holt, *Sanctified Violence: Holy War in World History* (Indianapolis, IN: Hackett Publishing, 2021).

[21] Bruce Hoffman, "Holy Terror: The Implications of Terrorism Motivated by a Religious Imperative," *Studies in Conflict and Terrorism* 18 (1995): 271–84; John J. Carlson, "Religion and Violence: Coming to Terms with Terms," *Blackwell Companion to Religion and Violence*, ed. Andrew R. Murphy (Malden, MA: Wiley-Blackwell, 2011), 7–22; John R. Hall, "Religion and Violence: Social Processes in Comparative Perspective," in *Handbook of the Sociology of Religion*, ed. Michele Dillon (Cambridge: Cambridge University Press, 2003), 359–81; Charles Selengut, *Sacred Fury: Understanding Religious Violence*, 3rd ed. (Lanham, MD: Rowman & Littlefield, 2017), 1–12.

all against all that threatens social collapse until it is spontaneously transformed via "the scapegoat mechanism" into the violence of all against one. Collective unity is rebuilt by the direct animosity, alienation, and possibly even annihilation of the Other.[22] "Collective cruelty is, of course, neither new nor confined to the West. Muslims, Jews, Hindus, Buddhists, and Christians continue in our day to perpetrate acts of violence and cruelty. But it is the secular modern state's awesome potential for cruelty and destruction," Talal Asad writes, "that deserves our sustained attention."[23] According to Hannah Arendt, "The very substance of violent action is ruled by the means-end category, whose chief characteristic, if applied to human affairs, has always been that the end is in danger of being over whelmed by the means which it justifies and which are needed to reach it."[24]

Whether we wonder about the interplay of human belief and behavior, why does religion inspire modes of hatred and violence? Why do people in one religion hate people of another religion or sometimes even a member of the same religion? How and why do some religions inspire hatred from others that leads to violence?[25]

There has been a growing body of research, most notably by Rutger Bregman, which argues that, over the past 200,000

---

[22] Thomas Hobbes, *Leviathan* (Bristol, UK: Thoemmes Continuum, 2003); Jean-Paul Sartre and George Joseph Becker, *Anti-Semite and Jew* (New York: Schocken Books, 1948); and René Girard, *Deceit, Desire, and the Novel: Self and Other in Literary Structure* (Baltimore: Johns Hopkins University Press, 1976).

[23] Talal Asad, *Genealogies of Religion: Discipline and Reasons of Power in Christianity and Islam* (Baltimore: Johns Hopkins University Press, 1993), 305–6.

[24] Hannah Arendt, *On Violence* (New York: Harcourt, Brace, Jovanovich, 1970), 4.

[25] Paul Hedges, *Religious Hatred: Prejudice: Islamophobia and Antisemitism in Global Context* (London: Bloomsbury, 2021).

years of human history, we have been a species geared toward cooperation rather than competition, wherein we can and often will work together with family, friends, and even with strangers because of our innate capacity to empathize and sympathize with others.[26] Yet, critical race theology calls us to discuss how conflict and violence—which are not synonymous—mark a shared reality of the human condition, even as we seek means to reduce and possibly even remedy violent acts and events among human beings in general. "Violence," Carsten de Dreu explains, "is not the same as conflict—you can't have violence without conflict, but you can have conflict without violence. Conflict," he continues, "is a situation, while violence is a behavior."[27] During his speech upon receiving the Nobel Prize in Literature in Stockholm on December 10, 1950, William Faulkner explained how the wellspring of his life's work as a writer was greatly propelled by his efforts to speak to and about "the problems of the human heart in conflict with itself."[28] Whereas conflict will likely always haunt humanity in one form or another, actively resorting to violence neither must nor needs to be the only response to those disputes.

As horrific as violence between individuals sometimes can be, the potential for violence is much worse when it occurs in and among groups. The propensity for things to get out of hand through group violence increases tremendously, escalates much faster, and moves well beyond the confines of interpersonal disputes. In the context of an interpersonal dispute, the sole target

---

[26] Rutger Bregman, *Humankind: A Hopeful History* (New York: Little, Brown, 2020).

[27] Social Science Bites, "Carsten de Dreu on Why People Fight," *Social Science Space*, June 30, 2023, https://www.socialsciencespace.com/2023/07/carsten-de-dreu-on-why-people-fight/.

[28] William Faulkner, "Banquet Speech," Speech at the Nobel Banquet at the City Hall, Stockholm, Sweden, December 10, 1950, https://www.nobelprize.org/prizes/literature/1949/faulkner/speech/.

of one's aggression or resistance is the perceived antagonist. However, in intergroup violence ranging from the micro- to the macrolevel, people sometimes become so focused on "the enemy"—whosoever they are and however they are defined—that they can lose sight of their own moral discretion and even an innate sense of personal safety.

While discerning the root causes of sanctified violence can sometimes prompt vigorous debate, René Girard is cogent and compelling for making sense of the correlation of sacred beliefs and human conflicts. While fighting over the real or perceived scarcity of resources (food, water, minerals, land, or even potential mates as chief examples) is not unique to humans as a species, the open wherewithal to fight over intangible ideas and values is utterly unique to humans. Based on the ancient category of mimesis, Girard argues that the basic imitative predisposition is a primary, unconscious, intrinsic, and vital dynamism that forces human behavior and our ways of thinking. This idea was documented in Aristotle's *Poetics*, in which he wrote, "[The human] differs from the other animals in that [it is] far more imitative and learns [the] first lessons by representing things."[29] Violence, within the purview of mimetic theory, is never just an absolutely random act, discrete event, or even an external feat. Instead, violence is the consequence of a relationship in which two desires directed toward the acquisition and consumption of the same object are inevitably competitive. Girard calls the conflict that ensues from imitation "mimetic rivalry."[30] Girard has been among the most provocative

---

[29] Aristotle, *Poetics*, 1448b.1.

[30] Michael Kirwan, *Discovering Girard* (Cambridge, MA: Cowley Publications, 2005); Wolfgang Palaver, *René Girard's Mimetic Theory: Studies in Violence, Mimesis and Culture* (East Lansing, MI: Michigan State University Press, 2013); Wolfgang Palaver and Richard Schenk, eds., *Mimetic Theory and World Religions: Studies in Violence, Mimesis and Culture* (East Lansing: Michigan State University Press, 2017).

and innovative religious thinkers contemplating the interrelation of religion and violence in modern society and culture, and a critical race theology must seriously engage with his ideas and analyses as it examines the origins and evolution of religious violence.[31]

The attempted extermination and forced exodus of the Mormons is a key example of how sanctified violence has contributed to the US religious experience. Though typically seen as an outlier or oddity in the overall narrative of US religious history, reckoning with these events as more central to the story of Jacksonian America reveals a wholesale failure of popular democracy and religious freedom just as the young nation was entering an era of heightened episodes of religion and violence in American life. Under the Prophet Joseph Smith in the 1820s and the early 1830s, Mormonism swept across the nation. Documenting both the religion's spread and the increasingly anti-Mormon sentiment of their newfound neighbors, Adam Jortner explains that anti-Mormonism thrived on territorial rivalry, gossip, conspiracy theories, and outright lies about the backgrounds, beliefs, and behaviors of the Mormon newcomers.[32] The strange brew of rising violence in this situation culminated in mounting throngs of anti-Mormons who openly and aggressively viewed the Church of Latter-Day Saints (LDS) as a wholesale threat to American democracy. Despite the constitutional fact of church–state separation in the United States, much of the animus was rooted in theological claims regarding prophecy and divine revelation. In sum, angry residents deemed any attestation of prophecy and

---

[31] See René Girard, *Violence and the Sacred,* trans. Patrick Gregory (Baltimore: Johns Hopkins University Press, 1977); René Girard, *Things Hidden Since the Foundation of the World* (Stanford, CA: Stanford University Press, 1987); Charles Selengut, *Sacred Fury: Understanding Religious Violence* 3rd ed. (Lanham, MD: Rowman & Littlefield, 2017), 41–82.

[32] Adam Jortner, *No Place for Saints: Mobs and Mormons in Jacksonian America* (Baltimore: Johns Hopkins University Press, 2021).

divine revelation outside the parameters of mainline Protestant Christianity as antithetical to what it means to be American.

By 1833, anti-Mormon neighbors demanded that all the LDS members leave Jackson County, Missouri, voluntarily or else face the brunt of their wrath. When the Mormons refused to surrender to this intimidation, citing the First Amendment in their own defense, the anti-Mormons attacked their homes, held their leaders at gunpoint, and ostensibly performed one of America's most egregious acts of religious cleansing with open impunity. Jortner illustrates how this bloodthirsty anti-Mormon rampage reshaped the trajectory of Mormon history, marking a particularly troubling episode of American law and lawlessness that remains distinctive within the annals of American religion.

R. Laurence Moore famously identified Mormons as an exemplary group of "religious outsiders" within American history. According to Moore,

> The nineteenth-century historians treated other [religious] groups condescendingly or with open contempt. They never asked why Mormonism ... emerged in the first place and lingered so long and so prominently in public view ... To have placed these questions and points in the foreground would have been to suggest God made mistakes.[33]

Why did Mormonism as a religion spawn such visceral, vicious anger? What could these conflicts say about our contemporary struggles with religious liberty?

Contemporaneous to the emergence of the LDS and the resulting anti-Mormon violence, the nation witnessed the Nat Turner slave rebellion, the Trail of Tears, and the Texas Revolution as part of our blood-stained history of cruel conflicts between white Americans and African Americans, Native Americans, and

---

[33] R. Laurence Moore, *Religious Outsiders and the Making of Americans* (New York: Oxford University Press, 1986), 13.

Mexicans, respectively. The Mormon expulsion is so notable not because of the brutality or bellicosity demonstrated in the anti-Mormon attacks but because of the extent to which the persecution of the members of the LDS was a violent intraracial conflict between opposing groups of white Americans. It was not one of the bloody interracial clashes in the early nineteenth century that was predicated on white supremacist xenophobia against racial–ethnic minorities and international Others.

A century later, the 1921 Tulsa race massacre offers another salient example of sanctified violence. Over a twenty-four-hour period spanning May 31 and June 1, 1921, a violent white multitude descended upon the Deep Greenwood district of Tulsa, Oklahoma, widely known as "Black Wall Street," and burned the community to the ground. Earlier on May 31, 1921, Tulsa police officers arrested a young Black man named Dick Rowland, who lived in the Greenwood area and earned a living by shining shoes, for allegedly assaulting a young white woman, Sarah Page, who was working as an elevator operator. Amid the larger silence in scholarly and popular awareness that surrounds these devastating events, documentary evidence remains largely unclear about what happened during the brief encounter between the two teenagers.[34] Page screamed when Rowland entered the elevator. Once the local

---

[34] It is important to note that, while there are numerous texts whose publication coincides with the centennial anniversary of the massacre, namely, Scott Ellsworth, *The Ground Breaking: An American City and Its Search for Justice* (New York: Dutton, 2021); Daniel Isgrigg, *Pentecost in Tulsa: The Revivals and Race Massacre that Shaped the Pentecostal Movement in Tulsa* (Lanham, MD: Seymour Press, 2021); and Jerroyln Eulinberg, *A Lynched Black Wall Street: A Womanist Perspective on Terrorism, Religion, and Black Resilience in the 1921 Tulsa Race Massacre—Remembering 100 Years* (Eugene, OR: Cascade Books, 2021), there remains a profound dearth of scholarly books addressing and analyzing the hidden history surrounding the Tulsa massacre.

police arrived on the scene, Rowland was arrested immediately for attacking Page. While subsequent accounts say Rowland may have simply tripped and clumsily stumbled onto Page, local gossip spread rapidly among white Tulsans accusing Rowland of raping Page. While evidence of any crime committed by Rowland was extremely weak, an afternoon edition of the *Tulsa Tribune* promptly printed an inflammatory editorial that called for a lynching. Consequently, a hostile mob of armed white men converged outside the courthouse. It was later revealed that members of the vigilante mob had been deputized and armed by city officials. With thoughts of protecting Rowland once word of the planned lynching eventually reached Greenwood, members of the Black community, including many Black World War I veterans, armed themselves and went to the courthouse to protect Rowland from the lynch-mob. Being outnumbered and outgunned, these would-be defenders retreated to the city's Greenwood neighborhood, and the angry mob pursued them relentlessly.

Lynching Black people and other related cases of racist terrorism were a far too common occurrence throughout the United States during this period. As part of the racial imaginary known as the Jim and Jane Crow South, Tulsa was a highly segregated metropolis. Its Black voters were suppressed, and its Black residents were incessantly blamed for the city's growing problems. Sociologist George Edmund Haynes identified thirty-eight separate racial riots in which whites attacked Black people in widely scattered cities during the brutally bloody "Red Summer" of 1919. Haynes reported his findings on these events in the autumn of that year as a prelude to an investigation by the US Senate Committee on the Judiciary.[35] For many decades, the most comprehensive total

---

[35] "For Action on Race Riot Peril; Radical Propaganda among Negroes Growing, and Increase of Mob Violence Set out in Senate Brief for Federal Inquiry the War's Responsibility. Reds Inflaming Blacks. Industrial Clashes. I. the Facts—1919. II. the Failure of the States. III. A National Problem.

of lynchings was housed in the Tuskegee Institute's archives, which tabulated 4,743 people who were murdered at the hands of American lynch mobs between 1881 and 1968.[36] According to the Tuskegee estimates, 3,446, roughly 72 percent, of lynching victims were African American men. More recently, the Equal Justice Initiative (EJI), which relied heavily on Tuskegee's data in building its own statistical model, integrated other sources, such as newspaper archives and other historical records, to arrive at a total of 4,084 racial terror lynchings in twelve southern states between the end of Reconstruction in 1877 and 1950, and another three hundred in other states.[37] According to EJI, nearly 25 percent of all lynching victims were accused of sexual assault despite the fact that most of these accusations of Black men raping white women were false.[38] In the period from 1911 to 1921, twenty-three Black Oklahomans were lynched by white mobs.

In Oklahoma particularly, a sense of frontier lawlessness lingered across the state. In 1920, a mob of hundreds of white Tulsans stormed the county courthouse to take a white prisoner, a

---

IV. Consequences of Lynching. V. the Danger," *New York Times*, October 5, 1919, https://www.nytimes.com/1919/10/05/archives/for-action-on-race-riot-peril-radical-propaganda-among-negroes.html.

[36] Because of the very nature of lynchings—summary vigilante executions that occurred outside the constraints of court documentation—there was no formal, centralized tracking of the phenomenon. As a result, a verifiable number of lynchings will always be dramatically underreported and therefore an accurate record will never be fully possible.

[37] "Lynching in America: Confronting the Legacy of Racial Terror," https://lynchinginamerica.eji.org/report/.

[38] Jamiles Lartey and Sam Morris, "How White Americans Used Lynchings to Terrorize and Control Black People," *The Guardian*, April 26, 2018, https://www.theguardian.com/us-news/2018/apr/26/lynchings-memorial-us-south-montgomery-alabama.

drifter named Roy Belton, into their own hands. They lynched him that night, facing almost no interference from the police. In the following days, Tulsa's police chief, John Gustafson, said that "the lynching of Belton will prove of real benefit to Tulsa and vicinity."[39] Residents of Deep Greenwood, regardless of background, knew quite well that, if the Tulsa police were not going to protect white residents from lynching, no one was going to protect Black Tulsans. This knowledge prompted Black war veterans and other concerned citizens to rally to defend Rowland's life at that crucial moment.

The massacre began when the impromptu lynch mob merged with and were aided by local Ku Klux Klan members. The attackers were galvanized under the growing influence of the Klan's program of "One Hundred Per Cent Americanism," marked by "uniting native-born [white] Christians for concerted action in the preservation of American institutions and the supremacy of the white race."[40] This large mob was estimated to number upward of several thousand white men and boys as they attacked the Greenwood residents with murderous intent, outnumbering the

---

[39] Randy Krehbiel, "Tulsa Race Massacre: A Pair of Lynchings Year before Massacre Shook Tulsa," *Tulsa World*, July 4, 2022, https://tulsaworld.com/tulsa-race-massacre-a-pair-of-lynchings-year-before-massacre-shook-tulsa/article_72a4115e-541c-54b6-b765-79d3276c6f4b.html.

[40] National Park Service-US Department of the Interior, *1921 Tulsa Race Riot Reconnaissance Survey: Final* (November 2005), https://www.nps.gov/parkhistory/online_books/nnps/tulsa_riot.pdf; Rory McVeigh, "Structural Incentives for Conservative Mobilization: Power Devaluation and the Rise of the Ku Klux Klan, 1915–1925," *Social Forces* 77, no. 4 (1999): 1461–96; Chris Gavaler, "The Ku Klux Klan and the Birth of the Superhero," *Journal of Graphic Novels and Comics*, 4, no. 2 (2013): 191–208; Gustaf Forsell, "Blood, Cross and Flag: The Influence of Race on Ku Klux Klan Theology in the 1920s," *Politics, Religion & Ideology* 21, no. 3 (2020): 269–87; Kelly J. Baker, "The Artifacts of White Supremacy, "*Religion & Culture Forum* June 14, 2017, https://voices.uchicago.edu/religionculture/2017/06/14/813/.

community's armed Black defenders by a ratio of approximately twenty to one, if not more. Far from being helpless victims, Tulsa's Black populace fought with bravery against the brutality of white invaders, but they were greatly outnumbered and outgunned. Witnesses said that shootings and other related acts of violence against Black Tulsans occurred with reckless abandon from the early morning, throughout the night, and into the next day. Additional reports stated that people saw airplanes fly over Deep Greenwood, wantonly attacking innocent Black bystanders by shooting at and even dropping firebombs on them from above.

At the end of the bloodbath, the white mob had destroyed thirty-five square blocks of Greenwood, burning down over twelve hundred homes, over sixty businesses, a school, a hospital, a public library, and a dozen churches. Hundreds of residential homes that had not burned were looted by the invaders. Some estimates put the death toll at three hundred, while others believe the actual body count was probably even higher. Many fled, while thousands more were captured and taken prisoner. At best, Tulsa Police took no action to prevent the massacre, and, at worst, there were credible eyewitness reports indicating that there may have been some police officers who actively participated in the violence and subsequent chaos. "Vigilantes ... under the color of law, destroyed the Black Wall Street of America," said former state Rep. Don Ross. "Some known victims were in unmarked graves in a city-owned cemetery and others were hauled off to unknown places in full view of the National Guard."[41]

As a manifestation of sanctified violence, the Tulsa massacre's devastating death toll and various other modes of harm can never be fully repaired. City, state, and federal officials, as well as prominent civic leaders, not only failed to invest in and rebuild the

---

[41] Oklahoma Commission to Study the Tulsa Race Riot of 1921, *Tulsa Race Riot: A Report by the Oklahoma Commission to Study the Race Riot of 1921* (Tulsa, OK, 2001), viii.

once-thriving Greenwood community but actively blocked efforts to do so for decades after the massacre. No one has ever been held responsible for these crimes, the overwhelming impact of which Black Tulsans still feel today. Efforts to secure justice in the courts have failed due to the statute of limitations. Ongoing racial segregation, discriminatory policies, and structural racism have left Black Tulsans, particularly those living in North Tulsa, with a lower quality of life and fewer opportunities.

Plumbing the depths of the tragedy of and trauma resonant from the Tulsa massacre reveals how this horrific event has twisted and tainted the coexistence of white and Black Tulsans alike. As historian Scott Ellsworth notes, over a century ago, Tulsa was awash in oil money at the height of these boom years, and that prosperity translated into the development of an impressive urban skyline that included numerous ornate churches across the city.[42] Daniel Isgrigg extols Tulsa as an important epicenter of Pentecostalism in the United States and acknowledges the racist bifurcation of Charismatic Christianity resulting from the racial segregation that has led to the obscuring of the tradition's Black roots both locally and nationally. In its earliest days emerging from the Azusa Street missions, Black Pentecostal revivals in Greenwood District helped establish important churches there. Later, well-known worldwide ministries were launched from Tulsa that impacted millions around the globe. Even as he describes the untold story of a resilient Black Pentecostal community that suffered the 1921 Tulsa massacre, Isgrigg's narrative seems more geared on a triumphalist outcome hurrying toward a proverbial "happy ending" focused on reconciliation rather than wrestling

---

[42] Scott Ellsworth, "The Tulsa Race Riot," *Tulsa Reparations: John Hope Franklin Center for Reconciliation*, https://tulsareparations.z19.web.core. windows.net/TulsaRiot1Of3.htm; Scott Ellsworth, *Death in a Promised Land: The Tulsa Race Riot of 1921* (Baton Rouge: Louisiana State University Press, 1982).

a bit more with the moral failures at stake among the white Pentecostals for possible sins of both commission and omission.[43] While he recognizes the racial–ethnic discrimination that has led to the erasure of Black Pentecostals from the church's broader history, he appears much less willing to condemn the ethical disparities of the white Pentecostals that contributed to the near eradication of Tulsa's Black community.

While Isgrigg hurriedly tries to move past the tragedy of racist terrorism in order to amplify a triumphal narrative of Black resiliency in the wake of 1921 massacre, a critical race theology approaches the events and aftermath of the Tulsa massacre through a critically self-aware reflection more akin to Robert P. Jones's diagnosis in *White Too Long*.[44] Jones asks his fellow white Christians to make a harsh yet honest reevaluation of their identity, history, and faith in recognition of a complex and complicit past infused with white supremacy. Informed by critical race theology, this self-critical reflection can enable white Christian denominations—from the mainline to the marginal—to at least recognize, if not outright reckon with, their own failures in both a historic and contemporary sense. In so doing, they can grapple with how a complicity with racism and violence has enmeshed them into their visions of both church and state.

When critical race theology encourages vital self-critical reflection on complicity in sanctified violence, we cannot only look to decades and centuries past. Mass shooting events and domestic terrorist attacks have become an increasingly prevalent aspect of our shared experience as a nation and a people over the past quarter century. Defining "mass public shootings" as incidents where four or more individuals were killed by a single shooter within a twenty-four- hour period, an estimated 158 mass

---

[43] Isgrigg, *Pentecost in Tulsa,* 53–71.

[44] Robert P. Jones, *White Too Long: The Legacy of White Supremacy in American Christianity* (New York: Simon & Schuster, 2020).

shootings occurred between 1976 and 2018, an average of 3.7 each year.[45] In recent years, they have become more commonplace, with an average of twenty occurring each year between 2009 and 2020.[46] Due largely to the unprecedented psychological stresses and unique challenges posed by the global COVID-19 pandemic, gun-related fatalities skyrocketed to record highs nationwide in 2020, with more than 45,000 people in gun-related deaths that were reported that year, a 15 percent increase over the previous year.[47] Data compiled on gun violence and related deaths have revealed that those rates have only gotten worse in subsequent years.[48]

Approaching gun violence as *sanctified* violence means understanding the processes that sanctify these events and tragedies in the public imagination. Whether addressing accidental weapon discharges, violent crimes involving firearms, shootings of unarmed citizens by either law enforcement officers or armed vigilantes, or mass shootings as terroristic acts, lobbying wings of organizations like the National Rifle Association (NRA) have actively shut down all serious conversations of gun control in recent decades, refashioning an association of hobbyists into a public relations firm for death-dealing atrocities.

Some of these mass shootings are fueled by underlying ideological agendas while others are motivated by personal grievances. As a nation, we have witnessed mass shooting events that have targeted Black churchgoers at a Wednesday night Bible study in Charleston, South Carolina; Jewish worshippers in a Pittsburgh, Pennsylvania,

---

[45] Grant Duwe, "Patterns and Prevalence of Lethal Mass Violence." *Criminology and Public Policy* 19, no. 1 (2020): 17–35.

[46] "Mass Shootings," Everytown, https://www.everytown.org/issues/mass-shootings/.

[47] "Gun Violence and COVID-19 in 2020: A Year of Colliding Crises," Everytown Research and Policy, https://everytownresearch.org/report/gun-violence-and-covid-19-in-2020-a-year-of-colliding-crises/.

[48] Gun Violence Archive (2023), https://www.gunviolencearchive.org/.

synagogue; Latinx shoppers at a Walmart in El Paso, Texas; Black customers at a Buffalo, New York, grocery store; Asian massage therapists at metro Atlanta, Georgia, spas; Latinx schoolchildren in an Uvalde, Texas, elementary school; and Sikhs peacefully gathered in an Oak Creek, Wisconsin, temple. Other mass shooting events seem terrifyingly random. Addressing the sanctifying of this violence, we must face two intertwined concerns: the misplaced notion that guns alone can solve the nation's addiction to sanctified violence and the gun lobby's uncanny ability to dissemble its way past any constructive criticism of America's obsession with gun culture.

In *The Violence Project: How to Stop a Mass Shooting Epidemic*, Jill Peterson and James Densley approach mass shootings as a psychologist and a sociologist, respectively. They examine why mass public shootings occur and, more importantly, how they might be prevented in the future. They establish the root causes of mass shootings as a means of figuring out how to stop them by examining hundreds of data points in the life histories of more than 170 mass shooters—from their childhood and adolescence to their mental health and criminal motives. Peterson and Densley identify four commonalities among mass shooters: (1) survivors of childhood abuse and exposure to traumatic experiences; (2) a crisis in days and weeks prior to the shooting; (3) following a "script" or ideology, often found in media or online; and (4) opportunity.[49] Rather than merely the obligatory offering of "thoughts and prayers" for the victims and loved ones of mass shootings, Peterson and Densley share their data-driven solutions for exactly what we must do at the individual level, in our communities, and as a country, to put an end to these tragedies that have defined our modern era.

In the March 27, 2023, shooting at Covenant School in Nashville, Tennessee, the shooter, Audrey Elizabeth Hale, was able to breach the locked doors of the school fully armed with tactical

---

[49] Jill Peterson and James Densley, *The Violence Project: How to Stop a Mass Shooting* (New York: Abrams Press, 2022).

gear, two rifles, and a handgun. After killing three students—
Evelyn Dieckhaus, Hallie Scruggs, and William Kinney—and
three adult members of the school's staff—Cynthia Peak, Mike
Hill, and Katherine Koonce—Hale was eventually shot and killed
by the Metro Nashville Police Department (MNPD) officers.[50]
In the immediate aftermath of the incident, the MNPD held a
press briefing and identified the shooter as a twenty-eight-year-old
former student of the school who was a "white female." They later
clarified that the shooter identified as a transgender male.[51]

In their zealous effort to find any reason other than lax
gun laws and soaring gun sales for this senseless bloodshed,
many conservative politicians and pundits twisted the fact that
the shooter had been misgendered in the initial reports to spew
transphobic vitriol and advance anti-LGBTQIA+ agendas in the
public sphere. These commentators enthusiastically condemned
Hale as a "transgender killer," a politically charged phrase that
incorrectly suggested that Hale was a serial killer who targeted
transgender people. The contrary was true: the shooter was a killer
who happened to be a transgender person.

More than a semantic difference, the phrase was echoed by
ruthlessly retrograde political forces who repeatedly craft and use
buzzwords, catchphrases, and sound bites in the media to oppress
huge swaths of humanity. Focusing on and vilifying Hale's sexuality
further, these right-wing observers then characterized the shooter
as one who "targets Christian school[s]." The motive for the

---

[50] Kelsey Beyeler, Logan Butts, D. Patrick Rodgers, Stephen Elliot,
and Matt Masters, "Covenant School Shooting Leaves Seven Dead
in 'Targeted Attack'," *Nashville Scene*, March 28, 2023, https://www.
nashvillescene.com/news/pithinthewind/covenant-school-shooting-
leaves-seven-dead-in-targeted-attack/article_32dc2cd6-cd6d-11ed-932a-
5b19d521176f.html.

[51] Beyeler, Butts, Rodgers, Elliot, and Masters, "Covenant School
Shooting Leaves Seven Dead in 'Targeted Attack'."

massacre was still murky and undetermined at that time. Hale, the investigation revealed, was an alum of the Covenant School and, therefore, targeted their alma mater because of familiarity rather than its ecclesial affiliation.

Lastly, the writings that law enforcement found on Hale's social media accounts were the writings of an emotionally disturbed individual that led to the murder of seven human beings—three children and four adults, including the shooter. But the writings, the "manifesto" did not slaughter those people on March 27. The two assault rifles, the handgun, and the ample ammunition that the shooter easily bought and readily brought with them did that.

Following the Covenant shooting, Elie Mystal argued,

> We live like this because of the Republican Party. These school shootings are not tragedies. They are choices made by our government. Every other country on Earth has violent people with a motive to do harm to others. Every other country has people with mental health issues. Every other country has access to media and art that glorifies or trivializes violence. But these school shootings don't happen in every other country, because every other country doesn't have easy, nearly unfettered access to weapons of mass murder.[52]

The sanctifying of gun violence in this country has made access to these weapons and ammunition easy. The sanctifying of gun violence has made the pursuit for answers about and solutions to the problems of violence into grand unspeakable mysteries. The sanctifying of gun violence has made this event, as tragic as it was, dangerously common.

---

[52] Elie Mystal, "Republicans Want You to Forget Their Complicity in the Nashville Shooting," *The Nation: Politics*, March 29, 2023, https://www.thenation.com/article/society/nashville-shooting-conservative-reaction/.

Landmark legislative actions at the state level and judicial decisions at the federal level have emboldened the NRA and larger gun lobby's efforts to transform US societies into a gun-owner's utopia. Following Tennessee's passage of a "Stand Your Ground" law in 2007 and the US Supreme Court's 5–4 decision in *District of Columbia v. Heller* in the summer of 2008, gun and ammunition sales saw a meteoric rise during the Obama presidency. More state legislatures, including Tennessee's, expanded legal access to guns in the 2010s. In addition to legal access, Tennessee quite literally makes tons of guns. According to data from the Bureau of Alcohol, Tobacco, and Firearms, 185,000 guns were produced in Tennessee in 2021. Most of these weapons were manufactured by Beretta, the famed Italian gun maker, after moving their US headquarters to Gallatin, Tennessee, in 2016. Likewise, the iconic US firearms manufacturer Smith & Wesson relocated its headquarters to eastern Tennessee in 2023 after more than a century of being based in Massachusetts. Both companies proudly touted Tennessee's strong gun lobby as the basis for moving their bases of operation to enjoy the state's gun-friendly political climate.[53]

According to Jonathan Metzl, many people express a need to purchase and own a gun in response to triggering events that "are about the breakdown of community infrastructure, the lack of investment in civic space, lack of trust in communal structures. We need to take people's concerns about fear and safety seriously and really try to address them."[54] Metzl's triggering events and call to take seriously people's concerns are vital for a critical race theology that works to understand the vast complex of death that I call *sanctified violence*. These are

---

[53] Eli Motycka, "Under the Gun: Nashvillians Learn to Live in an Armed Society," *Nashville Scene*, November 2, 2023, https://www.nashvillescene.com/news/coverstory/gun-laws-ownership-nashville-tennessee/article_96e33978-7758-11ee-9337-77b53ef113e6.html.

[54] Motycka, "Under the Gun."

on-the-ground concerns that demand life-giving constructive responses amid a death-dealing world.

For several decades, the NRA and other pro-gun extremist interests have been the prime movers in defining the terms of the gun ownership debate on the state and national levels. Yet, the killings at Covenant School churned Nashville beyond belief, shifting the political calculus at the State Capitol, where pro-gun GOP lawmakers have held supermajorities in the House and Senate. While vigils and prayer services were being held in Nashville, the Tennessee chapter of Moms Demand Action, a gun safety advocacy group, organized immediate, sustained protests that rallied outside of the State Capitol seeking gun safety legislation.[55] After leading a protest for gun safety legislation on the House floor in April 2023, Rep. Justin Jones (D-Nashville) and Rep. Justin Pearson (D-Memphis) were expelled by House Republicans from the legislature. A similar resolution to expel Rep. Gloria Johnson (D-Knoxville) failed by a single vote. Acting more like lawbreakers than lawmakers, the blatant abuse of power by the Tennessee's Republican politicians surprisingly drew national attention. Protesters and observers in attendance chanted their support of the trio while calling Republican lawmakers "fascists" as they entered the chamber. With audience sections above the chamber filled to overflowing, additional supporters watched the proceedings on televisions in the lobby as well as on their phones. "The fact that this vote is happening is shocking, undemocratic and without precedent," White House press secretary Karine Jean-Pierre said. "Across Tennessee and across America, our kids are paying the price for the actions of Republican lawmakers."[56] Within a matter

---

[55] "Nashville Shooting: Live Updates," *New York* Times, July 3, 2023, https://www.nytimes.com/live/2023/03/28/us/nashville-school-shooting-tennessee#nashville-shooting-victims.

[56] Stephen Elliot, Connor Daryani, and Kelsey Beyeler, "Republicans Vote to Expel Reps. Jones and Pearson; Johnson Expulsion Fails,"

of days, the "Tennessee Three" (as Jones, Pearson, and Johnson eventually were dubbed by the media) even had a special meetings with Vice President Kamala Harris and President Joe Biden, who supported a renewed call for an assault weapons ban and the revitalization of America's democratic values.[57] Despite the highly duplicitous, partisan, and antidemocratic effort by the Republicans to oust the Tennessee Three from the state legislature, Pearson and Jones were later reinstated on an interim basis by local officials who adhered to the overwhelming desires of their constituents. They eventually won special elections to finish their terms.

In August 2023, state legislators returned to Nashville for a special legislative session called by Governor Bill Lee, who announced the session amid harsh public reaction against the state's lax gun laws. In a press release issued on May 8, 2023, the governor said the session was intended to "keep Tennessee communities safe and preserve the constitutional rights of law-abiding citizens." Moreover, Lee's response to the recent shooting implied a potential revision of Tennessee's legal protections for firearms, a move that would be in direct conflict with the conservative credo of unlimited access to guns that has become sacrosanct in Tennessee over the past two decades. Unfortunately, once news coverage of the school shooting decreased and the black-and-red "I stand with Covenant" lawn signs began to fade, state lawmakers passed only one piece of legislation related to guns, a vague hodgepodge of statutes exempting firearm safety products from sales taxes, enabling Tennesseans to request free state gun locks and mandating

---

Nashville Scene, April 6, 2023, https://www.nashvillescene.com/news/pithinthewind/republicans-vote-to-expel-reps-jones-and-pearson-johnson-expulsion-fails/article_9ddb9945-a179-56ff-a42f-340af7ef6a0e.html.

[57] Josh Boak, Aamer Madhani, and Chris Megerian, "Biden Thanks 'Tennessee Three' for 'Standing up,'" Associated Press, October 10, 2023, https://apnews.com/article/biden-tennessee-three-lawmakers-pearson-jones-johnson-bb74e4bdb9628d53d64d13acf004248c.

safe-storage content in handgun training courses.[58] After reframing the session as a crime-focused work session, Lee delivered closing remarks. Despite all the ensuing chaos and controversy that erupted because of the shooting, Lee praised Covenant School parents for being a part of the public "engagement process," which became an exercise in futility.[59]

While Richard Hofstadter posed the question in the wake of assassinations and social turmoil of the 1960s, it has even greater resonance in our moment: "Why is it that in all other modern democratic societies those endangered ask to have such men disarmed, while in the United States alone they insist on arming themselves?"[60] Unable to rely on law enforcement and legislators to implement and enforce any gun control laws, some Americans have decided to risk gun ownership to help manage the fear and anxiety of living in a nation awash with weapons. While mass shootings have eroded many Americans' shared sense of security, it is also the frequency of intimate partner violence, retaliatory gun violence, accidental gun firings, gun-related criminal activity, and suicide by firearm that are killing people in growing numbers. The recent US Supreme Court decision *New York State Rifle & Pistol Association Inc. v. Bruen* (2022) has weaponized the court's Second Amendment extremism (pun fully intended). The majority opinion argued that a New York State law that required applicants for unrestricted concealed-carry licenses to demonstrate a special need for self-defense violated the Fourteenth Amendment by

---

[58] "Video: Gov. Lee Statement on Public Safety Special Session," Tennessee: Office of the Governor, August 29, 2023, https://www.tn.gov/governor/news/2023/8/29/video--gov--lee-statement-on-public-safety-special-session-0.html.

[59] "Video: Gov. Lee Statement on Public Safety Special Session."

[60] Richard Hofstadter, "America as a Gun Culture," *American Heritage* 21, no. 6 (October 1970), https://www.americanheritage.com/america-gun-culture.

preventing law-abiding citizens with ordinary "self-defense" needs from exercising their Second Amendment right to keep and bear arms in public for the purposes of protection.[61]

There are more guns in this country than people, mostly concentrated in the hands of "super-owners," a term used by Jonathan Metzl in *Dying of Whiteness: How the Politics of Racial Resentment Is Killing America's Heartland* (2019). As both a sociologist and psychiatrist, Metzl argues that struggling white voters tend to support politicians whose policies are increasingly endangering the voters' own lives. According to Metzl, there is a "politics of racial resentment" that purportedly claims to uphold the conservative values of security and austerity but is predicated on the psychological appeal rooted in white supremacy. The tragic irony, as Metzl indicates, is that the grievances and backlash by politics of white resentment "demand that working poor and middle-class white Americans vote against their own biological self-interests."[62] On issues with life-or-death consequences, chief among them being gun safety and health care, states where leaders once strove toward ideological moderation and compromise have now embraced extremist views as well as legislation that literally endangers their most vulnerable citizens. Even more, "the kinds of mortal trade-offs white Americans make in order to defend an imagined sense of whiteness," Metzl contends, has created "a narrative about how 'whiteness' becomes a formation worth living and dying for, and how, in myriad ways and on multiple levels, white Americans bet their lives on particular sets of meanings associated with whiteness, even in the face of clear threats to mortality or to common sense."[63]

---

[61] New York State Rifle & Pistol Association Inc. v. Bruen, 597 U.S. (2022).

[62] Jonathan Metzl, *Dying of Whiteness: How the Politics of Racial Resentment Is Killing America's Heartland* (New York: Basic Books, 2019), 10.

[63] Metzl, *Dying of Whiteness*, 270.

What makes this argument even more harrowing is evidence that white communities have embraced far-right ideas as inseparable from their own identities. As I have argued in previous chapters, right-wing politicians use dog whistle politics and coded rhetoric to convince white voters that their policies safeguard the position, privilege, and power of white citizens within the American social hierarchy. The rhetoric of white grievance politics has been so effective that the new laws have had unmistakably detrimental or chronically lethal effects on white communities. Metzl argues that white people support these policies and policymakers as a way of retaining vestiges of "lost white privilege" against the encroachment of Black, Indigenous, and People of Color (BIPOC) communities achieving greater social access. Subsequently, these aggrieved white people are willing to suffer and die to keep others who they have deemed undeserving and undesirable from enjoying a better quality of life.

Exploring the sanctification of gun violence reveals a deep history of the extent to which white people have gone to keep a qualitative difference between themselves and the undesirable Other. This history can be instructive for a critical race theology that faces many different forms of sanctified violence today. The Second Amendment was ratified originally to help land-owning white men arm themselves against Native Americans, enslaved African peoples, and anyone else they perceived as a threat to their property. In the centuries since the nation's founding, the mentality of a majority-white, majority-male electorate has only reinforced the furthest extremes of gun ownership, in turn fueling a cultural obsession with the Second Amendment as a sacred right.

Sanctifying violence like gun violence depends on domination of cultural norms and priorities by the nonstate actors like voters, corporate lobbyists, and affinity groups like communities of faith. Different from state-enacted violence like that explored in an earlier chapter, sanctified violence culturally ensconces violent acts, events, and actors by manipulating municipal, state, and federal regulations to reinforce systems of dominance and oppression. There are more stringent rules and regulations on most amusement park rides than on the possession and ownership of firearms in this country. Assessed through critical race theology's examination of sanctified violence, that sort of disparity can be understood more clearly. Rather than exercise concern for human well-being, white supremacy focuses on legal liability.

The 2005 Protection of Lawful Commerce in Arms Act (PLCAA) has served as an effective end-run against citizens being able to sue gunmakers and retailers for any damage done by their products.[64] Unlike other industries, including automakers, pharmaceutical companies, fast food chains, and tobacco companies, the gun industry and gun trade are protected from lawsuits because no injury or death by a firearm is a manufacturing or design flaw. A gun is intentionally designed to wound, maim, or kill. Responsibility and accountability for gun violence, then, is refocused on the due diligence and assurances that only trained and trustworthy individuals can acquire and use these products. Gun violence has been sanctified precisely for the death-dealing power over the Other that the gun can give its user. Yet, in his pithy summation of the societal impact of "the politics of whiteness," Michael Eric Dyson insists "it's killing us, and, quiet as it's kept, it's killing you, too."[65]

Effective use of sanctified violence by dominant groups—whether those groups are numerically greater than their opposition or not—happens in many ways, but it is aimed at neutralizing the Other and all real and perceived rival power centers within a society. The goal of neutralization tempts dominant groups—white

---

[64] Protection of Lawful Commerce in Arms Act of 2005, Pub. L. No. 109-92, 119 Stat. 2095 (2005).

[65] Michael Eric Dyson, *Tears We Cannot Stop: A Sermon to White America* (New York: St. Martin's Griffin, 2017), 44.

conservatives in this country—to create a scapegoat to justify their sinister objectives. As Girard has argued, in this way, they are able to blame the Other for all the nation's problems. According to Girard, the scapegoat mechanism demands some level of unconsciousness among the nation's populace. The victim cannot be considered as innocent. Girard shows that "to be genuine, in order to exist as a social reality, as a stabilized viewpoint on some act of collective violence, scapegoating must remain nonconscious. Persecutors do not realize that they chose their victim for inadequate reasons, or perhaps for no reason at all, at random."[66] As Kwame Anthony Appiah contends in *Cosmopolitanism*, "When you do something that harms someone else, you must be able to justify it."[67]

From Plato's *Republic* and Augustine's *City of God*, one is reminded how much the body politic as a political reality—such as a city, kingdom, realm, and/or nation-state—is considered metaphorically to be a physical body. Historically, this analogy originated in Greco-Roman philosophy with depictions of the sovereign typically as the body's head, and the analogy may also be extended to other anatomical parts. By the high and late medieval eras, however, the imagistic concept of "body politic" eventually expanded to include a jurisprudential significance and modern salience that would come to be identified with the legal theory of the corporation. Within the modern era, the English term *body politic* is sometimes used in modern legal contexts to describe a type of legal person, typically the state itself or a citizen or comparable entity connected to it.

---

[66] René Girard, "Generative Scapegoating," in *Violent Origins: Walter Burkett, René Girard, and Jonathan Z. Smith on Ritual Killing and Cultural Formation*, ed. R. G. Hamerton-Kelly (Palo Alto, CA: Stanford University Press, 1987), 78.

[67] Kwame Anthony Appiah, *Cosmopolitanism: Ethics in a World of Strangers* (New York: W. W. Norton, 2007), 151.

In Thomas Hobbes's theory of the state, the idea of modern body politic morphs beyond a human facsimile to becoming a divine substitute. In his classic philosophical treatise *Leviathan* (1651), Hobbes famously argues that life in the state of nature is "nasty, brutish, and short," resulting in nothing less than an egotistic state of "war of all against all."[68] With all human beings scrambling and scraping to maximize their own self-interests and material interests out of an innate desire for self-preservation, Hobbes (along with John Locke) asserts that the only way to prevent perpetual chaos was for people to agree in a "social contract," surrendering their natural rights to a sovereign state that, in turn, would allow them to keep law and order as well as protect existing property rights. According to Hobbes, life governed under a volitional regime was deemed "a necessary evil" believed to be much better than life in the state of nature. Hobbes maintained that sovereignty was absolute and the head could certainly not be "of lesser power" than the body of the people. Yet, with the social contract, he emphasized that the body politic—Leviathan, the "mortal god"—was fictional and artificial rather than natural, derived from an original decision by the people to constitute a sovereign.[69]

For critical race theology to impact life in the United States, we must recognize the important influence that a Hobbesian theory of the emergent nation-state as a body politic has exercised on

---

[68] Thomas Hobbes, *Leviathan, or the Matter, Forme, & Power of a Common-wealth Ecclesiasticall and Civill* (London: Andrew Crooke, 1651; Prepared for the McMaster University Archive of the History of Economic Thought, by Rod Hay), 78, 191.

[69] Katherine Bootle Attie, "Re-Membering the Body Politic: Hobbes and the Construction of Civic Immortality," *ELH* 75, no. 3 (2008): 500, 502; Quentin Skinner, *From Humanism to Hobbes: Studies in Rhetoric and Politics* (Cambridge: Cambridge University Press, 2018), 342–43.

subsequent political thinkers.[70] For John Locke, the chief defect in the state of nature is that it lacks a common judge to interpret the law of nature and a government to impose sanctions against violators. While right or wrong are eternally so—*a priori* to the existence of law—governments ultimately come into existence to use their laws to enforce what is naturally and morally right. Furthermore, Locke asserted that the natural right to private property precedes the social contract because individuals extend their own personalities into the objects produced from the state of nature. Valid claims to property can only be mediated under the watchful eye and forceful arm of the state. Samuel von Pufendorf recapitulated Hobbes's explanation of the origin of the state as a social contract and equally extended his notion of personhood, arguing that the state must be a specifically moral person with a rational nature and not simply coercive power.[71]

By the eighteenth century, Hobbes's theory of the state as an artificial body politic gained wide acceptance in Britain, continental Europe, and the North American context.[72] Writing during the American Revolutionary War, British reformist John Cartwright

---

[70] Laurens van Apeldoorn and Robin Douglass, eds., *Hobbes on Politics and Religion* (New York: Oxford University Press, 2018); Gabriel L. Negretto, "Hobbes' *Leviathan:* The Irresistible Power of a Mortal God," https://gabrielnegretto.com/wp-content/uploads/2016/04/Hobbes_Leviathan_The-Irresistible_Power_of_a_Mortal_God.pdf; Ben Jones, "The Natural Kingdom of God in Hobbes's Political Thought," *History of European Ideas* 45, no. 3 (2019): 436–53; Devin Stauffer, "'Of Religion' in Hobbes's *Leviathan*," *Journal of Politics* 72, no. 3 (2010): 868–79; Alan Cromartie, "The God of Thomas Hobbes," *Historical Journal* 51, no. 4 (2008): 857–79; Peter Geach, "The Religion of Thomas Hobbes," *Religious Studies* 17, no. 4 (1981): 549–58.

[71] Quentin Skinner, *From Humanism to Hobbes: Studies in Rhetoric and Politics* (Cambridge: Cambridge University Press, 2018), 365–66.

[72] Skinner, *From Humanism to Hobbes*, 352, 365–66, 370–71.

emphasized the artificial and immortal character of the body politic in 1780; arguing it was better conceived as a machine operating by the "due action and re-action of the ... springs of the constitution" than a human body, he determined "the body politic" was " not corporeal ... not formed from the dust of the earth. It is purely intellectual; and its life-spring is truth."[73]

Examining the radicalism of the American Revolution, Gordon Wood addresses the Founders' love–hate relationship with democracy as form of human governance. According to Wood,

> Democracy became for Americans more than the broader suffrage and the competitive politics of their system.... Democracy actually represented a new social order with new kinds of linkages holding people together. Not that in the new democratic society the monarchical influence of patronage and kinship was ever entirely lost or that the republican emphasis on affection and benevolence was ignored: no society or culture, however dynamic, could ever slough off the past completely.[74]

Part of critical race theology is an intentional wrestling with the past that cannot be sloughed off. For example, Founders such as James Madison held an apprehensive view of common citizens within a democratic republic as "but little superior to the untutored herd" that has lingered within more than two and a half centuries of American political thought.[75] This view stands in stark contrast

---

[73] Pasi Ihalainen, "Towards an Immortal Political Body: The State Machine in Eighteenth-Century English Political Discourse," *Contributions to the History of Concepts* 5, no. 1 (2009): 34–35.

[74] Gordon Wood, *The Radicalism of the American Revolution* (New York: Vintage Books, 1993), 232.

[75] Wood, *Radicalism of the American Revolution*, 235; James Madison, in *The Debates of the State Conventions on the Adoption of the Federal Constitution*, vol. 3, ed. Jonathan Elliot (Philadelphia, 1876), 536–37; "The Worcester

to the great reverence and regard for what Martin Luther King Jr. has called the "great wells of democracy," but the future of American electoral politics depends on entrusting the government to the governed.[76] According to John Dewey, all American citizens of good faith and true conscience who are genuinely concerned about the state of the nation need to "get rid of the ideas that lead us to believe that democratic conditions automatically maintain themselves, or that they can be identified with fulfillment of prescriptions laid down in a constitution."[77] In other words, democracy demands constant maintenance and restoration, or it will surely die.

Cultural insularity, moral rigidity, and institutional racism are a potent and highly toxic blend in today's body politic. Critical race theology recognizes how white nationalist political commitments have entwined with Evangelical Christian theological themes to produce a dangerous sectarianism. As Trump and others depict contemporary electoral politics as nothing less than blood sport, American conservatism has become completely out of touch

---

Speculator" (1787), in *American Political Writings during the Founding Era: 1760–1805,* vol. 1, ed. Charles S. Hyneman and Donald S. Lutz (Indianapolis: Liberty Fund, 1983); [Trenchard and Gordon], *Cato's Letters,* II, 35: Tillotson, quoted in Leon Guilhamet, *The Sincere Ideal: Studies on Sincerity in Eighteenth-Century English Literature* (Montreal: McGill Queen's University Press, 1974), 16; Ramsay, *Oration on American Independence,* in *Ramsay … Selections from His Writings,* ed. Brunhouse, 185; Thomas Jefferson, *A Summary View of the Rights of British America* (1774), in *Papers of Jefferson,* vol. 1, ed. Julian P. Boyd et al. (Princeton, NJ: Princeton University Press, 1950), 134; Gordon S. Wood, *Revolutionary Characters: What Made the Founders Different* (New York: Penguin Press, 2007), 141–72.

[76] Martin Luther King Jr., "I See the Promised Land," in *A Testament of Hope: The Essential Writings and Speeches of Martin Luther King Jr.,* ed. James M. Washington (New York: HarperOne, 1986), 286.

[77] John Dewey, *Freedom and Culture* (New York: G. P. Putnam's Sons, 1939), 34–35.

with the broad swath of Americans. "It is the strangest story," Michael Gerson writes, "how so many evangelicals lost their interest in decency, and how a religious tradition called by grace became defined by resentment."[78] We are experiencing a vision of white Christian nationalism as a cultural and political project that is rooted historically in Southern defenses of chattel slavery and "Lost Cause" religiosity as well as Jim and Jane Crow policies to justify white supremacy.

In her study of the rise of the Religious Right, Anthea Butler analyzes show how Republicans spent the last sixty years within the realm of US presidential politics either directly or indirectly appealing to the racism of white Evangelicals.[79]

> Because conservative evangelicalism embraces patriarchal culture imbued with a persecution complex, its leaders will always have an excuse for excesses, transgressions, and sins. And sin for evangelicals is always personal, not corporate, and God is always available to forgive deserving individuals, especially ... if the sinner is a white man.[80]

As a renowned evangelist and confidant to US presidents, Billy Graham had a key role in promoting American exceptionalism

---

[78] Michael Gerson, "The Last Temptation," *The Atlantic*, March 11, 2018, https://www.theatlantic.com/magazine/archive/2018/04/the-last-temptation/554066/.

[79] Ibram X. Kendi, *Stamped from the Beginning: The Definitive History of Racist Ideas in America* (New York: Nation Books, 2016); Gary Dorrien, *Breaking White Supremacy: Martin Luther King, Jr. and the Black Social Gospel* (New Haven, CT: Yale University Press, 2018); Jemar Tisby, *The Color of Compromise: The Truth about the American Church's Complicity in Racism* (Grand Rapids: Zondervan, 2019); Jones, *White Too Long*; Anthea Butler, *White Evangelical Racism: The Politics of Morality in America* (Chapel Hill: University of North Carolina Press, 2021).

[80] Butler, *White Evangelical Racism*, 10–11.

and anticommunism to millions of followers while also espousing anti-Black racism by connecting whiteness with being a "true American" who "cloaked themselves in morality, respectability, and power."[81] J. Edgar Hoover spent the first decade of the FBI's existence honing his own mythic status in the popular imagination almost single-handedly through the Bureau's pursuit of some of the era's most infamous militants and notorious gangsters. While Hoover was not an Evangelical in his own religious identification, his growing throngs of Christian admirers anointed him as their political champion, believing he would lead America back to God. Following Butler's work, a critical race theology today is able to observe how evangelicalism throughout much of the twentieth century was not genuinely a religious group so much as "a nationalistic political movement whose purpose is to support the hegemony of white Christian men over and against the flourishing of others."[82] Today's nonspiritual fears of a "deep state"—a secretive cabal of unaccountable government officials working in a conspiratorial manner against the will of the people—can be tracked back to what Lerone Martin called Hoover's "anti-statist statism."[83]

FBI agents, under Hoover's leadership, routinely attended spiritual retreats and worship services, and therefore deliberately created an FBI religious culture that fashioned his "G-men" into soldiers and ministers of Christian America. Martin shows how prominent religious figures, such as Billy Graham, Bishop Fulton Sheen, and countless other ministers from across the country, partnered with the FBI, laundering Bureau intelligence through

---

[81] Butler, *White Evangelical Racism*, 98.

[82] Butler, *White Evangelical Racism*, 138.

[83] Lerone A. Martin, *The Gospel of J. Edgar Hoover: How the FBI Aided and Abetted the Rise of White Christian Nationalism* (Princeton, NJ: Princeton University Press, 2023), 6.

their sermons, even as their faithful congregations crowned Hoover the adjudicator of true Evangelical faith and allegiance. These partnerships not only blurred the notion of church–state separation, they solidified the political norms of modern white evangelicalism, and they eventually contributed to the political rise of white Christian nationalism, establishing religion and race as the bedrock of the modern national security state.[84] They set the terms for today's state-enacted and sanctified domestic terrorist violence.

How are we supposed to live in a society where we must be so fearful and resentful? Throughout the twentieth and early twenty-first centuries, conservative politicians and other right-wing forces of demagoguery have exploited illiberalism, racism, patriarchy, xenophobia, revanchist politics, and rampant anti-intellectualism as tools of reactionary politicking in the United States. From the anti-Semitic machinations of Henry Ford in the 1920s to the pro-Nazi proclivities of Charles Lindbergh to the Nixon administration's Southern Strategy in the 1960s and 1970s to the heady "Shock and Y'all" days of the George W. Bush era in the early 2000s, we have seen how "backlash" politics that were once a white working-class mainstay eventually became a cultural cul-de-sac of worn-out tropes and white middle-class grievance politics. As the Cold War ended, many conservatives stopped genuflecting to

---

[84] Nelson Blackstock, *Cointelpro: The FBI's Secret War on Political Freedom* (New York: Vintage Books, 1976); James Kirkpatrick Davis, *Spying on America: The FBI's Domestic Counterintelligence Program* (London: Bloomsbury Publishing, 1992); Ward Churchill and Jim Vander Wall, *Agents of Repression: The FBI's Secret Wars Against the Black Panther Party and the American Indian Movement* (Boston: South End Press, 2002); Michael Friedly and David Gallen, eds., *Martin Luther King, Jr.: The FBI File* (New York: Carroll & Graf, 1993); Clayborne Carson, ed., *Malcolm X: The FBI File* (New York: Carroll & Graf 2012); William J. Maxwell, ed., *James Baldwin: The FBI File* (New York: Arcade Books, 2017).

democracy and freedom and used emergent forms of media—cable news and talk radio most especially—to spread their grievances.

Anthea Butler offers a powerful insight into how so much of this consternation is happening because they, particularly white Evangelical men, could only see themselves and their politics as "rooted in biblical admonitions and piety."[85] She further argues that these groups have convinced themselves that "the racism that underlay their religious movement could be waved away through belief, theology, and denial."[86] Therefore, when they are confronted about their past offenses and abuses of power, white Evangelical men often feel enraged and persecuted rather than demonstrating any interest in being held accountable.[87] For critical race theology, pursuing accountability engages concepts of sin, evil, innocence, and complicity.

Within mimetic theory, there is a rich and storied history in religion and theology to address humans striving to control their more desperate and dangerous desires toward wickedness. When we witness someone's experience as a worst-case scenario, it becomes incredibly difficult to reimagine concepts of sin and evil differently. The 2022 Netflix series *Dahmer—Monster: The Jeffrey Dahmer Story* controversially depicted Jeffrey Dahmer, the infamous cannibalistic serial killer, with a possibility for sympathy. If one could sidestep the more sensationalistic and salacious elements of the series, this televised portrayal of Jeffrey Dahmer is a mirror that provides a glimpse into a dark, twisted facet of America's soul. A cultural production like this gives viewers a unique opportunity to explore concerns about theodicy or "the problem of evil." Are people born evil or do they become that way? Why do bad things happen to good, innocent people? Why does a benevolent and loving God allow people to commit evil acts? Should we really have

---

[85] Butler, *White Evangelical Racism*, 99.

[86] Butler, *White Evangelical Racism*, 99.

[87] Butler, *White Evangelical Racism*, 145.

sympathy for such a monster? What do the worst people among us deserve from the innocent?

Whenever the topic of theodicy arises, any theologian worth their salt appreciates how thorny it is contemplating issues such as evil and malice as part of the human condition. In this regard, one most certainly sympathizes with the Apostle Paul's declaration in Romans 7:15, "I do not understand what I do. For what I want to do I do not do, but what I hate I do." Like its antecedents in certain branches of classical Hellenistic thought, Pauline Christianity demonstrates life in dualistic terms, split between "the Spirit" and "the flesh." Paul warns his readers not to gratify the desires of the flesh; gratifying the flesh can lead to some terrible things aside from temporary pleasure. Could this be what Friedrich Nietzsche meant by stating, "Whoever fights monsters should see to it that in the process he does not become a monster. And when you look long into an abyss, the abyss also looks into you."[88] There's certainly that option. If we see our opponents, rivals, or even enemies as "monsters," as less than human, it becomes possible to dispose of them. Monsters, almost by definition, don't change. If past is prologue, we can skirt around ethical considerations and abdicate moral responsibility to others if we simply change the category. Yet, all nonwhite and/or non-Christian peoples are considered, as Kathryn Gin Lum poignantly states, as "historyless heathens and stagnating pagans" from a white Christian nationalist worldview.[89] Whenever we categorize our fellow humans as something other than human, only greater levels of evil ensue.

When writing about actual monstrosities in *City of God*, Augustine of Hippo recognizes that if anyone is born of a human,

---

[88] Friedrich Nietzsche, *Beyond Good and Evil: Prelude to a Philosophy of the Future* (Chicago: Henry Regnery, 1955), 146.

[89] Lum, Kathryn Gin, "The Historyless Heathen and the Stagnating Pagan: History as Non-Native Category?" *Religion and American Culture: A Journal of Interpretation* 28, no. 1 (2018): 52–91.

they are a human. No matter how monstrous they look or act, they deserve to be afforded the same respect and dignity offered other humans. Christian tradition contends that, if a person is a human, they have humanity and all the rights and privileges that come with that. In that case, we are only left with the God of forgiveness. The failures of society, family, education, government, and even religion all play a role in crafting monsters. But the monsters are just humans whether we like it or not. If they are human, then they can be redeemed. And if the worst people can be redeemed, then there is hope for us all.

In *Moral Man and Immoral Society*, Reinhold Niebuhr addresses the situation this way:

> In the task of that redemption the most effective agents will be men [and women] who have substituted some new illusions for the abandoned ones. The most important of these illusions is that the collective life of [humankind] can achieve perfect justice. It is a very valuable illusion for the moment; for justice cannot be approximated if the hope of its perfect realization does not generate a sublime madness in the soul. Nothing but such madness will do battle with the malignant power and "spiritual wickedness in high places." The illusion is dangerous because it encourages terrible fanaticisms. It must therefore be brought under the control of reason. One can only hope that reason will not destroy it before its work is done.[90]

This Niebuhrian notion—a sublime madness in the soul—is a wonderful crystallization of what the great and grand tradition of social protest and civil disobedience has brought forth in American life and thought. In contrast to Lewis F. Powell Jr.'s depiction of young people protesting for social justice as demonic harbingers of

---

[90] Reinhold Niebuhr, *Moral Man and Immoral Society: A Study in Ethics and Politics* (New York: Charles Scribner's Sons, 1932), 277.

doomsday, Rev. Dr. Martin Luther King Jr. waxed enthusiastically about the revolutionary potential of the youth and what it meant for a just society.[91] In a 1968 speech entitled "A New Sense of Direction," King said,

> When they took their struggle to the streets, a new spirit of resistance was born. Inspired by the boldness and ingenuity of Negroes, white youth stirred into action and formed an alliance that roused the conscience of the nation. It is difficult to exaggerate the creative contributions of young Negroes. They took nonviolent resistance, first employed in Montgomery, Alabama, in mass dimensions, and developed original forms of application—sit-ins, freedom rides, and wade-ins. To accomplish these, they first transformed themselves ... Leadership passed into the hands of Negroes, and their white allies began learning from them. This was a revolutionary and wholesome development for both.[92]

---

[91] Powell, who eventually became a US Supreme Court justice, sent a secret memorandum to the US Chamber of Commerce entitled "Confidential Memorandum: Attack on American Free Enterprise System" (more commonly known as the "Powell Memo"). This infamous document was Powell's effort to alert corporate leaders and private-business owners to any critiques of the "free enterprise system," with his steadfast belief that these critiques were not only coming from leftists but, even more alarming to him, "from perfectly respectable elements of society: from the college campus, the pulpit, the media, the intellectual and literary journals, the arts and sciences and from politicians." Lewis F. Powell, Jr., "The Memo" (1971), *Powell Memorandum: Attack on American Free Enterprise System* 1, https://scholarlycommons.law.wlu.edu/powellmemo/1.

[92] Martin Luther King Jr. "A New Sense of Direction" (1968), Carnegie Council for Ethics in International Affairs, April 30, 1970,

Narrating the trajectory of his branch of the civil rights struggle from Montgomery to the March on Washington to Memphis, King rightly pointed to a world historical transformation in which young people were developing their capacity to embody the changes for which they were calling, a phenomenon that occasioned the Powell memo and motivated the reactionary agendas of the right. There is hardly any way to exaggerate the extent to which Black freedom movements and the writings of progressive Black intellectuals have been major inspirations for many social justice movements, global liberation struggles, and their accompanying cultural shifts.[93] Black artists, activists, and intellectuals have profoundly influenced the women's, LGBTQIA+, Asian American, Latinx, Indigenous, decolonization, prison abolitionist, antiwar, and antipoverty movements worldwide for decades.[94]

---

https://www.carnegiecouncil.org/media/article/a-new-sense-of-direction-1968.

[93] Gayraud Wilmore, *Black Religion and Black Radicalism: An Interpretation of the Religious History of African Americans* (Maryknoll, NY: Orbis Books, 1998); Vincent G. Harding, *Hope and History: Why We Must Share the Story of the Movement* (Maryknoll, NY: Orbis Books, 1990); Cedric Robinson, *Black Movements in America* (New York: Routledge, 1997); Robin DG Kelley, *Freedom Dreams: The Black Radical Imagination* (Boston: Beacon Press, 2003); Manning Marable, *Race, Reform, and Rebellion: The Second Reconstruction in Black America, 1945–1982* (Jackson: University Press of Mississippi, 1984); Deborah Gray-White, *Too Heavy a Load: Black Women in Defense of Themselves, 1894–1994* (New York: W. W. Norton, 2000); Stacey Floyd-Thomas and Anthony B. Pinn, eds., *Liberation Theologies in the United States: An Introduction* (New York: New York University Press, 2010); Nikole Hannah-Jones, *The 1619 Project: A New Origin Story* (New York: OneWorld Publishing, 2021); Keeanga-Yamahtta Taylor, *From #BlackLivesMatters to Black Liberation* (Chicago: Haymarket Books, 2016).

[94] John David Skrentny, *The Minority Rights Revolution* (Cambridge, MA: Belknap Press of Harvard University Press, 2002).

Throughout our history as a nation, protest has been rooted in the recognition that every human being should have an undeniable right and access to fundamental goods just by virtue of their willingness to share in the common good of the United States: daily meals of healthy food; clean drinking water; decent affordable housing; safe communities and communal spaces; universal health care and mental health services; free and quality education; fuller civic engagement with the principles and practices of our democratic republic; employment or entrepreneurial opportunities that provide a decent paycheck and dignified personhood; leisure time so folks fully can enjoy creative artistic expressions, regular vacations, sports, romances, holiday celebrations, and spiritual experiences. Making these desired goals an essential set of requirements of any humane society are not questions of access to available resources but questions of political will.

Protest is not the act of communal whining, collective nagging, or organized begging. It is the heart and soul of any true democratic society insofar as it is the most immediate, intense, and impassioned form of direct political participation. From the Stamp Act Congress to Seneca Falls Convention to The Steel Strike of 1919 to the Selma marches to the Stonewall Rebellion to the South Central uprising to the Standing Rock protectors to the Sister Marches following Trump's inauguration to the 2020 Summer of Racial Reckoning, the primacy of protest in American society and culture has a long and legendary historical record of ordinary citizens engaging in extraordinary efforts to resist oppression and remake our nation into a more just and equitable society. Faced with cascades of chaos, callousness, corruption, and cruelty in the white Christian nationalist movements, we can only withstand such an assault by holding onto our hope.

When one thinks of the turbulent nature of the last few years, one might genuinely ask, "Why bother with the notion of hope?" After the many terrifying events that we have had to witness over the past few years, it might seem unfathomable to have faith in humanity in such difficult and desolate times. Yet, the moral imperative is upon us to affirm our contributions to this society, our humanity, and our resilience in the face of deadly modes of oppression and hopelessness.[95] Long before hashtagging social media campaigns prompted people to remember the meaning and worth of human life, protest movements gave evidence of and bore witness to everyday ordinary folk who took hold of radical visions and hope. They, we, boldly went into the street to show how to live and fight and love as if one's life truly matters. The call for Black lives to matter in our present hour is a rallying cry for ALL human beings striving for freedom, justice, equality, and dignity. The compassionate humanism that undergirds critical race theology moves us to recognize our deep need for a political strategy, a social justice movement, and a moral outlook that seeks to coordinate and redeploy human power to rebuild, revitalize, and democratize civil society. We can redeem the failures of the first two Reconstruction eras and demand that we as a people and a nation must strive toward the fulfillment of a new one.

Hope entails a quest for an intellectual paradigm as well as spiritual framework that could help us, as W. B. Yeats once stated, "to hold in a single thought reality and justice."[96] "Optimism is the belief that things will be better," Rabbi Jonathan Sacks says; while "hope is the faith that, together, we can make things better. Optimism is a passive virtue; hope, an active one."[97] For critical race theology, liberation is the incarnation of human hope and the manifestation

---

[95] Alice Walker, "Watching You Hold Your Hatred," in *Hard Times Require Furious Dancing: New Poems* (Novato, CA: New World Library, 2010), 58–59.

[96] W. B. Yeats, *A Vision* (London: MacMillan, 1937), 24–25.

[97] Jonathan Sacks, *To Heal a Fractured World: The Ethics of Responsibility* (London: Bloomsbury Academic, 2013), 166.

of divine imagination. Any individual or institution that stands in the way of liberation always and ultimately does so at their own peril.

The struggle for liberation demands journeying together. In *Theology in the Capitalocene,* Joerg Rieger writes, "There is nothing more dangerous to the dominant status quo than solidarity. Yet solidarity appears to be almost impossible to conceive in progressive circles."[98] A little bit later, Rieger asserts, "Solidarity does not have to mean uniformity, sameness, or marching in lockstep, as it frequently does on the right. Disagreements are not necessarily detrimental to solidarity, and neither do all disagreements amount to the proverbial [circular] firing squads."[99] Working with Rieger's crucial project, critical race theology can bolster and be bolstered by deep solidarity by weaving three concepts and practices for our life together: specificity, sincerity, and sympathy.

The post-everything notion that power is everywhere and nowhere all at once renders no one responsible. This is a misguided myth that threatens the most vulnerable and marginalized among us. Critical race theology insists on exploring the specific to derive the means to discern and decipher universal truths. Thinking about the religious Left at its pinnacle within recent history, figures such as Martin Luther King Jr., Saul Alinsky, Cesar Chavez, Dolores Huerta, Michael Harrington, James and Grace Lee Boggs, Dorothy Day, Bayard Rustin, and Malcolm X, among others, made their cases for economic justice and social transformation based on delving deeper into their own cultural and religious realities. To place this point in sharper context, as pioneering Black socialist and product of the African Methodist Episcopal (AME) Church, A. Philip Randolph was treated as an unwanted and unwelcome dark stepchild of the American organized labor movement, yet he was most successful in executing two of the most fruitful and fateful

---

[98] Joerg Rieger, *Theology in the Capitalocene: Ecology, Identity, Class, and Solidarity* (Minneapolis: Fortress Press, 2022), 141.

[99] Rieger, *Theology in the Capitalocene,* 142.

labor actions this nation has witnessed: 1943 and 1963 March on Washington for Jobs and Freedom.

Many of the folks who are actively trying to engage in social justice work in both sacred and secular modalities harbor great skepticism about any iteration of optimism rooted in "trust" as naiveté at best and hypocrisy at its worst. Even if we shift our focus from an idealistic worldview of intersectional harmony to one more defined by material incentives for affinity and advocacy groups, the specter of a political economy that does not adhere to its own purported values creeps around us. In her book *The Sum of Us*, Heather McGhee agrees with the critique and refers to what she calls solidarity dividends: "gains available to everyone when they unite across racial lines, in the form of higher wages, cleaner air, and better-funded schools."[100] The problem, which hinges very much on the divide-and-conquer versus unite-and-conquer axis that Rieger depicts quite clearly, is that those of us without privilege and power in this current world order are victims of the proven and persistent history of bad faith that the architects and agents of white supremacy demonstrate as they kill even millions of white-identified folks in order to ensure the preservation of the status quo.

To lift sincerity as a value for solidarity and, ultimately, hope, critical race theology recognizes the profound erosion of trust in any sense of optimism and ostensible good will among millennials, Generation Z, and younger comrades. We older generations have left them a potential mountain of apocalyptic crises in our wake. They know this full well and have no reluctance in letting it be

---

[100] Heather C. McGhee, "The Way Out of America's Zero-Sum Thinking on Race and Wealth," *New York Times*, February 13, 2021, https://www.nytimes.com/2021/02/13/opinion/race-economy-inequality-civil-rights.html; Heather C. McGhee, *The Sum of Us: What Racism Costs Everyone and How We Can Prosper Together* (New York: OneWorld, 2021), 255–89.

known that they have been handed a sorrowful harvest with much less time and fewer resources by which to grapple with these biological, ecological, sociological, and theological disasters. When thinking about the history of squandered good will and missed opportunities for American coalition politics and interracial class unity, I think of the rise of the original Populist movement in the late nineteenth century. As chronicled by the likes of W. E. B. Du Bois in *Black Reconstruction*, C. Vann Woodward's *Strange Career of Jim Crow*, and Steven Hahn's *A Nation under Our Feet*, the categorical failure of the People's Party—the original Populists—as a vital and viable third national party in US electoral politics was not because pervasive poverty and social inequality had been resolved—because they have not—but because the trust and truthfulness necessary to forge stronger bonds of communal politics and cooperative economics were undermined by a retreat by white Populists to their own vision of racial identity over class interests. Critical race theology prioritizes sincerity in our solidarity as a strong resistance to the racial identity interests that are advanced in white Christian nationalism then and today.

Consumption, comparison, competition, and cruelty forestall any hope for generating genuine sympathy for other human beings who are suffering "separate but equal" class-based oppression. My emphasis here is on the matter of sympathy as it involves understanding from your own perspective. Empathy involves putting yourself in the other person's shoes and understanding why they may have particular feelings. In becoming aware of the root cause of why a person feels the way they do, we can better understand and provide healthier options in our movement for liberation. Each one of us helps to make this world come together, but, ultimately, we can only make it through this world together.[101] Therefore, it is vital to make the world and our lives in it as livable

---

[101] Peter Berger, *The Sacred Canopy: Elements of a Sociological Theory of Religion* (Garden City, NY: Doubleday, 1967), 1–10.

as humanly possible, and this will require a tremendous movement of sympathy and empathy.

Everyone faces flaws, fears, and failures in trying to be who they ought to be, but the blessings and benefits of this life are finding a way forward in being who we truly are in this world. While facing desperate odds, it is crucially important to recognize when, where, and why becoming the agent of one's own experience is fueled by our ability to realize how options can become opportunities. Life is about choices and chances. This obviously lends itself to existences wherein we make our choices and we take our chances. As much as we function within God's plan, God's will, and God's method, the ability to recognize our choices and chances to guide our consequences so that we can minimize our regrets and resentments. When granted the opportunity, take a chance to make a choice. If life, love, and liberation are not at the core of your religion, why are you in your religion? What remains in any community of faith or spiritual practice that is divorced from or utterly devoid of these elements is nothing more than death, hate, and slavery. There must be an honest recommitment to the prospect that, while God has clearly created human diversity, it has been humans who have curated adversity amongst us.

Because critical race theology insists that "hope" is not an attitude but an action, to let up in the fight of one's life even by a little bit is already to lose it entirely. Hope devoid of activity is little more than delayed despair. Pauli Murray was a dynamic witness to the action of hope.[102] In addition to a pioneering legal career,

---

[102] Pauli Murray was the first woman to graduate from the Howard University School of Law and had worked on Thurgood Marshall's legendary legal team that dismantled "separate but equal" legislation, enabling the 1954 *Brown v. Board of Education* decision. As an activist, Murray had been arrested for refusing to move to the back of the bus decades before the civil rights and women's rights movements of the 1960s and 1970s came into full bloom. Even as she personally and

advocacy work, and ministerial leadership, Murray published two autobiographies and a volume of poetry. An adaptation of one of Murray's poems sends forth this critical race theology into the world.[103]

Let us pray:

Dear God our Creator, we come before you now in a time when
    Hope is a crushed stalk
    Between clenched fingers
    Hope is a bird's wing
    Broken by a stone.
    Hope is a word in a tuneless ditty—
    A word whispered with the wind,
    A dream of forty acres and a mule,
    A cabin of one's own and a moment to rest,
    A name and place for one's children
    And children's children at last ...
We humbly ask you in our own form and fashion for
A world where the air is safe to breathe and the water is
    clean to drink

---

publicly challenged the strict confines of normative gender identity, Murray formed the National Organization for Women, in part out of a belief that civil rights—and dare we say *human* rights—were about the whole person. Murray was an advocate for civil rights of all kinds, especially racial and gender equality, identifying as what we now know to be transgender long before LGBTQIA+ rights became part of the public consciousness. Finally, Murray became the first female-identified African American to be an ordained priest in the Episcopal Church in 1977, seven days after the Episcopal Church established this possibility as official policy.

[103] Debie Thomas, "Dark Testament Verse 8." *Journey with Jesus*, 2024, https://www.journeywithjesus.net/poemsandprayers/1869-dark-testament-verse-8.

and where our neighbors study war no more and no one has
to be a refugee in their own land or a prisoner in their
own home
As we prepare to live into the purpose that you created for
and called us into, we give thanks that
Hope is a song in a weary throat.
Give us a song of hope
And a world where we can sing it.
Give us a song of faith
And a people to believe in it.
Give us a song of kinship and kindness
And a country where we can live it.
Give us a song of hope and love
And a child's heart to fully hear it.
And all those who would say Amen.

Acknowledgments

This book project first emerged as a possibility when Stacey and I had a visit with dear friends, Rev. Dr. Frederick Douglass Haynes III and First Lady Debra Peek-Haynes of Friendship West Baptist Church in Dallas, TX, in the summer of 2021. While the final product does not fully capture the contours of that dinner conversation over one evening they suggested, this book largely has been guided by Pastor Haynes's injunction as a peerless scholar-minister-activist: "If you don't have justice for all then you don't have justice at all!" I am thankful for their encouragement, kindness, and compassion as friends and family to whom I am eternally grateful for them sharing food for thought, body, and soul with me.

Without a doubt, when thinking on some of the most landmark texts dealing with Black religion in general and the Black Church in particular, Orbis Books looms large in my scholarly consciousness. I express my wholehearted gratitude to my editor at Orbis Books, Thomas Hermans-Webster, as well as managing editor Maria Angelini, who did such an excellent job bringing this book to fruition by guiding the book from inception through to the final stages of production with varying degrees of inspiration, perspiration, and sheer determination, but never left me in a state of isolation or frustration. Furthermore, I offer special thanks to Robert Ellsberg, publisher extraordinaire, for believing in the merits of this book to join this hallowed literary roster as the lead volume of the Ethics and Intersectionality Series in theological ethics. I am deeply humbled and honored by this act of faith.

An earlier iteration of this book's introduction was published as "Making America Possible Again: Towards a New Social Gospel in the 21st Century" in *Journal of Religious Leadership* Vol. 20, No. 2 (Autumn 2021), 24-36. I am grateful for the journal's permission to adapt the article for this book, to Lisa Withrow for her editorial guidance on the article, as well as Robert K. Martin for his invaluable feedback as well as permission to revise this article for the book. Likewise, Chapter 4 began as a revised version of an essay first published in *Kalfou: A Journal of Comparative and Relational Ethnic Studies* Vol. 4, No. 1 (2017), 30-39. I also want to express my thanks to *Kalfou*'s editor, Rosa Elfman, for permission to revise this article for the book. Although they were fine in their original iteration, I have these included revised versions of these previously published materials because here it finds a new audience as well as an alternate contextual framing and intentionality previously unavailable. Also, these materials are presented here because they advance the purposes of this book in crucial ways. When combined with the new chapters, these pieces are more than the sum of their parts; they represent discussions I have not yet fully developed elsewhere in my writings. It is my hope that, taken together, they respond to longstanding questions and challenges to some of my worldview as well as chart possible pathways for the future of this work.

While researching and writing this book, I have been blessed with the support of colleagues, friends, and family too numerous to mention, but I must acknowledge a "great cloud of witnesses" such as Willie James Jennings, Kelly Brown Douglas, John L. Jackson Jr., Yolanda Pierce, Blanche B. Cook, Alexis Wells-Oghoghomeh, Herbert R. Marbury, Valerie Bridgman, Teresa Fry Brown, George Lipsitz, Gary Dorrien, Marla Frederick, Barbara D. Savage, Paul C. Lim, Phillis Sheppard, Laurel C. Schneider, emilie m. townes, Theresa Smallwood, Yara González-Justiniano, M. Shawn Copeland, W. David Nelson, Mark Toulouse, David K. Kim, Christopher Driscoll, Forrest E. Harris Sr., Graham B. Reside, Alexandra Chambers, Stephen G. Ray Jr., Renita J. Weems, Jaco

Hamman, Brad R. Braxton, Joerg Rieger, Brooke Ackerly, Lee H. Butler Jr., Volker Küster, Dorothea Küster, Daniel R Brunstetter, Scott Hagley, J. Kameron Carter, Melanie Jones Quarles, Evan Rosa, Laura M. Cheifitz, D. Jamil Grimes, Aundrea Matthews, Damien Durr, Royal Todd, Tatayana Richardson, and Edward Vogel, whose ideas, insights, and inventiveness over the years as colleagues, compatriots, and conversation partners has been challenged and changed me in countless ways.

In addition to my gratitude for the foreword to this volume by the prolific and profound scholar Michael Eric Dyson, I am thankful to him for the generosity of his genius spent in poignant conversation, rigorous debate, critical encouragement, and good humor to help me think through many of the issues addressed in this volume. I also want to state my unyielding gratitude to Anthony B. Pinn, whose creativity, courage, conviction, and collaboration over the years both as a scholar and a dear friend has been incomparable. Lastly, I want to extol my deep and abiding respect and appreciation to Peniel Joseph, who helped spark my interest in critical race theory back in graduate school so many years ago. To this day, Niel's razor-sharp mind and radical passions have crafted impressive, inspiring scholarship that continually fuels my thinking in this book and beyond.

Unquestionably, this book often was written tearfully in loving memory of my mother, Desrine Thomas, and my mother-in-law, Lillian Floyd, who both shuffled off this mortal coil far too soon in January and December 2017 respectively. Although their physical presence is so sorely missed, their spiritual essence continues to profoundly enrich and empower me, my family, friends, and countless others whose lives they touched during their sojourn amongst us. Also, I sadly celebrate the memories of my former students Alaenor London, Omar Archer, and Jerrolyn Eulinberg, who I was blessed to know before they made their all-too-early journey to join the ancestors.

Finally, I leave my deepest and most heartfelt gratitude to my wonderful partner in all things, Stacey Floyd-Thomas, and our brilliant, beautiful, and blessed daughter, Lillian. I dedicate the book to Stacey because no one is more responsible for this book's existence than she is. Over nearly three decades of life, labor, and love, Stacey's steadfast faith, abiding love, and boundless wisdom always keeps me grounded even as she has spent that time making impossible dreams into glorious realities. As the greatest example of our collaboration, Lillian is simply the most refreshing, remarkable person I have ever known because of her incredible capacity to find new ways to make me think, laugh, and truly love this extraordinary world in which we live. More than anything, the love, grace, and mercy they exude constantly has made my thinking, being, and acting so much better. I hope this book reflects that truth.

Index